Fred Feldman is an important philosopher who has made a substantial contribution to utilitarian moral philosophy. This collection of ten previously published essays plus a new introductory essay reveals the striking originality and unity of his views.

Feldman's version of utilitarianism differs from traditional forms in that it evaluates behavior by appeal to the values of accessible worlds. These worlds, in turn, are evaluated in terms of the amount of pleasure they contain, but the conception of pleasure involved is a novel one and the formulation of hedonism is improved. In Feldman's view, pleasure is not a feeling but a propositional attitude. He also deals with problems of justice that affect standard forms of utilitarianism.

The collection is ideally suited for courses on contemporary utilitarian theory.

D1291032

Utilitarianism, hedonism, and desert

CAMBRIDGE STUDIES IN PHILOSOPHY

General editor ERNEST SOSA (Brown University)

Advisory editors
JONATHAN DANCY (University of Keele)
JOHN HALDANE (University of St. Andrews)
GILBERT HARMAN (Princeton University)
FRANK JACKSON (Australian National University)
WILLIAM G. LYCAN (University of North Carolina at Chapel Hill)
SYDNEY SHOEMAKER (Cornell University)
JUDITH J. THOMSON (Massachusetts Institute of Technology)

RECENT TITLES

Utilitarianism, hedonism, and desert

ESSAYS IN MORAL PHILOSOPHY

Fred Feldman

The University of Massachusetts at Amherst

CAMBRIDGE
UNIVERSITY PRESS

BJ
1012
F434
1997

PUBLISHED BY THE PRESS SYNDICATE OF THE UNIVERSITY OF CAMBRIDGE
The Pitt Building, Trumpington Street, Cambridge CB2 1RP, United Kingdom

CAMBRIDGE UNIVERSITY PRESS
The Edinburgh Building, Cambridge CB2 2RU, United Kingdom
40 West 20th Street, New York, NY 10011–4211, USA
10 Stamford Road, Oakleigh, Melbourne 3166, Australia

www.cambridge.org
Information on this title: www.cambridge.org/9780521591553

© Fred Feldman 1997

First published 1997

Typeset in Bembo

Library of Congress Cataloging-in-Publication Data
Feldman, Fred, 1941–
Utilitarianism, hedonism, and desert : essays in moral philosophy
/ Fred Feldman.
p.   cm. – (Cambrdige studies in philosophy)
Includes bibliographical references and index.
ISBN 0-521-59155-4 (hb). – ISBN 0-521-59842-7 (pbk.)
1. Ethics.   2. Utilitarianism.   3. Hedonism.   I. Title.
II. Series.
BJ1012.F434   1997
170 – dc21   96–49898
                                                      CIP

*A catalog record for this book is available from
the British Library.*

ISBN-13 978-0-521-59155-3 hardback
ISBN-10 0-521-59155-4 hardback

ISBN-13 978-0-521-59842-2 paperback
ISBN-10 0-521-59842-7 paperback

Transferred to digital printing 2005

Contents

Acknowledgments

Throughout the time during which I was working on the essays included here, I was blessed with the opportunity to collaborate with a remarkable number of outstanding students. Many of them were thinking about issues related to the ones that interested me. All of them were generous with criticism and suggestions. I think here especially of Eva Bodanszky, Ben Bradley, Earl Conee, David Cowles, Judi DeCew, Neil Feit, Bob Frazier, Ishtiyaque Haji, Paul MacNamara, Ned Markosian, Owen McLeod, Kevin Moon, Eric Moore, Neil Schaefer, Ted Sider, Erik Wielenberg, and Michael Zimmerman. I owe a special debt of gratitude to Owen McLeod for encouraging me to put together this book, and for giving me wise and knowledgeable guidance.

I am also grateful to a number of colleagues who provided criticism and encouragement in connection with various essays in the collection. These include Dennis Cooley, David Copp, Irwin Goldstein, Michael Jubien, Jaegwon Kim, Noah Lemos, Jeff McMahan, Ingmar Persson, John Troyer, and Peter Vallentyne. My brother, Richard Feldman, has been a steady and reliable source of critical comment and emotional support throughout my career. I suspect that he is not fully aware of how profoundly grateful I am to him. Many others are mentioned in footnotes of acknowledgment in the essays.

I owe a special debt of gratitude to Roderick Chisholm, whose work originally sparked my interest in these issues. I continue to be inspired by Chisholm's philosophical insights and his extraordinary personal commitment to truth and clarity.

I am especially grateful to Ernest Sosa, the General Editor of the Cambridge Studies in Philosophy, for his guidance and encouragement.

This book is dedicated, with sincere thanks, to all the students who participated in the the search for The Good in the ethics seminars over the past two decades at The University of Massachusetts at Amherst.

Sources

"World Utilitarianism," in *Analysis and Metaphysics*, ed. by Keith Lehrer (Dordrecht: Reidel, 1975), 255–271. Reprinted with kind permission of Kluwer Academic Publishers, Inc.

"On the Extensional Equivalence of Simple and General Utilitarianism," *Noûs* 8 (March 1974), 185–194. Reprinted by permission of Blackwell Publishers, Inc.

"The Principle of Moral Harmony," *The Journal of Philosophy* (March 1980), 166–179. Reprinted by permission of *The Journal of Philosophy*.

"On the Consistency of Act- and Motive-Utilitarianism: A Reply to Robert Adams," *Philosophical Studies* 70 (1993), 201–212. Reprinted by permission of *Philosophical Studies*.

"Two Questions about Pleasure," in *Philosophical Analysis: A Defense by Example*, ed. by David Austin (Dordrecht: Reidel, 1988), 59–81. Reprinted with kind permission of Kluwer Academic Publishers, Inc.

"Mill, Moore, and the Consistency of Qualified Hedonism," in *Midwest Studies in Philosophy, Volume XX: Moral Concepts,* ed. by Peter French, Theodore E. Uehling, Jr., and Howard K. Wettstein (Notre Dame, Indiana: University of Notre Dame Press, 1996), 318–331. Reprinted by permission of University of Notre Dame Press.

"On the Intrinsic Value of Pleasures" *Ethics* 107 (April 1997): 448–466.

"Adjusting Utility for Justice: A Consequentialist Reply to the Objection from Justice," *Philosophy and Phenomenological Research* LV, 3 (September 1995), 567–585. Reprinted by permission of *Philosophy and Phenomenological Research*.

"Desert: Reconsideration of Some Received Wisdom," *Mind* 104 (January 1995), 63–77. Reprinted by permission of Oxford University Press.

"Justice, Desert, and the Repugnant Conclusion," *Utilitas: A Journal of Utilitarian Studies* 7, 2 (November 1995), 189–206. Reprinted by permission of *Utilitas* and Edinburgh University Press.

Introduction

For as long as I can remember, it has seemed obvious to me that our fundamental moral obligation is to do the best we can – to make the world as good as we can make it. Naturally, I was delighted when I discovered that many others – the utilitarians – maintained approximately the same view. However, my delight turned to consternation when I began to look more closely at the philosophical literature on utilitarianism. One tremendous problem was that the received formulations of the view fail to express the utilitarian insight. Indeed, most received formulations fail to express any insight – they are simply incoherent, as Hector-Neri Castañeda showed in a series of brilliant papers published in the late 1960s and early 1970s.[1]

Utilitarianism has been linked to hedonism since the time of Bentham and Mill. The fundamental insight of hedonism ("pleasure is The Good") seemed attractive, too. Yet again when I took a look at the literature on hedonism I discovered near chaos. There was enormous confusion about the nature of pleasure, and equally great confusion about precisely what hedonists would want to say about pleasure, assuming that they could reach any agreement about what it is. I could not find a clear statement of the intended theory of value.

Furthermore, even if these underlying conceptual difficulties could be solved, it appeared that the resulting normative theory would surely confront the most troublesome of moral objections. For (if only it could be stated coherently!) act utilitarianism would undoubtedly imply something roughly equivalent to the idea that the morally right course of action is the one that leads to the best result. But critics had pointed out that

---

1. Some of the central papers are "A Problem for Utilitarianism," *Analysis* 28 (1968), 141–142; "Ought, Value, and Utilitarianism," *American Philosophical Quarterly* 6,4 (October 1969), 257–275; and "On the Problem of Formulating a Coherent Act Utilitarianism," *Analysis* 32, 4 (March 1972), 118–124. Other papers on this topic are cited in the Bibliography at the end of "World Utilitarianism."

sometimes the path to the best result involves the most outrageous of injustices. For example, it might be necessary to sacrifice innocent by-standers for the sake of the greatest good.[2] Did I really want to endorse a moral philosophy that required that we take any means necessary – no matter how unjust – in order to arrive at the best end?

In a series of papers written over a period of more than twenty years, I have presented my solutions to these three great problems. In "World Utilitarianism" and succeeding papers, I developed a simple, coherent formulation of the fundamental act utilitarian insight. In "Two Questions about Pleasure," I presented a clear and (as I see it) plausible conception of pleasure, and I subsequently presented a number of consistent forms of hedonism. In "Adjusting Utility for Justice," I described a systematic way in which considerations of justice may be incorporated into the value theory associated with act utilitarianism.

This volume consists of ten of these papers in moral philosophy. In these papers I present my solutions to the three problems just sketched. The book as a whole may be seen as a presentation of a novel form of utilitarianism, supported by a hedonistic axiology in which the value of pleasure is adjusted in order to take account of justice. Part I contains four papers on the formulation of act utilitarianism. Part II contains three papers on hedonism. Part III contains three papers on the adjustment of utility for justice – which I take to be receipt according to desert.

The papers were published over a period of many years. They were originally written as independent pieces, without much thought of their place in a larger scheme. As a result, it is sometimes not clear how the papers fit together. And there are some cases in which I no longer would put things quite as I did originally. Thus, it may be useful for me to say a few words here about the papers and their connections.

PART I. UTILITARIANISM

For more than a century following the publication of Mill's *Utilitarianism*, philosophers went about their business of attacking and defending this most attractive of normative theories. There was, of course, some debate about whether Mill is best understood as an act utilitarian or as a rule utilitarian.[3] But there was very little serious debate about the nature of

2. I cite a variety of sources for objections of this sort in fn. 3 of "Adjusting Utility for Justice."
3. One of the first important papers on this issue was J. O. Urmson's "The Interpretation of the Moral Philosophy of J. S. Mill," *Philosophical Quarterly* III (1953), reprinted in *Mill:*

the act utilitarian doctrine – the version most commonly ascribed to Mill. Philosophers thought they understood act utilitarianism.

In its typical formulation, act utilitarianism presupposes that on each occasion of moral choice, the agent confronts a set of alternative possible acts. For each possible act, there is a consequence. The consequence contains all the subsequent events that would occur as a result of the act if it were performed. Each consequence has a value determined by the amount of good and evil it contains. Act utilitarianism is standardly taken to be the view that the agent's moral obligation is to perform the act that has the best consequence.

Castañeda showed that any such standard form of utilitarianism is incoherent. Although Castañeda did not put it quite this way, I think it is fair to say that he came to the startling insight that utilitarianism *cannot be* the view that right acts always have the best consequences. This standard formula says something that utilitarians simply would not want to say, if only they were to think clearly about what it means.

Consider what act utilitarianism says about the behavior of a surgeon about to perform essential heart surgery. Perhaps the surgeon's alternatives are:

a1: Perform heart surgery on this patient.
a2: Don't perform heart surgery on this patient.

We may think (if this is a typical case) that because the consequences of a1 are far better (the patient lives; family and friends are relieved; the surgeon gets a handsome fee), utilitarianism implies that it is right – indeed, in this case obligatory – for the surgeon to perform a1. The right act in this case seems to be the one with the best consequence.

But a1 is a complex act. It is a sequence of thousands of smaller acts. If the surgeon performs a1, he will perform something like this sequence of steps on the unconscious patient: First, he ensures that the patient is properly prepped; then he makes a large incision in the patient's chest; then he slices through some muscles; then he cracks a few ribs; then he starts to work on some arteries or valves in the heart; and so on. Consider the surgeon's act of *cracking the ribs*. He does this to gain access to the heart, and surely in a typical case a utilitarian would want the surgeon to gain access to the heart.

But what are the *consequences* of that act? What are the *effects* of cracking

A Collection of Critical Essays, ed. J. B. Schneewind (Garden City, N.Y.: Doubleday, 1968), 179–189.

3

the ribs? It should be obvious that, as a result of that act of cracking ribs, the patient will experience a lot of pain when he later regains consciousness. The discomfort of recovery from heart surgery is due in large measure to the injuries to the ribs. So far as I can tell, cracking those ribs does not cause anything good – either for the surgeon or for the patient. It certainly does not *cause* the patient's heart condition to be improved. Yet – and this is the amazing fact – though cracking those ribs has no good results, and hence must be declared morally wrong by typical formulations of utilitarianism, it is a step in a more complex action (heart surgery) that is obligatory by the same standard!

(You mustn't think that the act of cracking those ribs is a necessary part of the best act, either. Keep in mind that it was possible for the surgeon to gain access to the heart by cracking some *other* ribs. Hence, that particular act of rib cracking was not a necessary part of a sequence that has the best consequences. Nevertheless, if this is a typical case in which surgery is the best option, this act of rib cracking seems to have some sort of utilitarian justification.)

Castañeda's insight is really quite simple: There are cases in which a complex act has better consequences than any of its alternatives, but *parts* of that act may have worse consequences than some of their alternatives. Act utilitarianism of the standard form implies in such cases that it is obligatory to perform the complex act but forbidden to perform its parts. This is surely a most surprising and unwelcome result. Imagine what would happen if there were a formalistic utilitarian advisor giving moral instruction to the surgeon: "By all means, do perform the surgery – it's your best option; but by all means, don't make that incision! Don't crack those ribs! You have better things to do just now."

Following the publication of Castañeda's papers, there was a flurry of replies in the literature.[4] A few critics claimed that there is something wrong with Castañeda's argument, but the overwhelming majority appreciated his point. They tried to reformulate utilitarianism so as to accommodate it. In many cases, the resulting reformulations of act utilitarianism turned out to be mind-numbingly complex theories subject to difficulties similar to the one Castañeda had discovered.

In my 1975 paper "World Utilitarianism" (Essay 1 of the present volume) I describe some of the problems with traditional formulations of act

---

4. Some of these are cited in the Bibliography at the end of "World Utilitarianism." For a more extensive discussion of this literature, see my *Doing the Best We Can* (Dordrecht: Reidel, 1986), 227–228.

utilitarianism. I then present a novel, simple, coherent version of the doctrine. Although the theory I propose is intended to express the utilitarian insight, it does so without appeal to the problematic notions of "alternatives" and "consequences."

Instead of assuming that on each occasion of moral choice the agent confronts a new set of alternative possible acts, I start with the idea of a "life history." In "World Utilitarianism," a life history for a person at a time is a set of acts still performable by that person as of that time and sufficiently rich that it will provide the person with things to do from the specified time until his or her death. I assume that for each such life history, there is a possible world that would be actual if the person were to live out the life history. I call these "life history worlds." Each such world has a value. The fundamental idea of world utilitarianism is that an action is morally permissible for a person as of a time if and only if the person performs the act in one of the best life history worlds still accessible to him or her as of the time.

In the surgery case described earlier, world utilitarianism implies that it is permissible for the surgeon to crack some ribs – because he performs heart surgery and hence cracks some ribs in the best worlds then accessible to him. On my view the consequences of rib cracking are irrelevant. What's relevant is that if the surgeon lives out his life in the best still possible way, he will have to crack a few ribs.

In a later paper in the volume – "On the Consistency of Act- and Motive-Utilitarianism" (Essay 4) – I present a much tidier formulation of world utilitarianism. The later formulation makes no appeal to a metaphysics of "acts," but I believe it has the resources to explain everything plausible about act utilitarianism. I try to explain all this in Section 5 of the later essay.

Arguments concerning formulations of utilitarianism often turn on claims about equivalence or inconsistency between different versions. A good example of this sort of argument arose when early forms of rule utilitarianism were first developed in an effort to avoid certain moral objections to act utilitarianism. In some cases, critics claimed that the new rule utilitarian formulations were "extensionally equivalent" to the old act utilitarian ones. Thus, these critics claimed, the new versions would be subject to exactly the same objections as the old. Defenders of the new formulations often insisted that their versions of the doctrine were indeed distinct from (and preferable to) the outmoded versions.

When I first became aware of these disputes, I was fascinated. I sought out and cataloged different forms of utilitarianism, trying to figure out which pairs were equivalent and which ones were distinct. As I studied the details of various formulations, I discovered that when formulations had different moral implications, it often happened that at least one of the formulations had different moral implications largely because it said something quite unintended and implausible.

Essay 2, "On the Extensional Equivalence of Simple and General Utilitarianism," illustrates this interest. Act (or "simple") utilitarianism (in traditional forms) requires a person to perform an act if the consequence of that particular act would be better than the consequence of any particular alternative. A corresponding form of rule (or "general") utilitarianism requires a person to perform an act if the consequence of *universal performance (to the greatest extent possible) of similar acts* would be better than the consequence of *universal performance (to the greatest extent possible) of acts similar to the alternatives*. David Lyons argued (in his *Forms and Limits of Utilitarianism*) that the requirements of the two theories would have to be the same.[5] He thought that if a certain set of alternatives is ranked in a certain way in terms of their own consequences, then they must be ranked in the same way in terms of the consequences of universal (to the greatest extent possible) performance.

In "On the Extensional Equivalence . . ." I show that the rankings need not be the same and that the implications of the theories may be different. Although I don't sufficiently emphasize the point in the essay, part of my aim was to show that rule utilitarianism (at least of the sort Lyons considered) makes the normative status of each action depend upon a wholly irrelevant factor – the number of others in position to perform relevantly similar acts. My hidden agenda in the essay was thus to pour cold water on rule utilitarianism – a style of utilitarianism that I have never found congenial.

Nineteen years after "On the Extensional Equivalence . . . ," in "On the Consistency of Act- and Motive-Utilitarianism" (Essay 4), I was still pursuing my fascination with the relations among forms of utilitarianism. In this case, I try to rebut Robert Adams's claim about the inconsistency of these two forms of utilitarianism.[6] My argument turns essentially on my claim that in order to be coherent at all, utilitarianism must be formulated approximately as I originally proposed in "World Utilitarianism." Once this is done with Adams's AU and MU, it becomes clear that these

5. David Lyons, *Forms and Limits of Utilitarianism* (Oxford: Oxford University Press, 1965).
6. Robert Adams, "Motive Utilitarianism," *The Journal of Philosophy* LXXIII, 14 (August 12, 1976), 467–481.

are perfectly consistent corollaries of the more general thesis that we ought to bring about whatever states of affairs occur in the best accessible worlds. Some defenders of the utilitarian approach have thought that one virtue of utilitarianism is this: If each person does his or her duty according to utilitarianism, then each does what's best for the group. If each does what's best for the group, then group welfare must inevitably be maximized. This has been thought to provide a sort of justification for utilitarianism.[7] In "The Principle of Moral Harmony" (Essay 3) I show that this line of thought is mistaken. Even when each does his or her best for the group, the group may fail to be best off.

"The Principle of Moral Harmony" focuses on a topic that continues to intrigue me – the connection (or lack thereof) between groups taken distributively and groups taken collectively. In "The Principle of Moral Harmony," the issue arises in this way: Suppose each member of a group does the best he or she can to maximize the welfare of his group; does it follow that the welfare of the group will be maximized? More exactly, does it follow that there is nothing *the group* could have done that would have made the group better off? By appeal to some examples, I try to show that it does not follow.[8]

PART II. HEDONISM

In most of my early papers on act utilitarianism, I was primarily interested in problems concerning the underlying structure of utilitarianism. I wanted to develop a coherent version of the theory that made the normative evaluation of behavior depend on the intrinsic values of accessible possible worlds. I deliberately avoided getting entangled in substantive debates about what in fact determines the values of worlds. However, it

---

7. The prime example is Bentham, who said, "The principle of utility is capable of being consistently pursued; and it is but tautology to say that the more consistently it is pursued, the better it must ever be for humankind." *Introduction to the Principles of Morals and Legislation*, in E. A. Burtt, ed., *The English Philosophers from Bacon to Mill* (New York: Modern Library, 1949), 796.
8. I have discussed this and related issues in a number of other papers and chapters. In "On the Advantages of Cooperativeness," *Midwest Studies* XIII (1988), 308–323, I try to show that it is not always in the interest of the individual to play his or her role in the group activity that is most in the interest of the group. In Chapter 5, "Rule Utilitarianism," of my *Introductory Ethics* (Englewood Cliffs, N.J.: Prentice-Hall, 1978), I formulate several versions of rule utilitarianism. In each case, I try to show that the proposed theory makes the normative status of actions depend upon something that is in fact normatively irrelevant. In Chapter 7, "Individual Obligation and Group Welfare," of *Doing the Best We Can*, I discuss interactions between individual and group obligation.

was apparent that in order to give the theory any real normative substance, I would eventually have to provide an axiology that would yield a ranking of possible worlds in terms of intrinsic value.

Since the time of Bentham and Mill, utilitarianism has been linked to *hedonism*. Indeed, some have gone so far as to *define* utilitarianism as the view that the right act is the one that maximizes the balance of pleasure over pain. Furthermore, hedonism is perhaps the oldest and most initially attractive of axiological views. It was therefore natural for me to give some attention to the idea that hedonism might serve as the axiology for my normative theory.

Just as act utilitarianism is often taken to be the simplest of normative theories, hedonism is often taken to be the simplest of axiological theories. In traditional forms, it is said to be the view that "pleasure alone is intrinsically good."[9] But as in the case of act utilitarianism, things are not as simple as they have appeared. In my view, a substantial part of the classic literature on hedonism, both pro and con, is marred by deep conceptual confusions. Philosophers have construed hedonism in a remarkable variety of ways – some of which are nonstarters. It is no wonder that there is so much disagreement about the *truth* of hedonism.

Perhaps the greatest source of confusion about hedonism is this: Some philosophers think that pleasure is a special sort of sensation. Moore and many others have assumed that to get pleasure is to *feel* a certain something – a special, indefinable, phenomenologically uniform sensation – the feeling of "pleasure itself."[10] These philosophers quite naturally assume that hedonism is the view that this feeling is the fundamental bearer of positive intrinsic value.

The remarkable fact is that there simply is no such feeling. Feelings of the most disparate sorts may correctly be called "pleasures." Sidgwick, Broad, Ryle, Brandt, and many others have made this clear. The implication is obvious: If we take hedonism to be the view that this uniform sensation is the sole bearer of positive intrinsic value, then we are driven to the conclusion that nothing intrinsically good has ever happened!

In Essay 5, "Two Questions about Pleasure," I develop my own conception of the nature of pleasure. Whereas virtually every other philosopher who has discussed this issue has started with the idea that pleasure must be some sort of sensory phenomenon, I start with the idea that the

---

9. Moore persistently formulates hedonism this way. See, for example, *Principia Ethica*, 61, 62, 63, and so on.
10. Moore commits himself to this conception of pleasure in *Principia Ethica*, 12–13.

fundamental hedonic phenomenon is a certain propositional attitude. This is the familiar attitude we express when we say that we are pleased that something is the case or that we "take pleasure in" some state of affairs. I offer no definition of this attitude, but I think we are all familiar with it. It is not a "feeling."

I try to show how we may explain "pleasurable feelings" by appeal to this propositional pleasure. My idea, roughly, is that a feeling (had by a person on some particular occasion) is a sensory pleasure if and only if the person who feels it on that occasion takes immediate propositional pleasure in the fact that he or she is then feeling it.

At the core of hedonism is the doctrine that *pleasure is intrinsically good*. We may call this the "Hedonic Thesis." As I indicated in "Two Questions about Pleasure," many philosophers agree that there is no such thing as "the feeling of pleasure itself." So what is the subject of the Hedonic Thesis? Philosophers in the tradition of Sidgwick maintain that when we say that a certain feeling is a pleasure, what we mean is that we have a certain attitude toward the experience – perhaps we like it for its own sake, or want to prolong it. On a typical version of this view – Richard Brandt's – the Hedonic Thesis is taken to mean that these *intrinsically liked experiences* are bearers of positive intrinsic value.

In "On the Intrinsic Value of Pleasures" (Essay 7), I show that if we understand intrinsic value in the classic Moorean way, any such interpretation of the Hedonic Thesis is unacceptable. The problem is that on the Sidgwickian conception, what makes an experience a pleasure is a certain *extrinsic* feature of that experience – it is liked in a certain way by the person who experiences it. Yet if such experiences are intrinsically good, they ought to be good in virtue of their *intrinsic* features.

I go on to present my propositional conception of pleasure (first defended in "Two Questions about Pleasure"). Making use of this concept, I describe a certain sort of state of affairs. These are "basic hedonic states" – states of affairs in which some person takes propositional pleasure to some degree at some time in the fact that he or she then is experiencing some feeling. I claim that the simplest coherent form of hedonism includes the view that states of affairs such as these are the fundamental bearers of positive intrinsic value. These are the things we ought to have in mind when we say that "pleasures are intrinsically good." If we understand pleasure in the proposed way, we will be able to make sense of the Hedonic Thesis. My view makes the intrinsic value of pleasures (construed as hedonic states) supervene entirely on *intrinsic* features of those states.

One of the great ongoing debates about hedonism is the debate concerning the question of whether there are different "qualities" of pleasure. Bentham is often cited as the father of the "no-qualities view." He said that quantity is all that matters. "Prejudice apart, the game of pushpin is of equal value with the arts and sciences of music and poetry. If the game of pushpin furnish more pleasure, it is more valuable than either."[11] Mill, on the other hand, said:

> It is quite compatible with the principle of utility to recognise the fact, that some *kinds* of pleasure are more desirable and more valuable than others. It would be absurd that while, in estimating all other things, quality is considered as well as quantity, the estimation of pleasures should be supposed to depend on quantity alone.[12]

Many subsequent authors have weighed in on one side of this debate or the other. In a famous passage in *Principia Ethica*, Moore claimed that Mill's qualified hedonism is inconsistent.[13] Moore seems to have thought that qualified hedonism implies both that pleasure is the *only* intrinsic good (because it is a form of hedonism) and that something other than pleasure is intrinsically good (because *quality* makes a difference, too). This, of course, would be a contradiction. Some commentators have agreed with Moore; others have sided with Mill.[14]

In "Mill, Moore, and the Consistency of Qualified Hedonism" (Essay 6), I rebut Moore's claim that Mill's hedonism is inconsistent. My argument turns on what may seem to be a fairly extensive exercise in preliminary stage setting. I devote a large portion of the essay to the formulation of a few sorts of hedonism. I try to show that once we state the various sorts of hedonism correctly, Moore's arguments simply evaporate.

In this case, too, there is a hidden agenda. My deeper aim here is to show, by appeal to a number of prominent figures, that standard formulations of hedonism are self-contradictory. This obviously undermines the effort to deal with the quality–quantity controversy: There's little point in trying to determine if "hedonism" is consistent with "qualified hedonism" if each view is independently self-contradictory. My deeper point is that the real meaning of hedonism has not been understood. A huge portion of the debate about hedonism has simply been at cross pur-

---

11. Jeremy Bentham, *The Rationale of Reward* in *The Works of Jeremy Bentham*, ed. John Bowring (New York: Russell & Russell, 1962), Vol. Two, 253.
12. J. S. Mill, *Utilitarianism*, ed. Oskar Piest (Indianapolis: Liberal Arts Press, 1957), 12.
13. G. E. Moore, *Principia Ethica*, 80.
14. I give rosters of the opposing sides in fnn. 5 and 6 of "Mill, Moore, and the Consistency of Qualitative Hedonism."

poses because there is so little understanding of the nature of the doctrine under consideration.

PART III. DESERT

It has long been recognized that one of the most serious substantive difficulties for utilitarianism concerns its implications for *justice*. Utilitarianism implies that we ought to bring about the outcome that contains the greatest total amount of value, regardless of the details of distribution. Yet sometimes this best outcome seems morally objectionable in virtue of the fact that the goods within it are so unfairly distributed. Starting in "World Utilitarianism," I suggested that there must be a way for the utilitarian to incorporate considerations of justice when evaluating outcomes.

In Essay 8, "Adjusting Utility for Justice" (which was published twenty years after "World Utilitarianism"), I present and defend an axiological theory that incorporates considerations of justice. It does this by adjusting raw values (positive or negative) in light of the desert (positive or negative) of the recipient of the value. I try to show how the classic "objections from justice" to utilitarianism can be overcome if we thus adjust utilities for desert.

Roughly, my idea is that when persons deserves a certain good – a pleasure, for example – then it is extra good for them to receive it. Its value is enhanced. On the other hand, when persons do not deserve a certain good but get it anyway, then it is not very good for them to receive it. Its value is "mitigated." Similar things happen in the case of evils – pains, for example. If persons deserve a certain pain, then it is not so bad for them to experience it. Its disvalue is mitigated. If a person does not deserve pain but gets it anyway, then their receipt of it is extra bad. The value of getting that pain is enhanced (made even worse).

My aim in all this is to formulate the axiology in such a way as to incorporate considerations of justice. If this can be done successfully, then we will be able to retain what I take to be the fundamental utilitarian thesis: We ought to make the world as good as we can make it. The trick is to find a way to adjust the values of the goods and evils of the world so as to reflect the extent to which the recipients deserve them. By doing this, we locate justice in the axiology rather than in the normative theory itself.

I appeal in "Adjusting Utility to Justice" to the classic conception of justice, according to which justice obtains when people get what they deserve. Thus, *desert* plays a crucial role in my axiology. Unfortunately,

11

the concept of desert is currently in bad repute. Since the publication of Rawls's *A Theory of Justice*, moral philosophers have been wary of appeals to desert.[15] Because I make explicit appeal to desert in my axiology, it is important for me to develop a clear understanding of the concept. In "Desert: Reconsideration of Some Received Wisdom" (Essay 9), I take some steps in this direction. I show that some central elements of the received view about desert are false.

One very popular idea is that desert arises only after the fact. For example, it is widely agreed that a person deserves punishment for a certain crime only *after* he or she has committed the crime. Similarly, it is widely agreed that a person deserves rewards for performing a certain good deed only *after* he or she has performed the deed. Many philosophers have assumed that what's true in these cases is universally true – true as a matter of the "logic of desert." But I show that there are cases in which desert arises before the fact. In light of these cases, we must be more cautious about sweeping claims concerning desert and time.

Another, perhaps even more popular idea is that desert arises only in cases in which people are responsible. It is widely agreed that a person deserves punishment for a crime only if he or she is morally responsible for the commission of that crime. Similarly, it is widely agreed that a person deserves a reward for a good deed only if he or she is responsible for the performance of that good deed. I try to show that there are cases in which desert arises in the absence of responsibility. Sometimes we are deserving in virtue of things for which no one bears any responsibility. My argument is designed to show that desert is not linked to responsibility (or freedom, or intention) in the way it has often been assumed to be linked.

In "Justice, Desert, and the Repugnant Conclusion" (Essay 10), I try to show that my desert-adjusted axiology is useful for other purposes. It may provide the basis for solving Derek Parfit's deeply troubling "repugnant conclusion."

---

15. "There is a tendency for common sense to suppose that income and wealth, and the good things in life generally, should be distributed according to moral desert. . . . Now justice as fairness rejects this conception." John Rawls, *A Theory of Justice* (Cambridge, Mass.: Harvard University Press, 1971), 310. I should mention that in my view, this passage from Rawls has been seriously misunderstood by many commentators. As I read it, Rawls is *not* here rejecting the view that justice is receipt according to desert. (He seems to endorse that view on p. 313.) Rather, I think he is merely saying in a misleading way that *moral virtue* is not the sole desert base.

12

SOME UNDERLYING THEMES

Moore begins the Preface to *Principia Ethica* with a wonderfully Moorean remark:

> It appears to me that in Ethics, as in all other philosophical studies, the difficulties and disagreements, of which its history is full, are mainly due to a very simple cause: namely to the attempt to answer questions, without first discovering precisely *what* question it is which you desire to answer.[16]

I believe that there is another, closely related source of "difficulty and disagreement" in ethics: It is that philosophers have set out to defend (or attack) certain doctrines without first discovering precisely *what* doctrine they desire to defend (or attack). Thus, Mill, Bentham, and many others have vigorously defended "utilitarianism" without succeeding in formulating the doctrine precisely. Others have just as vigorously attacked "utilitarianism" without making the details of the view entirely clear.

The situation with respect to "hedonism" seems to me to be even worse. There are several sources of difficulty. In the first place, as I have already mentioned, there is enormous confusion over the concept of *pleasure*. Some think that pleasure is a special sort of feeling or sensation. Others recognize that there is no such feeling; feelings of the most disparate sorts may correctly be called "pleasures." A second source of difficulty concerning hedonism arises from the fact that there is no consensus about how to formulate a theory of value. Some apparently think it satisfactory to say that hedonism is the view that "pleasure is the good" and then proceed directly to the battle.

Throughout the papers in this volume, I have struggled with what some other philosophers might view as merely preliminary matters. I have tried again and again to state the various theories clearly. My guiding instinct in all this is an aversion to "Rambo philosophy." I think we have a duty to see our theoretical targets clearly before we pull our argumentative triggers. In many cases, as I try to show in several of the papers, if we take the trouble to formulate the theory with sufficient care, the controversy surrounding it simply evaporates. It becomes *obvious*, for example, that qualified hedonism is a form of hedonism; it becomes *obvious* that act and motive utilitarianism are consistent.

Another central theme of these papers concerns the plasticity and re-

---

16. Moore, *Principia Ethica*, vii.

13

sourcefulness of some of the classic moral conceptions. I have tried to reveal something of the enormous potential of utilitarianism and hedonism. While retaining the core idea in each case, we can vary the details almost endlessly. As a result, each of these views can be modified so as to accommodate a staggering variety of moral intuitions.

Thus, for example, when critics attack utilitarianism, charging that it fails to account for justice, my inclination is to look for a way to accommodate what's important and true in the criticism. As I try to show in "Adjusting Utility for Justice," such accommodation is possible. Furthermore, I have suggested a pattern according to which other objections might be defused. In this particular case, my strategy involves tinkering with the axiology rather than adding side constraints, as some others have proposed.

As a result of all this, my view may be seen as a sort of hybrid of consequentialism and deontology. On the one hand, as a utilitarian, I steadfastly insist that we should make the world as good as we can make it. (How could it be otherwise?) But on the other hand, in my effort to deal with well-founded objections to traditional forms of consequentialism, I am happy to adjust the axiology so as to take account of such things as promises, rights, and past good and bad behavior. Thus, instead of rejecting the claims of deontology, I try to find a place for them in my fundamentally consequentialist scheme.

Part I

Utilitarianism

Essay 1

World utilitarianism

INTRODUCTORY COMMENTS

In "A Problem for Utilitarianism," Castañeda pointed out a difficulty for traditional formulations of act utilitarianism. A careless reader might think that Castañeda's problem is just a small one of interest primarily to deontic logicians. But that would be a mistake. The problem Castañeda discovered is deep and serious. He showed that act utilitarianism requires a thoroughgoing reconception.

On traditional formulations, act utilitarianism assumes that there are "concrete acts," and that most of these are never performed. They remain mere possibilities. Yet these concrete acts are supposed to be the fundamental bearers of normative status. Once we accept this metaphysical assumption, it is quite natural to go on to accept the idea that some of these concrete acts are complex and have simpler acts as parts. The act of tying my shoes this morning had as its parts the act of tying my right shoe and the act of tying my left shoe.

Castañeda discovered that traditional forms of act utilitarianism run counter to deep-seated moral intuitions about the normative status of complex acts and their parts. Suppose that the act of tying my shoes this morning had higher utility than any time-identical alternative. Nothing else I could have done during the same time period would have produced better results. Then act utilitarianism of traditional forms concludes that it was *obligatory*.

A deep-seated moral intuition tells us that if it was obligatory for me to perform the act of tying my shoes this morning, and if tying my left shoe is "half" of this act, then it was obligatory for me to perform the act of tying my left shoe this morning. But (and this is Castañeda's insight) there is no guarantee that the act of tying my left shoe had higher utility than its time-identical alternatives. It is possible that there was something better for me to do *at that moment*. Thus, tying my left shoe might not have been obligatory according to act utilitarianism. It might have been *forbidden* on typical formulations of that view in spite of the fact that it is part of a larger act that is obligatory on the same standard.

Once we recognize this point, we see similar cases everywhere. One important type involves *prerequisites*. In many cases, it is impossible to do a marvelously good thing without first taking some preliminary steps – the heart surgeon must crack a few ribs before he can repair the blocked artery in the heart. In many cases, such prerequisites have no good consequences of their own. They do not cause, or produce, or lead to anything of value. So, in many cases, they are forbidden on traditional formulations of act utilitarianism. Yet even the most hard-core utilitarian would recognize that such acts ought to have some sort of utilitarian justification.

In "World Utilitarianism" I formulate a theory that detaches the normative status of acts from their (individual) utilities. This is the first significant novelty of my view. An act may be morally obligatory no matter what its utility – even if there are time-identical alternatives that would produce much better results. What counts on this theory is that the act is part of the best life available to the agent. Intuitively, the idea is that what you ought to do as of a time is what you do in the best life then open to you; if you live the rest of your life in the best still possible way, you will do it. Parts of this life may be worse than time-identical parts of other lives that are, on the whole, less good.

The second significant novelty of my view is that all normative concepts are *time-relativized* on the proposed theory. Traditional forms of act utilitarianism purport to give necessary and sufficient conditions for an act's moral rightness. But as I show in the essay, a given act's normative status may change through time. On Monday, the act of *being in Bangor on Friday* may be morally right; on Thursday the same act may no longer be morally right. Indeed, on Thursday the same act may no longer be one of my options!

In "World Utilitarianism" I say that I have formulated a theory of "tensed" rightness. I think that is a mistake. Tenses play no role in the theory. (I say nothing about "was right," "is right," "will be right," "will have been right," and so on.) The appropriate term is "time-relativized." According to the theory, each normative concept is a relation among a person, a possible concrete act, and a time. A given act may have different normative statuses for the same person at different times.

One central feature of "World Utilitarianism" now seems wrong to me. I no longer accept an ontology of "possible concrete acts." I think all talk of "acts" can be replaced by more tractable talk of states of affairs.

18

Hence, I no longer believe that "possible concrete acts" are the fundamental bearers of normative status. Instead, I think that we should say that a person has a moral obligation, as of a time, to "see to the occurrence of" a state of affairs at a time.

I present a more up-to-date formulation of world utilitarianism in Section 5 of "On the Consistency of Act- and Motive-Utilitarianism," which is Essay 4 in this volume. For a much more detailed discussion, the interested reader is invited to consult the relevant passages of *Doing the Best We Can: An Essay in Informal Deontic Logic.*

1

World utilitarianism

Act utilitarianism, in some of its more popular forms, is often taken to be a perfectly straightforward doctrine. Critics of the doctrine frequently claim that, in certain cases at least, act utilitarianism is *morally* wrong. It is said that act utilitarianism implies that a certain act would be right in certain circumstances, but the considered, impartial judgment of reasonable moralists is that the act would not be right. Thus it is assumed that act utilitarianism has clearcut consequences, and it is alleged that some of these consequences are morally objectionable.

During the last ten years or so, more and more philosophers have been coming to believe that the situation is far worse than such criticism would suggest. They have come to believe that act utilitarianism, in these popular forms, suffers from a kind of formal incoherence. Arguments have been presented that apparently show that such principles can be made to generate inconsistent moral judgments, as well as judgments that conflict with principles that seem destined for a place in any acceptable deontic logic. Until these formal problems have been solved, it seems to me, moral criticism of act utilitarianism may be premature.

In this paper, I first present a fairly typical act utilitarian principle. Then I describe a variety of related formal objections that have been raised against it. I next introduce what I take to be a novel form of utilitarianism – world utilitarianism. I try to show that this form of utilitarianism succeeds in avoiding the formal objections that weigh so heavily against act utilitarianism. I proceed to try to develop world utilitarianism in greater detail. I conclude with a brief discussion of some possible objections to the view proposed.

I

As my 'fairly typical' act utilitarian principle, I shall take:

(AU) An act is right if and only if its utility is at least as great as that of any of its alternatives.

Associated with (AU) are the doctrines that an act is wrong if and only if it is not right; and that an act is obligatory if and only if it would be wrong to fail to do it.

As I see it, the main sources of unclarity in a principle such as (AU) are in the concepts expressed by 'act', 'utility', and 'alternative'. Let us consider these in turn.

We can draw a broad distinction between 'generic acts' and 'concrete acts'. Generic acts are kinds of action – such things as walking, stealing from the rich, and giving to the poor. These can be done over and over again, and are perhaps best thought of as properties, or perhaps as relations between people and times. Concrete acts are particular, dated, non-repeatable individuals such as the walk I took yesterday afternoon, the robbery committed last night in Amherst, and my wife's writing a check at noon today. (AU) is best construed as a theory about such concrete acts.

The utility of an act is the difference between the total amount of intrinsic good it would produce and the total amount of intrinsic evil it would produce.

Historically, utilitarianism has been associated with the idea that the only intrinsic good is pleasure and the only intrinsic evil is pain. We can make use of this historical association in the development of a sample utility calculus. First, we must assume that every episode of pleasure can be evaluated on three scales. One scale would measure the intensity of the pleasure, another would measure the duration of the pleasure, and the last would measure the 'quality' of the pleasure. On the basis of these measurements, three numbers will be assigned to the episode of pleasure. The product of these would be the 'hedonic value' of the episode.

Next we would have to find the sum of the hedonic values of all the non-overlapping episodes of pleasure that would be produced by the act. This sum would be the 'gross hedonic utility' of the act.

The 'doloric utility' of the act would be the sum of the doloric values of all the non-overlapping episodes of pain that would be produced by the act. The doloric value of each such episode would be the product of the episode's intensity, duration, and quality. If we subtract the doloric utility of the act from the gross hedonic utility of the act, the result is the 'net hedonic utility' of the act. Some hedonists may want to say that the utility of an act is the same as what I call its net hedonic utility. Nonhedonists, of course, will prefer to measure utility in some other way. Indeed, even some hedonists may have objections to this way of calculating utility. I offer it here primarily as an example.

However, whatever concept of utility we select, it should turn out that the utility of an act is a number, and that better acts have higher numbers. I will use 'U(a)' as an abbreviation for 'the utility of the act, a'.

The concept of alternatives has not received as much attention as it deserves. To my knowledge, the most carefully developed concept of alternatives is one proposed by Lars Bergström.[1] His proposal is that we first define the concept of the alternative set roughly as follows: a set, K, of possible concrete acts is an alternative set if and only if there is a person, S, and a time, t, such that (i) each member of K is such that, if it were performed, it would be performed by S; (ii) each member of K is such that, if it were performed, it would be performed at or during t; (iii) each member of K is such that S is able to perform it; (iv) it is not the case that there are any two members of K such that S is able to perform both of them together; and (v) it is not the case that S is able to avoid performing all the members of K.[2]

Now we can say that an act, a, is an alternative to an act, b, if and only if there is an alternative set, K, such that a is a member of K and b is a member of K. 'Aa, b' is a convenient abbreviation for 'a is an alternative to b'.

Making use of the notation suggested above, we can reformulate (AU) as:

(AU') Ra iff (b) (Aa, b ⊃ U(a) ≥ U(b)).

Associated with (AU') are the standard principles about wrongness and obligatoriness.

II

As I mentioned at the outset, we can distinguish between moral criticism, on the one hand, and formal criticism, on the other. I want next to consider three important and closely related formal criticisms of (AU').

(i) In an extremely provocative paper,[3] Hector-Neri Castañeda argued

---

1. See [2] and [5].
2. This account is not entirely unproblematic. For one thing, it is not clear *when* the agent is supposed to have the ability to perform the acts in the set. For another, it is not clear that alternatives have to be time-identical.
3. See [7].

quite effectively against the principle about obligatoriness associated with (AU'). If we abstract from his formulation, disregarding certain features that may not be relevant to our present concerns, then his argument becomes something like this: consider the following utilitarian principle, in which 'O*a*' abbreviates '*a* is obligatory':

(AU") O*a* iff (*b*) (A*a*, *b* ⊃ U(*a*) > U(*b*)).

It seems clear that if a person is obligated to perform a complex act composed of two parts, then he is obligated to perform each of the parts:

(DC) If O($a + b$), then O*a*.

Suppose, next, that some complex act ($a + b$), is obligatory for some person, S. (DC) implies that since ($a + b$) is obligatory, so is *a*. If these acts are alternatives, then we face the anomalous result, via two applications of (AU"), that U($a + b$) is both greater than and less than U(*a*). Obviously, something has gone wrong.

Some may feel uneasy about the introduction of conjunctive acts in Castañeda's argument. It seems to me, however, that there is no genuine basis for objection here. Most of the things we do are, in a fairly straightforward sense, complex. My act of tying my shoes this morning was composed of my act of tying my left shoe this morning, and my act of tying my right shoe this morning. Your act of reading this paper, similarly, is composed of your act of reading the first sentence, your act of reading the second sentence, etc.

Perhaps we would go too far if we said that for any acts, *a* and *b*, there is a complex act ($a + b$). Yet in many cases, several acts do seem to go together to form a complex act. When *a* and *b* do go together in this way as parts of some more complex act, then we can speak of the conjunctive act ($a + b$). So far as I can tell, all this talk of conjunctive acts can be avoided, if we like, in favor of perfectly unobjectionable, if somewhat vague, talk about 'complex acts' and their 'parts'. The fact that it relies on the concept of conjunctive acts, therefore, does not detract from the impact of Castañeda's argument.[4]

Castañeda's argument is not, however, entirely satisfactory. As Castañeda has pointed out,[5] the argument apparently assumes some concept of alternatives according to which alternatives need not be incompatible. Otherwise, *a* could not be an alternative to ($a + b$). Clause (iv) of the

4. For another point of view on this question see [16].
5. See [8], p. 258.

23

definition of alternative set presented above rules out this possibility. Perhaps the fact that it does rule out this sort of case provides some of the motivation for the adoption of that condition.

(ii) However, Castañeda's argument can easily be modified so as to reveal a genuine and deep-seated defect of (AU'). The argument goes as follows: suppose that at some time, t, an agent, S, has open to him an alternative set consisting of just a and b. Suppose that, of these, a has the higher utility. According to (AU'), it would seem that a is right and b is wrong. Next we must suppose that right after he does whichever of a and b he selects, S will face a new alternative set consisting of just c and d. Suppose further that whether S chooses to do a or b, he will in fact be choosing the first half of a complex act whose second part will have to be either c or d. Now consider the following set: $\{(a + c), (a + d), (b + c), (b + d)\}$. The complex acts in this set are (i) agent identical; (ii) time identical; (iii) performable; (iv) exclusive; and (v) exhaustive. Hence, this set constitutes an alternative set in the sense indicated above.

Furthermore, it apparently may be the case that, for example, $(b + d)$ is the best choice from this set − it may have higher utility than any of the other members. In this case, (AU') implies that $(b + d)$ is right. It follows by a principle similar to (DC) that b must be right, too. But we have already seen that b is not right. The upshot is that there may be many alternative sets available to an agent at a time, and a rather poor choice from one such set may be part of the best choice from another. An elegant version of this argument has been developed by Bergström.[6]

It is important to notice that this puzzle does not rely on the idea that alternatives can be compatible. For the wrongness of b is established by comparing the utility of b to the utility of b's (incompatible) alternative. The rightness of $(b + d)$ is also established by comparing its utility to the utility of its (incompatible) alternatives. Thus, we cannot so easily dismiss this example by appeal to some alleged misuse of the notion of alternatives. It apparently does show that on (AU'), it may be right to do a certain act, but wrong to do any of its parts.

(iii) In 'The Inconsistency of Utilitarianism', Harold Zellner presented an interesting argument that may turn out to be essentially the same as the one just described.[7] Suppose that at some time, S has alternatives a and b available to him. Suppose that a has the higher utility of the two. Suppose also that if S performs a, then he won't be able to perform some

---

6. See [5], pp. 242–243.
7. See [17].

later act, d, that would be an enormous boon to mankind, far greater in utility than anything else S will ever be able to do. However, if S does b, the alternative with less utility, he will be able to do d. Surely, we want to say that since d is so good, S should be permitted to do b in order to get himself into a position from which d will be possible. Thus, b seems to be right, even though it is wrong according to (AU').[8]

III

To meet these problems I propose a new form of utilitarianism, which I call 'world utilitarianism', or 'WU'. The basic ideas behind WU are very simple, although their development may appear slightly complex. First, I assume that at every moment of moral choice, each agent has available to him a rather large supply of 'life histories,' each of which is a set of acts exactly coinciding with all he has already done, and the rest of which he is still able to perform. Early in life, each agent has an enormous supply of these life histories. Later on, after he has made a lot of moral choices, he will have 'bypassed' many of them. They are no longer open to him. When his life is over, there will only be one life history left for him – the one he has actually lived out. Secondly, I assume that for each such life history, there is a possible world such that what happens in that world is what would happen, if the agent were to live out the life history. Each such world is a 'life history world' for the agent at the time. Third, I assume that we can assign utilities to these possible worlds. I shall describe one method of doing this, even though several are possible. My proposal, then, is that an act is right for an agent at a time if and only if he performs that act in an optimific life history world then open to him. An act is obligatory for an agent at a time if and only if he performs that act in every optimific life history world then open to him. An act is wrong for an agent at a time if and only if he performs it in no optimific life history world then open to him.

Perhaps it will already be clear – in a rough and ready way – how this proposal is supposed to circumvent the problems mentioned above.

(i) If some conjunctive act, $(a + b)$, is obligatory for some agent at some time, then he performs it in every optimific life history world then open to him. It follows, of course, that he performs a in every such world,

8. Another argument along these lines has been developed by Prawitz and Bergström. It relies on Bergström's concept of 'version' and 'quasi-version'. A clear example of it appears in [6].

and so *a* is also obligatory for him according to WU. The fact that *a* has lower utility than (*a* + *b*) and than some of its alternatives is irrelevant on WU, since the obligatoriness of the act does not depend upon its utility vis-à-vis the utilities of its alternatives. The obligatoriness of an act at a time depends upon whether or not the act is performed in every optimific world then open to the agent. In cases such as the one Castañeda has described, we must say that if a conjunctive act is performed in every suitable world, then each of its conjuncts is performed in each of those worlds, too. Hence, a modified form of DC is validated by WU.

(ii) The second puzzle is solved in a similar fashion. First we should recognize that the fact that *a* has higher utility than its only alternative, *b*, does not imply either that *a* is right or that *b* is not right. Nor does the fact that (*b* + *d*) has higher utility than its alternatives imply anything about its normative status. To show that (*b* + *d*) is right on WU, we would have to show that the agent performs it in an optimific life history world currently open to him. If this is the case, then he must also perform *b* in such a world. Hence, the problem derived from Bergström does not arise on WU.

(iii) The Zellner puzzle does not pose any threat to WU, either. If *d*, the 'boon to mankind', is in fact right for S at t, and *b* is a necessary condition for *d*, then *b* is right for S at t, too. Surely, if S performs *d* in an optimific life history world currently open to him, and he cannot perform *d* without first performing *b*, then he does *b* there, too. Hence, *b* is performed in an optimific world, and is right, even though it does not produce very much utility.

In order to develop my exposition of WU, it will be necessary to indicate some assumptions I make, and some terminology I employ. First, I assume that there is a domain of possible 'concrete acts', or 'act tokens'. I indicate such acts by the letters '*a*', '*b*', '*c*', etc., as well as by the more complex expressions '(*a* + *b*)', etc. which indicates the complex act composed of *a* and *b*. I also assume that each such act, *a*, is associated with an agent and a time, indicated respectively by 'S(*a*)' and 't(*a*)'. S(*a*) is the one who would perform *a*, if it were performed; t(*a*) is the time at which *a* would be performed, if it were performed. For many acts, the time of performance will be an interval, rather than a point. In such cases, t(*a*) will be the whole interval during which *a* would be performed.

A complete elaboration and defence of these assumptions about acts would, of course, be desirable. However, it will not be undertaken in this paper.

I shall also make use of an undefined ability concept, expressed by 'S has it in his power at t to perform a at $t(a)$'. The meaning of this expression strikes me as being fairly intuitive. We say, for example, that since nothing has yet happened that would rule it out, I now have it in my power to plant my garden on June 1, 1975. There is, after all, a 'course of action' that I can embark upon, and every part of which I would be able to perform at its appointed time, that would terminate with my planting of my garden at that time. Thus it seems that it is now in my power to plant my garden then. If I should go camping in the Yukon in May, 1975, thus making it impossible for me to get to Massachusetts by June 1, then I would no longer have it in my power to plant my garden on June 1.

Perhaps I can elucidate the concept of 'having it in power', as well as the associated concept of action, by describing some principles about power and action. First, since actions are associated with agents and times, no one ever has it in his power to perform an act associated with an agent other than himself. I cannot perform your acts, and you cannot perform mine:

(1) For any agent, S, if $S \neq S(a)$, then for any time, t, it is not the case that S has it in his power at t to perform a at $t(a)$.

Similarly, no one ever has it in his power to perform an act at any time other than the time associated with the act:

(2) For any time, t, if $t \neq t(a)$, then, for any agent, S, it is not the case that S has it in his power at any time to perform a at t.

(2) does not mean that the time of 'having power' must be the same as the time of the act. It only means that the time of 'performing' must be the same as the time associated with the act.

If an agent 'bypasses' an act, then he forever loses his ability to perform it. Thus, if I don't plant my garden on June 1, 1975, I shall never thereafter have it in my power to perform the act of planting my garden on June 1, 1975. Of course, I may yet have some other garden-planting acts in my power.

(3) If S does not perform a at $t(a)$, then for any time, t', if t' is later than $t(a)$, then S does not have it in his power at t' to perform a at $t(a)$.

Any act that an agent actually does perform is one that he will always be able to perform:

(4) If S performs a at $t(a)$, then for any time t, if S exists at t, then S has it in his power at t to perform a at $t(a)$.

27

This does not mean, of course, that S is able to perform *a* again, or at any times other than t(*a*). But (4) does imply this: if S in fact performed *a* in the past, then S now has it in his power to have performed *a* then.

If some act is in someone's power at some time, then it always was in his power. For example, if I now have it in my power to plant peas on April 1, 1975, then I have always had it in my power to plant peas on April 1, 1975. Thus:

(5) If S has it in his power at t to perform *a* at t(*a*), then, for any time, t', if t' is earlier than t, and S exists at t', then S has it in his power at t' to perform *a* at t(*a*).

What (5) says, in effect, is that we cannot gain new powers. However, it does not follow that we cannot lose powers. From the fact that S has a power now, it does not follow that he will always have it, or even that he will have it right up to the time of the act. In other words, this principle is false:

(6) If S has it in his power at t to perform *a* at t(*a*), and t' is later than t but earlier than t(*a*), then S has it in his power at t' to perform *a* at t(*a*).

The trouble with (6) is that it conflicts with the fact that we often rule out certain later choices as a result of earlier ones. I am now able to plant my garden on June 1, 1975. If I choose to go camping in the Yukon in mid-May, 1975, I may not have that garden planting power on May 31, 1975.

Now let us consider some principles about conjunctive acts. Surely, if I now have it in my power to perform (*a* + *b*), then I now have it in my power to perform *a*, and I now have it in my power to perform *b*. This is *not* to say that I must have it in my power to perform *a* without *b*, or that I must have it in my power to perform *a* no matter what else I do. But it is to say:

(7) If S has it in his power at t to perform (*a* + *b*) at t(*a* + *b*), then S has it in his power at t to perform *a* at t(*a*).

The converse of (7) is unacceptable. That is, we should reject this principle:

(8) If S has it in his power at t to perform *a* at t(*a*), and S has it in his power at t to perform *b* at t(*b*), then S has it in his power at t to perform (*a* + *b*) at t(*a* + *b*).

(8) is extremely dubious. For one thing, the fact that there are such acts as *a* and *b* does not guarantee that there is such an act as (*a* + *b*). For

another, even if there is such an act, it might be impossible for S to perform it. For example, I am now able to perform the act of driving to New York City tonight, and I am now able to perform the act of driving to Bangor, Maine, tonight. But I cannot perform both.

Let us turn, next, to the concept of the 'life history'. The basic idea here is simple. At any given moment during his life, a person has it in his power to complete his life in a variety of different ways. For each such way of completing his life, there is a whole series of acts that he would perform if and only if he were to complete his life in that way. Each such series of acts represents one possible way of traversing the time between the present and the time of death.

It would not be correct to say that a life history for a person at a time is just the set of all and only the acts that are in his power at the time. The problem here is that the various possible ways of completing a life will be incompatible. In one life history, I go to the Yukon in May of 1975. In another, I stay in Massachusetts to work on my compost pile during May of 1975. In no life history will I do both. Yet if we said that a life history contains all acts currently in my power, we would have to say that some life history for me now contains both.

But every act in any life history must be one the agent is still able to perform. To say this alone would not, of course, be sufficient. One or two acts do not constitute a life history. The set must be large enough to carry the agent through to the end of his life.

Perhaps we can capture the relevant concept in the following way. Let us say that an agent 'lives out' a set of acts, provided that he performs every member of that set. Now we can say that a life history for an agent at a time is a set of acts such that the agent has it in his power at the time to live out the set, but, if we add any other act to the set, then the agent will no longer be able to live it out:

(LH) K is a life history for S at t = df. (i) S has it in his power at t to live out K; and (ii) for any act, *a*, if *a* is not a member of K, then S does not have it in his power at t to live out the union of K and *a*

So, if K is a life history for me now, then K contains every act that I have already performed, and a lot of acts that I still can perform. Furthermore, while I can perform all of the acts in K, K is sufficiently large that no other act could be added to it without making it impossible for me to live it out. Thus, K is a history that is both 'maximal' and 'possible'.

Next, we need the concept of the 'life history world'. I assume that for every person, S, time, t, and life history, K, then available to him, there is exactly one possible world that is the one that would exist if S were to live out K. Everything that happens in that world is something that would happen if S were to live out K. Some of the things that happen in that world are, in some sense, 'consequences' of S's behavior there. Others are not. They are things that happen there anyway, independent of S's behavior. But from our point of view here in the real world, it is correct to say that what happens there is what would happen if S were to live out K. Any world that satisfies this condition is a 'life history world for S at t':

(LHW) w is a life history world for S at t = df. there is a set, K, such that K is a life history for S at t, and, for any event, e, e occurs in w if and only if, if S were to live out K, then e would occur.

We must not assume that at every moment of his life, an agent has open to him the same life history worlds that were open to him before. In fact, with every decision, we shed life history worlds. For example, a young person may now have open to him an indefinitely large supply of life history worlds in every one of which he becomes a doctor, and an indefinitely large supply of life history worlds in every one of which he becomes a lawyer. Once he decides to enter law school, however, he may no longer have any medical life histories open to him. And once he begins to specialize in corporate tax law, he may no longer have any life history worlds in which he becomes a criminal lawyer.

Each life history world available to a person at a time can be assigned a utility. There are many different ways in which this might be done, and I do not in fact have any favorite among them. I shall sketch a relatively simple one primarily to provide an example. Let us assume again that pleasure is the only intrinsic good, and that pain is the only intrinsic evil. Furthermore, let us assume that every episode of pleasure or pain can be split up into units of minimal duration, and that for each such unit, we can assign a number representing the quality and the intensity of the pleasure or pain. I prefer to consider pleasure episodes of minimal duration so as to avoid certain problems that might arise if pleasure episodes were allowed to overlap temporally. This is an assumption that may be dubious, but it is designed primarily to facilitate the illustration of a possible utility measure. The hedonic value of each minimal pleasure episode is the product of its intensity and quality. The gross hedonic value of a possible world is the sum of the hedonic values of all the nonoverlapping minimal episodes of pleasure that occur there.

The doloric value of a possible world, similarly, is the sum of the doloric values of all the non-overlapping minimal episodes of pain that occur there. The net hedonic value of a possible world is the difference between its gross hedonic value and its doloric value. The suggestion, then, is that the utility of a world, w, or $U(w)$, is the same as the net hedonic value of w.

A life history world for a person at a time is said to be an 'optimific life history world' for him then, if and only if there is no other life history world for him then that has a higher utility:

(OLHW) w is an optimific life history world for S at t =df. w is a life history world for S at t, and, for any world, w', if w' is a life history world for S at t, then $U(w) \geqslant U(w')$

It should perhaps be noted that a world may fail to be an optimific life history world for a certain person at one time, and yet may become an optimific world for him later. If, for example, I fail to do what is right for me to do on several occasions, then I may find that the world that is now the best life history world for me is one that formerly was fairly far down on the list. For it may happen that, as a result of these injudicious choices, every preferable world is now no longer a life history world for me. Such worlds, having been bypassed, are no longer in contention for the rank of optimific life history world.

The main thesis of WU can now be stated:

(WU)   It is right at t for S to perform a at t(a) if and only if there is a world, w, such that w is an optimific life history world for S at t, and S performs a at t(a) in w.

Associated with WU are the principles that an act is wrong for an agent at a time if and only if he performs it in no optimific life history world then open to him; and an act is obligatory for an agent at a time if and only if he performs it in every optimific life history world then open to him.

There are a number of features of WU that should be emphasized. First, WU is a proposed criterion of *tensed* rightness. A certain act that would be performed next year may be right for me now, but may not be right for me next week. In assuming that normative concepts are tensed in this way, I depart from some traditional utilitarians. Moore, for example, said with respect to Brutus's murdering of Caesar, that if

... this action of his was right then, it must be equally true now, and will always be true, that this particular action of Brutus's was right, and it never

31

can have been and never will be true that it was wrong. . . . If it was once true that it was right, then it must always be true that it was right.[9]

Moore's assertion may seem plausible, but I think that certain considerations weigh heavily against it. Lennart Åqvist has claimed, for example, that a version of the "contrary to duty imperatives" puzzle can be solved by the use of the notion of tensed obligatoriness. His example is somewhat complicated.[10] The following case, based on his, should serve to illustrate the point. Suppose a patient is ill, and that his doctor can choose between two main courses of treatment. He can either give the patient medicine A today, and then give him medicine A again tomorrow, or he can give him medicine B today and again tomorrow. Suppose the course of treatment with B would cure the patient, but would produce some unpleasant side effects, while the course of treatment with A would cure the patient without any side effects. Suppose, finally, that mixing the treatments would be fatal to the patient, a delightful person who spreads cheer wherever he goes. In this case, let us agree, prior to the time at which he gives any medicine, it is right for the doctor to give A on the first day, and it is right for the doctor to give A on the second day.

Suppose, however, that the doctor fails to do what is best. For whatever reason, he gives the patient B on the first day. It seems clear that it is no longer right for him to give A on the second day – that would kill the patient. Once the doctor has failed to do his duty, and has given B on the first day, the rights and wrongs of the case seem to change.

In the context of WU, this example would be described as follows. Prior to the time at which he gives any medicine, the doctor gives A on both days in the best life history world then open to him. As soon as he gives B, the world in which he gives A on both days ceases being a life history world for him. Thus, what's right for him then is what he does in the best remaining life history world. That, clearly, would be a world in which he gives B on the second day. For every remaining life history world in which he gives A on the second day is a world in which he kills the patient.[11]

9. See [10], p. 51.
10. See [1]. The view discussed in Section 5 of [1] is similar to WU.
11. Defining the tenselessly wrong in terms of the tensed wrong is not easy. Three plausible, but defective, definitions are: a is wrong $=$ df. (t) (t is earlier than $t(a) \supset$ it is wrong for $S(a)$ at t to perform a at $t(a)$); a is wrong $=$ df. (Et) (t is earlier than $t(a) \supset$ it is wrong for $S(a)$ at t to perform a at $t(a)$); a is wrong $=$ df. (t) (t is earlier than $t(a)$ & S has it in his power at t to refrain from performing a at $t(a) \supset$ it is wrong for S at t to perform a at $t(a)$).

The trouble with the first definition is that it makes many very bad actions non-

IV

Let us turn, now, from exposition to evaluation. It seems to me that WU is open, or may appear to be open, to three main objections.

(i) First of all, I think it can be shown that, according to WU, all past actions are now obligatory for their agents. Thus, if S performed some nasty deed, *a*, yesterday, then it is now obligatory for S to have performed *a* then. This follows from the fact that *a* is performed in every life history world for S today. Hence it must be performed in every optimific life history world for S today.

This consequence of WU does not please me, but it does not show WU to be totally unacceptable, either. For we are free to say that *a*, which is obligatory for S now, was wrong at virtually every time prior to t(*a*). That is, right up to the time at which *a* became 'inevitable' for S, it was wrong for S to perform *a* at t(*a*). Perhaps this suggests that in some yet to be defined sense, *a* is tenselessly wrong.

Furthermore, even though all past deeds are now obligatory, their agents may still merit punishment and blame for having performed them. After all, WU is a form of utilitarianism, and is naturally associated with a utilitarian theory of punishment. Thus, if I did some bad deed yesterday, and punishment would be worthwhile, then it may be obligatory for you to punish me today, even though what I did yesterday is now obligatory for me.

(ii) A second objection to WU is that it is virtually impossible for anyone to make use of this theory in an attempt to figure out what he ought to do. We have very little information about all these possible worlds, and their relative utilities. Hence, it might be said that WU is useless.

It seems to me that this objection is misguided. WU is not intended

---

wrong. For we may want to say that an action is wrong even though the agent did something before it that made it inevitable. Hence, there will be times prior to the performance of the action at which the action, nasty though it may be, nevertheless is done in every optimific life history world for the agent. The trouble with the second definition is that it makes just about everything we do wrong, unless we are living out the best life history that has ever been open to us. That's asking too much. The third definition is much more plausible, but I think it may be open to the following objection: Suppose S has it in his power to perform either of two utterly atrocious acts, or else a very good one. Suppose he rules out the good one, and then does the better of the two atrocious ones. We may want to say that what he did was wrong. But since the better of the two atrocious acts was, for a little while, the best choice open to him, it wasn't wrong at every time at which it could be avoided. Hence, we have to say that it wasn't wrong. But I think it was.

to serve as a practical guide to action, or as a moral advisor. It is intended to serve as an account of the connections between the deontic concepts of rightness, wrongness, and obligatoriness, on the one hand, and the concepts of intrinsic good and evil, on the other. Failure to serve as a practical guide in no way detracts from WU's ability to explicate these connections.

(iii) Finally, I want to acknowledge that I think WU is open to serious moral objections – it takes no account of fairness or justice; it provides no explanation of the obligatoriness of certain non-optimific, but 'practice-bound' acts, such as the keeping of promises; and it does not validate certain deep-seated views about the morality of punishment. Thus, it might be objected that there is no point in presenting the theory, since it is known to be false.

I believe there may be some good reason to formulate WU, even though it is morally unacceptable. One such reason is this: Act utilitarianism is a historically important, profoundly attractive doctrine. It undoubtedly deserves our close and careful attention. Yet, in the past, it has never been formulated in such a way as to be free of serious non-moral defects. Among these defects are the ones I have tried to avoid in my formulation of WU. If I have succeeded, then perhaps we have taken a step toward providing a coherent version of an important and plausible moral doctrine. That, perhaps, is sufficient.

But it also seems to me that, with certain modifications, WU might turn out to be morally acceptable. What I have in mind, primarily, are modifications to the utility measure for possible worlds. If there were some way to assign higher utilities to worlds in which justice reigns, and promises are kept, then at least some of the objections to WU could be answered. But that's a job for another occasion.

BIBLIOGRAPHY

[1] Åqvist, Lennart, 'Improved Formulations of Act Utilitarianism', *Noûs* **3** (1969), 299–323.
[2] Bergström, Lars, *The Alternatives and Consequences of Actions*, Stockholm, 1966.
[3] Bergström, Lars, 'Alternatives and Utilitarianism', *Theoria* **34** (1968), 163–170.
[4] Bergström, Lars, 'Utilitarianism and Deontic Logic', *Analysis* **29** (1968), 43–44.
[5] Bergström, Lars, 'Utilitarianism and Alternative Actions', *Noûs* **5** (1971), 237–252.

[6] Bergström, Lars, 'On the Formulation and Application of Utilitarianism', *Noûs*, **16** (1976), 121–144.

[7] Castañeda, Hector-Neri, 'A Problem for Utilitarianism', *Analysis* **33** (1973), 141–142.

[8] Castañeda, Hector-Neri, 'Ought, Value, and Utilitarianism', *American Philosophical Quarterly* **6** (1969), 257–275.

[9] Castañeda, Hector-Neri, 'On the Problem of Formulating a Coherent Act Utilitarianism', *Analysis* **32** (1972), 118–124.

[10] Moore, G. E., *Ethics*, London, 1912.

[11] Moore, G. E., *Principia Ethica*, Cambridge, 1962.

[12] Prawitz, Dag, 'A Discussion Note on Utilitarianism', *Theoria* **34** (1968), 76–84.

[13] Prawitz, Dag, 'The Alternatives to an Action', *Theoria* **36** (1970), 116–126.

[14] Sobel, Howard, 'Utilitarianisms: Simple and General', *Inquiry* **13** (1970), 394–449.

[15] Sobel, Howard, 'Value, Alternatives, and Utilitarianism', *Noûs* **4** (1971), 373–384.

[16] Westphal, Fred, 'Utilitarianism and Conjunctive Acts', *Analysis* **32** (1972), 82–85.

[17] Zellner, Harold, 'The Inconsistency of Utilitarianism', read at Eastern Division Meetings of American Philosophical Association, December, 1972.

[18] Zellner, Harold, 'Utilitarianism and Derived Obligation', *Analysis* **32** (1972), 124–125.

Essay 2

On the extensional equivalence of simple and general utilitarianism

INTRODUCTORY COMMENTS

Traditional forms of act utilitarianism were subjected to a variety of moral objections. Among these, two of the most important concerned examples involving promises and punishment. Objectors pointed out that if act utilitarianism were true, then it would be morally permissible to break a solemn promise whenever doing so would have even a tiny bit more utility than doing otherwise. They also pointed out that if act utilitarianism were true, then it would be morally permissible to punish an innocent victim whenever doing so would maximize utility. Particularly lurid and counterintuitive examples blossomed in the literature. These results were deeply disturbing.

Some utilitarians were moved by objections such as these to abandon act utilitarianism in favor of rule utilitarianism. They suggested that we go wrong in focusing on the utilities of individual acts and their individual alternatives. Instead, we should focus on the results of *general* or *universal* performance of acts relevantly like the ones in the original alternative set.

It was claimed that morally permissible acts are ones that have something like this feature: General performance of acts relevantly like them would have higher utility than general performance of acts relevantly like their alternatives. Such views were classified as forms of rule utilitarianism. Their advocates (including such luminaries as John Rawls in "Two Concepts of Rules") claimed that these theories did not have the same offensive results as act utilitarianism. These theories allegedly implied that it would be wrong to break a promise even if it happened to have high utility; that it would be wrong to punish an innocent man, even in the odd case where it would be for the best.

Many forms of rule utilitarianism were proposed. Many of them were interesting but at bottom elusive. Some, such as the one sketched by J. O. Urmson in "On the Interpretation of the Moral Philosophy of J. S. Mill," were obviously and hopelessly confused. (For a much more exten-

36

sive discussion of some forms of rule utilitarianism, see Chapter Five of my *Introductory Ethics*.)

In his *Forms and Limits of Utilitarianism*, David Lyons introduced new clarity and rigor into the literature on this controversy in utilitarianism. The book established a new standard for clear thinking on its topics. Perhaps the most exciting line of argument in the book is devoted to showing that if the objections reveal something wrong with act utilitarianism, then they reveal something wrong with rule utilitarianism, too. This because corresponding forms of act and rule utilitarianism are "extensionally equivalent" – they have exactly the same normative implications.

In Essay 2, I try to show that Lyons's argument fails. The fundamental problem is that there are two factors that influence the generalized utility of an act. One is the amount of utility that would be produced by each relevantly similar act. The other is the number of such relevantly similar acts that would be performed if everyone did the same. Lyons thought that for any set of alternatives, the second number would be a constant. But I think he was mistaken. As a result, a given act might have a very high generalized utility not because each relevantly similar act has high utility, but because there are many relevantly similar acts. "If everyone did the same, *very many* would do the same."

In the essay, I devote a lot of effort to showing that Lyons's argument for extensional equivalence fails. In the final paragraph I hint at a deeper point: At least some forms of rule utilitarianism make the normative status of individual acts turn on a completely irrelevant factor. That factor is the number of others in a position to perform relevantly similar acts. Where this number is sufficiently high, the generalized utility of the act becomes correspondingly high. But no reasonable person would think that this has any bearing on the question of whether the original act is morally right.

Perhaps if I were to write this essay again from scratch, I would place greater emphasis on this latter point. It now seems more important than the criticism of Lyons's argument. Rule utilitarianism of the sort discussed by Lyons seems to me to be a moral monstrosity. It makes the normative status of my alternatives depend in part upon how many others, for each of the alternatives, can do likewise. If advocates of the theory had only reflected carefully on this feature prior to publication, the theory would never have seen the light of day.

2

On the extensional equivalence of simple and general utilitarianism

In *Forms and Limits of Utilitarianism* (Oxford: 1965), David Lyons presents an impressive defense of the thesis that each form of simple utilitarianism is "extensionally equivalent" to its general utilitarian analogue. An act is judged to be right on a simple principle if and only if it is judged to be right on the corresponding general principle. Lyons' thesis implies that each version of generalized utilitarianism has exactly the same merits and defects as the version of simple utilitarianism it is meant to replace.

While I feel that something like Lyons' view may ultimately turn out to be correct, I also believe that important parts of his argument are defective. One relatively minor problem arises in the defense of the claim that "non-comparative" principles are extensionally equivalent. Another, more serious, problem arises in connection with the claim that the same is true of "comparative" principles. In order to discuss these parts of Lyons' argument, it will be necessary to explain some technical terms, and review some of the background.

I

The "simple utility" of an act, *a*, is the total net utility that would result if *a* were performed. We can use *"S(a)"* to abbreviate 'the simple utility of *a*'. The "generalized utility" of an act, *a*, is the total net utility that would result if all acts relevantly similar to *a* that can be performed, were performed. We can use *"G(a)"* to express this value.

Without a clear concept of "relevant similarity" the notion of generalized utility is rather empty. Lyons devotes considerable attention to the problem of developing an account of "relevant similarity". First, let us say that a property is *teleologically significant* if and only if acts having it produce utility or disutility in virtue of the fact that they have it. Now we can say that, for purposes of utilitarian generalization, acts are *relevantly similar* if and only if they have exactly the same teleologically significant properties. Furthermore, we can say that a *general utilitarian description* of an act is one that contains mention of all and only teleologically significant properties of the act. Thus, relevantly similar acts will have the same general utilitarian description.

A utilitarian principle is "comparative" if it assesses the value of each act by comparing its utility (simple or general) with the utility (simple or general) of its alternatives. "Non-comparative" principles lack this feature. Thus, we can formulate a pair of non-comparative principles, one simple and one general:

(S_2) An act, a, is right iff $S(a)$ is positive.
(G_1) An act, a, is right iff $G(a)$ is positive.

Now some comparative principles:

(S_2) An act, a, is right iff (x) (if x is an alternative to a, then $S(x)$ does not exceed $S(a)$).
(G_2) An act, a, is right iff (x) (if x is an alternative to a, then $G(x)$ does not exceed $G(a)$).

II

Lyons presents an extensive, subtle argument for the conclusion that analogous non-comparative principles are extensionally equivalent. He argues, in effect, that since acts are relevantly similar only if they have the same teleologically significant properties, and since acts produce utilities and disutilities in virtue of their teleologically significant properties, relevantly similar acts must produce the same utility or disutility. In other words, if an act, a, is relevantly similar to an act, b, then $S(a) = S(b)$.

We can use "$n(a)$" to indicate the number of such acts that would be performed if all acts relevantly similar to a that can be performed, were performed. Lyons argues that since each act relevantly similar to a has the same simple utility as a, it follows that $G(a)$ is equal to $S(a)$ times $n(a)$. Lyons puts this point by saying that "linearity obtains" or that the G/S relation is linear.

Since $n(a)$ has to be positive, $G(a)$ is positive if and only if $S(a)$ is positive, negative if and only if $S(a)$ is negative, and zero if and only if $S(a)$ is zero. In light of this, Lyons claims that "linearity entails that there is no qualitative difference between the generalized and the simple utilities of given acts" (p. 115). From this it follows that an act is right on (S_1) if and only if it is right on (G_1). Lyons concludes that "all analogous non-comparative principles are extensionally equivalent" (p. 115).

III

Now, perhaps, we are in a position to discuss the first difficulty for Lyons' thesis. Lyons has presented an argument to show that (S_1) and (G_2) are extensionally equivalent. But his claim is somewhat stronger. He claims to have shown that *every* non-comparative simple principle is extensionally equivalent to its general analogue. I believe that there are some exceptions to this stronger claim.

We can formulate a pair of principles based on the idea that there is a certain amount of utility, call it K, such that an act is right if and only if its utility exceeds K. Perhaps K is the amount of utility that would be produced by staying in bed or by tending your own garden. The actual value of K is irrelevant, so long as it is a positive constant. Now consider:

(S_3) An act, a, is right iff $S(a)$ exceeds K.
(G_3) An act, a, is right iff $G(a)$ exceeds K.

These principles are alike in every respect except that where (S_3) refers to simple utility, (G_3) refers to generalized utility. Furthermore, no mention is made in either about the utilities of alternatives. Therefore, (S_3) seems to be the non-comparative, simple utilitarian analogue of the non-comparative, general utilitarian principle, (G_3).

If (S_3) and (G_3) are analogous non-comparative principles, they constitute a counterexample to Lyons' claim. For surely there can be an act, a, such that $S(a)$ does not exceed K, but $G(a)$ does. All that is required is that $n(a)$ be large enough to make the product of $S(a)$ and $n(a)$ exceed K. If a is performed, only a little utility will be produced – far less than K. But if all acts relevantly similar to a that can be performed, are performed, then quite a lot of utility will be produced – far more than K. Thus, (S_3), together with the imagined facts, entails that a is not right, while (G_3), together with the same imagined facts, entails that a is right. Clearly, (S_3) is not extensionally equivalent to (G_3).

One way to deal with this problem would be to develop a somewhat more precise account of what it means to say that utilitarian principles are "analogues". On such an analysis, (G_3) might not be the analogue of (S_3). The development of such an analysis is, obviously, of considerable interest even apart from its impact on this, rather minor, difficulty.

40

Lyons also claims that analogous comparative principles are extensionally equivalent. Here, it seems to me, problems of a more serious kind arise. Let us consider, as our pair of comparative principles:

(S_2) An act, a, is right iff (x) (if x is an alternative to a, then $S(x)$ does not exceed $S(a)$),

(G_2) An act, a, is right iff (x) (if x is an alternative to a, then $G(x)$ does not exceed $G(a)$).

The following is an example in which (S_2), together with certain purported facts, implies that a certain act is right, but (G_2), together with the same purported facts, implies that this act is not right.

Suppose a man is faced with three alternatives. He can give a bone to an Irish Wolfhound (call this act a_1); he can give the bone to a Cocker Spaniel (call this act a_2); or he can keep the bone for himself (call this act a_3). Suppose further that it is a law of nature that Irish Wolfhounds always get a considerable amount of pleasure from being given bones and that it is also a law of nature that Cocker Spaniels always get some pleasure, but not quite so much, from being given bones. Suppose further that pleasure is the only intrinsic good and that no other pleasures are relevant to the example. Apparently, the only teleologically significant property of a_1 is that it would be a case of giving a bone to an Irish Wolfhound, and the only teleologically significant property of a_2 is that it would be a case of giving a bone to a Cocker Spaniel. Since a_3 would produce no utility or disutility, it has no teleologically significant properties.

As the example has been stated, $S(a_1)$ exceeds $S(a_2)$ as well as $S(a_3)$. We are assuming that these are the only alternatives open at the time, and so (S_2) tells us that a_1 is the right act.

However, since there aren't very many Irish Wolfhounds, not very many people are in a position to give a bone to an Irish Wolfhound. In order to perform an act relevantly similar to a_1, one must perform an act that has the property of being a case of giving a bone to an Irish Wolfhound. Thus, not many people are in a position to perform acts relevantly similar to a_1. Therefore, $n(a_1)$, or the number of such acts that would be performed, if all acts relevantly similar to a_1 that can be performed, were performed, is rather low.

According to the linearity principle, which we are granting Lyons, $G(a_1)$ is the product of $S(a_1)$ and $n(a_1)$. Since $n(a_1)$ is so low, $G(a_1)$ is rather low, too. If everyone in a position to give a bone to an Irish Wolfhound were to do so, the total net utility thereby produced would be fairly low, even though each Wolfhound thus pleased would obtain considerable utility.

On the other hand, since there are so many Cocker Spaniels, many others are in a position to perform an act relevantly like a_2. If each were to do so, quite a lot of utility would be realized. In other words, since $n(a_2)$ is so high, $G(a_2)$ is very high even though $S(a_2)$ is not too high.

We can assign arbitrary, but properly related, numerical values to S, n, and G for each of the alternatives on the basis of this information:

act	S-value	n-value	G-value
a_1	10	2	20
a_2	5	5	25
a_3	0	—	0

Clearly, $G(a_2)$ exceeds $G(a_1)$. Thus, (G_2), together with the imagined facts, yields the conclusion that a_1 is not right – there is an alternative whose generalized utility exceeds the generalized utility of a_1. This is a case, then, in which the result yielded by (S_2) diverges from the result yielded by (G_2). So we seem to have a counterexample to Lyons' thesis.

But Lyons argues that cases such as this one cannot arise. In effect, he claims that if a_1, a_2, and a_3 were genuine alternatives, then their n-values would have to be the same. If the n-values are held constant, then the generalized utilities of the alternatives relate to each other in the same way as do the simple utilities.

Here is Lyons' argument for the conclusion that the n-values of gen-uine alternatives must be equal:

> I would argue that (the value of n) is a constant, in effect, in such cases. Notice that each of the acts, a_1, a_2 . . . , a_m, has a complete general utilitarian description, 'A_1', 'A_2', . . . 'A_m'. But it is an essential part of the circum-stances surrounding a_1, for example, that acts like a_2, . . . , a_m are open. The causally and teleologically significant features of the circumstances sur-rounding a_1 would be different if (some of) these alternatives were not open and others were. In other words, included (or implicit) in the description 'A_1' of a_1 is a reference to the *kinds* of alternatives open. The descriptions 'A_1', 'A_2', . . . , 'A_m' are *internally related*. From this it follows that, for any given set of n alternatives, the value of n for the several kinds of acts is the same when the acts are completely relevantly described. (p. 117)

Lyons' argument is a bit sketchy, but its main outlines seem to be as follows: if an act didn't have some of the alternatives it does in fact have, then the circumstances surrounding the act would have different teleologically significant properties. From this, Lyons infers that the property of having just the kinds of alternatives it in fact has is a teleologically significant property of each act. He puts this point by saying that the general utilitarian description of the act, the description that mentions all and only teleologically significant properties of the act, must contain reference to the kinds of alternatives open. Therefore, if two acts are relevantly similar, they must have the same kinds of alternatives.

Lyons presumably meant to continue, arguing perhaps in this way for the conclusion that alternatives cannot have different n-values. Suppose there are two acts, a_1 and a_2, such that the n-value of a_1 exceeds the n-value of a_2 even though a_1 and a_2 are alternatives. Then there must be some act, x, relevantly similar to a_1 but which would be performed by someone for whom at that time no act relevantly similar to a_2 is an alternative. In this case, a_1 would have the property of being performed by someone for whom an act like a_2 is open, but x would not have this property. But, as Lyons has already argued, such "alternative-properties" are teleologically significant and so must be had or lacked in common by a_1 and x, since they are assumed to be relevantly similar. Thus, a_1 and x cannot differ in this way. The assumption that a_1 and a_2 are alternatives with differing n-values thus leads to contradiction. Alternatives must have the same n-value.

The argument bears on our example in this way: we thought that the only teleologically significant property of a_1 was the property of being a case of giving a bone to an Irish Wolfhound. But Lyons would say that it is an "essential part of the circumstances surrounding" a_1 that there is also a Cocker Spaniel within bone-giving distance. This, too, is teleologically significant. Thus, for an act to be relevantly similar to a_1, it would have to have the property of being a case of giving a bone to an Irish Wolfhound when a Cocker Spaniel is also within bone-giving distance. Equally, a_2 has the teleologically significant property of being a case of giving a bone to a Cocker Spaniel when an Irish Wolfhound is also within bone-giving distance. Any act relevantly like a_2 would have to have this property in common with a_2.

Thus, if Lyons is right, we erred in thinking that $n(a_2)$ exceeds $n(a_1)$. In fact, since there are so few Irish Wolfhounds, very few people are in a position to give a bone to a Cocker Spaniel when an Irish Wolfhound is also within bone-giving distance. And this is what must be done, if an act relevantly similar to a_2 is to be performed. To be exact, the number of opportunities for giving a bone to a Cocker Spaniel when an Irish Wolfhound is also within bone-giving distance is equal to the number of opportunities for giving a bone to an Irish Wolfhound when a Cocker Spaniel is within bone-giving distance. In other words, $n(a_1) = n(a_2)$. Thus, the value of n in our example should have been held constant. If we had held n constant, (S_2) and (G_2) could not have yielded divergent results. Thus, Lyons would say, the counterexample fails to refute the thesis of extensional equivalence.

V

Lyons' argument for the equivalence of the n-values of alternatives is based, in large measure, on the thesis that alternative-properties are teleologically significant. While Lyons is surely right in suggesting that alternative properties are genuine properties of acts (cf. pp. 30–61), it seems to me that he is wrong in claiming that every such property is teleologically significant. In fact, I think we can show that some alternative properties are not teleologically significant. Consider an act that has a few alternatives, but produces no utility or disutility. Since this act has alternatives, it has alternative-properties. But since it produces no utility or disutility, it does not have any teleologically significant properties. Therefore, the alternative-properties had by this act are not teleologically significant.

Furthermore, even if we restrict ourselves to acts that do produce utility or disutility, there is no reason to suppose that all alternative-properties are teleologically significant. Recall that a teleologically significant property is one in virtue of which any act that has it produces utility or disutility. Obscure as this notion may be, it seems clear that in any standard case we would not want to say that an act that produces some utility or disutility produces it in virtue of the fact that the person who performed it could have done something else instead! In any standard case, an act that produces some utility or disutility would produce just that utility or disutility whether or not a certain alternative were open.

When we are interested in the *rightness* or *wrongness* of an act, we may want to consider what alternatives were open to the agent. Indeed, that is the basic point behind the comparative utilitarian principles. However, when we are interested in the *utility* or *disutility* produced by an act, we do not generally have to consider the alternatives. We only consider the causal consequences of the act, and the value or disvalue of these consequences. Thus, an act's rightness or wrongness may depend, in part, on its alternative-properties, but its utility or disutility, in general, does not.

Admittedly, there are some odd cases in which an act produces certain

44

utility or disutility because, among other things, it has certain alternatives (cf. pp. 59–60). In these odd cases, the relevant alternative-property may be teleologically significant. An example of such a case may be constructed as follows: suppose a certain Irish Wolfhound gets an extra measure of pleasure from being given a bone whenever the person who gives the bone could have given it to a Cocker Spaniel instead. Perhaps due to some bizarre psychological quirk, the Wolfhound is especially pleased whenever an act of bone-giving has the alternative-property: being performed by someone who could have given the bone to a Cocker Spaniel instead.

Suppose someone performs the act, a_4, of giving a bone to this Wolfhound, and suppose further that when he performed a_4 he could have given the bone to a nearby Cocker Spaniel instead. His act, a_4, has a rather complex teleologically significant property: being a case of giving a bone to a dog who enjoys being given bones by people who could have given those bones to Cocker Spaniels instead, and being performed by a person who could have given the bone to a Cocker Spaniel instead. It is reasonable to suppose that a_4 produces some of its utility in virtue of the fact that it has this, admittedly odd, property.

Clearly, however, it is not the case that *every* act involves some individual with a relevantly similar quirk. Surely most acts produce their utility or disutility in virtue of properties that have nothing to do with what alternatives are open. No general reason has been given to suppose that all, or even most, alternative-properties are teleologically significant. In the original example described above in Part IV, no such property is teleologically significant.

It appears, then, that the act, a_1, of giving the bone to the Irish Wolfhound produces utility purely in virtue of the fact that it is a case of giving a bone to an Irish Wolfhound. At any rate, there is no reason to suppose that this act would have produced different utility if some of its alternatives had not been open, and others had been. Its alternative-properties are not teleologically significant.

So it turns out that we can, after all, give a complete listing of the teleologically significant properties of an act without mentioning every one of its alternatives. Thus, Lyons' claim that the descriptions of alternatives are "internally related" is false. This being so, we must conclude that the n-values of alternatives may diverge as they appear to do in the example. The upshot is that analogous comparative principles can give divergent results.

In conclusion, I would like to point out one possible source of mis-

45

understanding. I have attempted to show that Lyons' argument for the equivalence of simple and general utilitarianism is defective. I have been concerned to defend the view that principles such as (S_2) and (G_2) can give divergent results. But I have not claimed that where these principles diverge, the generalized principles are always closer to the truth than the simple ones. I have not here attempted to defend any version of generalized utilitarianism. Indeed, it seems to me that the example described in Part IV provides strong reason for us to suspect that generalized principles make the rightness of an act depend upon an utterly irrelevant consideration – how many others are in a position to do something relevantly similar.

Essay 3

The principle of moral harmony

INTRODUCTORY COMMENTS

Since time immemorial, moral philosophers have been drawn to the idea that morality is justified by its social benefits. The idea surfaces in many forms. Some, for example, have suggested that a society's morality is a system of rules adopted by the society for the purpose of coordinating the behavior of the members; if the members obey the rules, the society as a whole will be best off. Such views are versions of the Principle of Moral Harmony, or "PMH." My aim in this essay is to show that such principles are false.

PMH has special relevance to utilitarianism because an advocate of act utilitarianism might appeal to PMH in an effort to justify act utilitarianism. The reasoning might go like this: If everyone in a group were to act in accord with the demands of act utilitarianism, the group would be best off. No other normative theory can in this way guarantee to maximize group benefits. In other words, act utilitarianism is the only normative theory that generates obligations sure to conform with PMH. Therefore, there is a reason to advocate and believe in act utilitarianism above all other normative theories.

However popular such thinking might be, I am convinced that it is deeply misguided. The greatest mistake, as I see it, is the assumption that a normative theory needs or could be given this sort of justification. But it would be hard to demonstrate that justification is impossible or unnecessary. In "The Principle of Moral Harmony" I establish a slightly less dramatic point: that any such attempted justification of act utilitarianism fails because act utilitarianism in fact does *not* generate obligations sure to conform with PMH.

Act utilitarian advocates of PMH may be guilty of something like the fallacy of composition. Suppose that we have a bunch of acts, $\{a^1, a^2, \ldots, a^n\}$; suppose that these are acts to be performed by different members of a group at the same time; suppose that each act maximizes utility. It may seem that in such a case the collective act $(a^1 + a^2 + \ldots + a^n)$ must also maximize utility. One moral of "The Principle of Moral Harmony" is that the conclusion does not follow. Even when each member of the group does his or her best, the group may fail to do its best.

The issues discussed in this essay were subjected to a more extended and slightly more formal treatment in Chapter 7, "Individual Obligation and Group Welfare," in my book *Doing the Best We Can*.

3

The principle of moral harmony

With a few exceptions, moral philosophers seem to be agreed that, at the level of the individual, morality doesn't necessarily pay. Hardly anyone who thinks about it seriously would maintain that doing what he morally ought to do invariably benefits the agent more than would some worse alternative. However, when we rise from the level of the individual to the level of the social group, we find that the reverse is true. Quite a few moral philosophers seem to believe that when all the members of a social group do what they morally ought to do, the group as a whole does benefit more than it would have from the performance of any worse alternative set of actions. I shall say that any such view is a version of the Principle of Moral Harmony (PMH). These doctrines are the subject of this paper.

My procedure here is as follows: first I sketch some of the main forms of PMH, and some of the main uses to which it has been put. I then attempt to show that some of the most plausible forms of PMH are false. After attempting to deal with some possible objections, I conclude by assessing the significance of what I have shown.

I

PMH may be formulated in a wide variety of ways. One version is suggested by Berkeley in *Passive Obedience*.[1] Berkeley held that God has brought it about that certain sorts of action are morally right. God's judg-

Earlier versions of this paper were read at several places, including SUNY at Fredonia, DePauw, Vanderbilt, Ohio, and Northern Illinois Universities. I am grateful to many of the participants in the discussions for useful comments. Many other friends read and commented on the paper. I am grateful to all of them, especially Eva Bodanszky, Earl Conee, and Terry Horgan.
1. George Berkeley, *Passive Obedience*, in Mary W. Calkins, ed., *Berkeley: Selections* (New York: Scribner's, 1929), pp. 427–469.

ments about the rightness of these actions are expressed in a set of moral rules, or precepts. Berkeley calls the set of these rules "the law of nature." Concerning it, he says:

> The law of nature is a system of such rules or precepts as that, if they be all of them, at all times, in all places, and by all men observed, they will necessarily promote the well-being of mankind, so far as it is attainable by human actions (239).[2]

In this form, PMH tells us that if everyone always does his duty, mankind as a whole is as well off as it can possibly be. So Berkeley's version of PMH applies only to the case in which we have universal duty doing. In this case, he seems to be saying, we are best off. It should be noted that this version of PMH does not have any direct bearing on the question whether large-scale, but nonuniversal, duty doing promotes welfare more or less than smaller-scale duty doing.

Bentham's version of PMH seems to make just this point. Bentham apparently held that the principle of utility tells us what our duties are. To "pursue" this principle is to do the acts it tells us to do – in other words, to do our duties. Bentham says:

> The principle of utility is capable of being consistently pursued; and it is but tautology to say that the more consistently it is pursued, the better it must ever be for humankind.[3]

So Bentham apparently wished to maintain that if most of us were to do our duty most of the time, "humankind" would be better off than it would be if fewer of us were to do our duty less of the time. More generally, his position seems to be that the greater the extent to which we do what we should, the better off we'll be.

Some contemporary philosophers have affirmed versions of PMH, too. Stephen Toulmin, for example, claims that the "function of morality" is "to correlate our feelings and behavior in such a way as to make the fulfillment of everyone's aims and desires as far as possible compatible."[4] This statement is open to a variety of interpretations, and the context does not make clear just which one Toulmin meant to affirm. Of these, however, the following seems to me to be reasonable, and it may be the one

2. It may be interesting to compare Berkeley's view with Leibniz's. See especially paragraphs 83–90 of the *Monadology*.
3. Jeremy Bentham, *Introduction to the Principles of Morals and Legislation*, in E. A. Burtt ed., *The English Philosophers from Bacon to Mill* (New York: Modern Library, 1949), p. 796.
4. *The Place of Reason in Ethics* (New York: Cambridge, 1950), p. 137; parenthetical page references to Toulmin will be in this book.

Toulmin had in mind. First we can say that the "fulfillment value" of a state of affairs for a society is the extent to which that state of affairs leads to the fulfillment of the aims and desires of members of that society. We can understand these aims and desires to be the ones they actually have, although ones they might have had under various counterfactual circumstances could also be considered. In any case, Toulmin's statement suggests the view that the fulfillment value for society S of the state of affairs in which everyone in S does what is morally right is at least as great as the fulfillment value for S of any other state of affairs the members of S could bring about.

Kurt Baier, Hector-Neri Castañeda, and others have also suggested versions of PMH.[5] So it isn't hard to find moral philosophers who affirm PMH, in one form or another. Furthermore, many of these philosophers go on to make use of PMH in their work. Let us consider some of the main uses to which this doctrine has been (or might be) put.

Various moral philosophers, including Kurt Baier and Brian Medlin, have appealed to PMH in connection with attempts to refute ethical egoism.[6] An argument against this form of egoism, based on PMH, might go as follows: sometimes interests conflict in such a way that, if each participant in a group attempts to maximize self-interest, the group as a whole will be worse off. Thus, if each member does what egoism says to do, the group does not do as well as it would if they performed some alternative combination of actions. However, according to PMH, morally right actions cannot have this feature. Doing them must always maximize group welfare. Hence, egoistic actions are not morally right, and egoism is allegedly refuted.

This argument can be clarified by means of an example. Suppose there is a small community living around a lake. Let the community be called 'S', and suppose the members are Vincent, Margaret, George, and Mary. Suppose each produces a moderate amount of garbage, and, as things stand, each takes his own garbage to the community dump a few miles away. Vincent, we may suppose, recognizes that he has two main alternatives with respect to his garbage: he can either (a) take it to the dump,

---

5. Baier, *The Moral Point of View*, abridged ed. (New York: Random House, 1965), see especially pp. 106–109; parenthetical page references to Baier are to this book. Castañeda, *The Structure of Morality* (Springfield, Ill.: Charles C. Thomas, 1974). J. L. Mackie, *Ethics* (New York: Penguin, 1977), see esp. ch. 5.
6. Baier, *op. cit.*, pp. 95/6. Medlin, "Ultimate Principles and Ethical Egoism" in David Gauthier, ed., *Morality and Rational Self-Interest* (Englewood Cliffs, N.J.: Prentice-Hall, 1970), pp. 56–63.

or (b) secretly throw it into the lake. Suppose he could get away with throwing it into the lake, no harm would come from doing so, and he would thereby avoid a bothersome trip to the dump. Egoism says he morally ought to throw his garbage into the lake.

However, egoism tells Margaret, George, and Mary the same thing. Each of them, according to this view, should take advantage of his or her neighbors, and use the lake as a dump. But, if they all did so, the lake would soon be polluted, they would all be worse off, and the community would suffer. PMH says that morally right actions never have this feature. Their joint performance must be maximally beneficial to the community. Hence, it has been argued, egoism must be wrong.

PMH also figures prominently in some discussions of the question, Why should I be moral? Baier claims that one of the main functions of morality is to provide us with a systematic way of resolving conflicts of interest. "By the moral point of view," he says, "we mean a point of view which furnishes a court of arbitration for conflicts of interest" (96). Baier goes on to claim that the acceptance of a moral system "is in the interest of everyone alike" (106–109). His point seems to be that social groups benefit from having moralities since the moral rules provide an especially good way of resolving conflict. Thus, if each of us does what the rules specify, the group as a whole will be better off than it would have been if each of use had behaved in some other way. In light of this, each member of the social unit has an overridingly good reason to "be moral." Each of us should act in accord with the moral rules of our society, Baier seems to argue, because the group will be best off if we do (see 148–162).

Other philosophers make use of PMH in their attempts to give an account of the nature of morality. This is an interesting puzzle: what is it that makes a set of rules a set of *moral* rules rather than, for example, a set of rules of etiquette or prudence? One suggestion is that moral rules must be designed to serve a certain function. Toulmin, as we have seen, says that the function of morality is "to correlate our feelings and behavior in such a way as to make the fulfillment of everyone's aims and desires as far as possible compatible" (137). He goes on to claim that "what makes us call a judgment 'ethical' is the fact that it is used to harmonize people's actions" (137). So Toulmin would apparently want to appeal to a version of PMH in an attempt to explain what morality is. The morality of a society is a set of rules adopted by that society for the purpose of resolving "lower-level" conflicts, and thereby "harmonizing" people's actions.

Thus, a form of PMH might be said to be true in virtue of the meaning of the term 'ethical'.[7]

PMH might also figure in an argument for act utilitarianism. For purposes of argument, we can assume that the "well-offness" of a society may be considered to be the same as the total amount of utility enjoyed by the members of the society. Act utilitarianism tells each of us to do what maximizes utility. It may seem obvious that if each of us does what act utilitarianism tells us to do, our society will be best off.[8] PMH says that morally right actions have this feature, too. Hence, we may want to conclude that the acts act utilitarianism tells us to do are one and all morally right. In other words, act utilitarianism is true.

So PMH has been formulated in a variety of ways, and has been (or might be) put to a variety of philosophical uses.

II

Now let us consider some of these doctrines a bit more critically.

Bentham maintained that "it is but tautology to say that the more consistently [the principle of utility] is pursued, the better it must ever be for humankind." I take this to mean that the greater the extent to which we individually do what maximizes utility, the better off we'll be collectively. Let's call this PMH$_2$.

Even if we evaluate our collective "well-offness" strictly in terms of how much utility we collectively enjoy, this is surely no tautology. It seems clear enough that two moderately bad wrong actions may have a much less bad total impact on our collective well-offness than one moderately good right action together with an absolutely horrendous wrong one. Yet the extent to which we do our duty when we do it not at all is apparently less than the extent to which we do our duty when we do it once. So Bentham's principle is no tautology.

To see this in a more concrete case, consider the following possibility. Suppose Vincent has his choice of three alternatives, v_1, v_2, and v_3, and Margaret has her choice of two: m_1 and m_2. Suppose these acts are unconnected, and have the following utilities:

---

7. It might be instructive to compare this view with that proposed by Castañeda in *The Structure of Morality*, ch. 8.
8. This view is criticized below, pp. 175ff.

$$v_1 \quad +2 \qquad\qquad m_1 \quad +2$$
$$v_2 \quad -5 \qquad\qquad m_2 \quad -5$$
$$v_3 \quad -10{,}000$$

If the group composed of Margaret and Vincent (we can consider it to be the set, $\{M, V\}$) does the group act $\{v_2, m_2\}$, it does two wrong actions. The group as a whole suffers a utility deficit of -10 (given some natural assumptions). Yet if the group does $\{v_3, m_1\}$, then they at least do one right action. Yet the group is much worse off. It suffers a utility deficit of $-9{,}998$. I can see no reason to suppose that similar results would be impossible in the case of a much larger group (even humanity as a whole) or over a much longer period of time (even eternity). Thus, I have to reject PMH_2.

A more plausible form of PMH might be developed by focusing on a single moment and a single social group. Consider the set of actions the members of the group would perform if each were to do something that's morally obligatory for him or her then. Won't the group as a whole be better off as a result of that than it would have been as a result of any alternative set of actions for the group including some wrong ones? This view, which we may call PMH_3, may seem attractive, especially to those who look favorably upon utilitarianism. Nevertheless, it seems to me that this version of PMH is false, too. Let us consider an example.

Suppose a group of adults has taken a group of children out to do some ice skating. The adults have assured the children and their parents that, in case of accident, they will do everything in their power to protect the children. Each adult in the party is a good skater and swimmer. Suppose, finally, that, while they are out skating, it just so happens that all the adults are spread out around the edge of the pond. A lone child is skating in the middle, equidistant from the adults. Suddenly, the ice breaks, and the child falls through. There is no time for consultation or deliberation. Someone must quickly save the child. However, since the ice is very thin, it would be disastrous for more than one of the adults to venture near the place where the child broke through. For if two or more were to go out, they would all fall in and all would be in profound trouble. In fact, let us suppose, no one goes to the aid of the child, and it is only after hard and painful efforts that the child manages to scramble out of the water.

In my view, every one of the adults in this example has failed to do his or her moral duty. Each of them is such that he or she morally ought to have gone to the aid of the child. This intuition is supported by virtually every plausible moral theory I can think of. On act utilitarianism, for example, it is clear that each adult should have saved the child. For each adult faced roughly two main alternatives: to attempt to save the child or not. Since no one did attempt to save the child, and no one's attempt would have provoked anyone else to try, each adult is such that if he or she had attempted to save the child, he or she would have done so successfully and alone. Hence, attempting to save the child maximizes utility for each adult. On Ross's theory, it seems plausible to say that each should have attempted to save the child. For each promised to do so, thus creating a prima facie duty to do so. I can see no overriding prima facie duty that lets anyone off the hook. So each seems to have an all-in duty to save the child. Various forms of Kantianism, it seems to me, may plausibly be thought to imply that each adult ought to have gone to the aid of the endangered child.

I prefer, however, to let the example stand or fall with reflective moral intuition, rather than with some controversial normative theory. My moral intuition tells me that this is a case in which each adult should have gone to the aid of the child. In my view, this is closely related to the stipulated fact that each of the adults does this in all the best possible worlds accessible to him or her at the time.

It is also quite clear, I think, that this example refutes PMH_3. For here we have a case in which there is a time at which, if each member of the social group were to do what in fact is his or her moral duty, then the group as a whole would be much worse off than it would have been if only one were to do what in fact is his or her duty. For it is clear that if all were to go out on the thin ice, many would get cold and wet. Indeed, we may even suppose that all of them, including the child, would fail to survive. That result is enormously worse than the result of just one doing his or her duty. For in that case only two get cold and wet, and all survive. Thus, PMH_3 is false. It is not the case that a group is inevitably better off if everyone does his or her duty.

The ice-skating example illustrates a sort of case that refutes many forms of PMH. The important aspects of the case may be illustrated in a simple utility matrix. In this matrix, we show a case in which there are two agents, V and M. V has two choices, v_1 and v_2, and M has two choices, m_1 and m_2. We may think if v_1 and v_2 as representing, respectively, V's going out on the ice, and V's remaining on the edge of the pond. Similarly for m_1 and m_2. The numbers in the matrix represent the amounts of utility that would result from the joint performance of the relevant actions.

$$M$$

	m_1	m_2
v_1	A_{-100}	B_{+100}
v_2	C_{+100}	D_{-50}

V is on the left spanning the rows.

In fact, let us suppose that m_2 is performed. Then V may choose between doing v_1 and thereby helping to produce + 100 units of utility (square B) or doing v_2, and thereby helping to produce −50 (square D). Clearly, act utilitarianism implies that v_1 is the morally right choice.

Let us also suppose that v_2 is in fact performed. Then M may choose between doing m_1 and thereby helping to produce + 100 (square C) or else doing m_2 and thereby helping to produce − 50 (square D). Clearly, m_1 is obligatory, at least on utilitarian grounds.

The upshot is that m_1 and v_1 are reasonably thought to be obligatory, even though $\{m_1, v_1\}$ is clearly the worst group action of the lot. Given some innocent and natural assumptions (such as that the actions here are timewise identical and that the agents in the example ought to do the acts that have the best results), this shows that PMH$_3$ is false.

Reflection on this utility matrix may shed some light on the connection between PMH and act utilitarianism. In my view, there are cases in which the implication of these doctrines conflict. We must not assume that if each of a set of actions is utility-maximizing (and so individually right according to act utilitarianism) then the group action composed of them will also be utility-maximizing (and so right according to a version of act utilitarianism applicable to group actions).

When we assign a utility to an action, we consider how much pleasure and pain it would produce, if it were performed. In other words, we consider how much pleasure and pain it does produce in "the nearest possible world" in which it is performed. It may be that in the nearest world where an action v_1 is performed, it produces a lot of pleasure and no pain. It may be that in that world another action m_1 is not performed. Furthermore, it may be that in the nearest world in which m_1 is performed, it produces a lot of pleasure and no pain, and v_1 is not performed. It is consistent with these assumptions to stipulate further that in the nearest world in which $\{m_1, v_1\}$ is performed, it produces a lot of pain and no pleasure. The utility of a group action bears no interesting relation to the sum of the utilities of the actions composing it.

A utilitarian might want to insist that the utility of a group action has to be equal to the sum of the utilities of its components. This seems to me to be straightforwardly false, as I have tried to show. Something like it, however, may be true. We should note that actions have their utilities contingently. It makes sense to speak of the utility an action would have had, under various counterfactual circumstances. We may want to say that the utility of a group action is equal to the sum of the utilities its components would have had, if they had been performed together. In this way, we focus on the nearest world in which the group action is performed, and maintain that the utility produced by the collective act must be distributed among its parts. This view seems to me to be reasonable, although I am not entirely convinced that it is true.[9]

So if a utilitarian wants to extend his normative theory so as to make it apply to group actions, he or she must be wary of assuming that utility-maximizing group actions are invariably composed of utility-maximizing components. Thus, the utilitarian must be wary of saying that morally right group actions are invariably composed of morally right components. In fact, I can see no straightforward way to connect the normative status of a group action with that of each of its components. An act can be right for a group to perform, and each component thereof wrong for its agent, and vice versa.[10]

III

Some might claim that my ice-skating example seems to work only because it is a case in which in fact everyone fails to do his or her duty. Furthermore, it might be claimed, PMH_3 is a principle about what happens when everyone does his or her duty. Hence, the example might be thought not to run counter to PMH_3, properly understood.

I'm not moved by this sort of objection. In the ice-skating example, each of the adults ought to perform a certain action. PMH_3 tells us that, if they were all to perform these actions, the group as a whole would be best off. I have claimed that, if they were to perform these actions together, the group would be far worse off. I admit that, had some of them behaved differently, some of these actions would not have been obligatory, Nevertheless, as it stands, the example does run counter to PMH_3.

---

9. So far as I know, the best discussion of this topic is still to be found in David Lyons, *Forms and Limits of Utilitarianism* (New York: Oxford, 1965).
10. For an interesting twist on this point, see Gerald Barnes, "Utilitarianisms," *Ethics*, LXXXII, 1 (October 1971): 56–64.

In any case, it may be instructive to consider a revision of PMH$_3$. Let us formulate a version that applies only to cases in which everyone in the example in fact does what's obligatory. This may suffice:

PMH$_4$: If there is a society S and a time t such that every member of S does something he or she morally ought to do at t, then S as a whole is better off than it would have been if some members had done something wrong instead of what they did.

This principle is of less interest than PMH$_3$, since it applies only to cases in which all the members of some society do what they should. Nevertheless, I think PMH$_4$ is false. I shall assume a version of utilitarianism for ease of exposition here, and present and analyze a purported counterexample.

Suppose the residents of the village are plagued by mosquitoes. Suppose there is only one way in which they can get rid of the mosquitoes. Each of the residents would have to fumigate his or her yard with a special insecticide, and they would all have to do it simultaneously at noon. If some but not all of them were to fumigate, terrible results would ensue. In this case, universal cooperation is essential. Suppose no one else is in fact going to fumigate at noon (although each of them easily could). Suppose nothing Vincent can do will make any of the others cooperate. Vincent has two main choices: he can fumigate at noon, or he can refrain from fumigating at noon. Clearly, if he fumigates, he does so alone and so helps to produce very bad results. If he does not fumigate at noon, nothing especially bad will happen, but the mosquitoes will not be killed. So it seems that Vincent ought to refrain from fumigating.

Similar arguments apply to each of the rest. Each of them ought to refrain from fumigating at noon. Suppose noon comes, and no one fumigates. Each of them does what he or she ought to do.

Now consider the relevant group action they perform at noon. This action is composed of several acts of nonfumigation, and each such act is morally obligatory. Yet it should be clear that the group as a whole had an alternative that would have had enormously better results. They could have got rid of the mosquitoes. So PMH$_4$ is refuted. In this example, every member of the group in fact does what he or she ought to do, and yet the group is not best off.[11]

---

11. As we saw above, Berkeley apparently maintained that if everyone eternally does what's morally right, the "well-being of mankind" will be maximized. Let's call this PMH$_1$. One obvious problem with this view is that it lacks practical relevance. It is too late to actualize the only case to which it applied. Beyond that, however, I think we can now

This case has a structure slightly different from that of the ice-skating case. Its essential features can be represented in another utility matrix. Here we simplify again, assuming that the society has only two members, and that each member has only two choices:

$$
\begin{array}{c c c c}
 & & \multicolumn{2}{c}{M} \\
 & & m_1 & m_2 \\
V & v_1 & A_{+100} & B_{-100} \\
 & v_2 & C_{-100} & D_{+50} \\
\end{array}
$$

If we assume that m_2 is in fact performed and view the matrix from V's point of view, we see that V has two choices: he can do v_1 (fumigate alone), which will yield -100 (square B), or he can do v_2 (refrain from fumigating), which will yield $+50$ (square D). Clearly, v_2 is by far his better choice.

If we also assume that v_2 is in fact performed and view the matrix from M's point of view, we see that she has two choices: she can do m_1, which will yield -100 (square C), or she can do m_2, which will yield $+50$ (square D). Clearly, m_2 is her better choice.

Yet the group action $\{m_1, v_1\}$ is preferable from the standpoint of group welfare. The group $\{M, V\}$ would be much better off if $\{m_1, v_1\}$ were performed than it would be if $\{m_2, v_2\}$ were performed. Yet, as we have seen, $\{m_2, v_2\}$ contains two obligatory actions, each of which in fact was performed. I think this sort of example shows that PMH$_4$ goes wrong.

Another sort of objection to my ice-skating example may be based on the view that I have failed to distinguish between conditional obligation and absolute obligation. Thus, some may grant that Vincent has a conditional obligation to save the child if no one else does, but they may want to deny that Vincent has an absolute obligation to save the child. These objectors could go on to claim that the same is true of each of the other adults in the example. Each conditionally ought to save the child if no one else does, but none absolutely ought to save the child.

If this claim is correct, then my alleged counterexample does not work. For PMH$_3$ does not say anything about group actions composed of merely

see that this principle, too, is no conceptual truth. For there might be a world whose whole history consists of what goes on in our community at noon. There everyone "eternally" does his duty. Yet the group would have been better off if they had all acted otherwise.

conditionally obligatory individual actions. Furthermore, it would appear that no bad results would ensue if each adult in the example were to go to the aid of the child if no one else did. For, if they all did that, then exactly one would go to the aid of the child, and group welfare would be maximized.

This objection obviously raises some serious issues, and I can't attempt to settle them here.[12] Nevertheless, I want to sketch an answer.

In the first place, I grant that Vincent conditionally ought to go to the aid of the child if no one else does. Similarly for the rest. Secondly, I admit that no bad results would be produced by the joint fulfillment of these conditional obligations. Nevertheless, I also believe that each adult absolutely ought to go to the aid of the child. I've given some reasons for thinking this to be true. Each promised. Each is such that nothing else he or she could do would produce better results. Each has a non-overridden prima facie duty to do so. I think it is clear that the results of the group action composed of all these acts of going to the aid of the child would be terrible. So I feel that I have presented a legitimate counterexample to PMH$_3$.

Moreover, I believe that it can be shown that if each adult has a conditional obligation to go to the aid of the child if no one else does, and no one has it in his power to make any of the others go, then each has an absolute obligation to go to the aid of the child. To see this, let us focus on Vincent, and see what he ought to do, absolutely and conditionally.

It is agreed that Vincent ought to go to the aid of the endangered child if no one else does. It is also agreed that in fact no one else does. However, from these two premises we may not infer that Vincent absolutely ought to go to the aid of the child. We cannot detach an absolute obligation from a conditional obligation and its condition.

Yet in the case at hand I believe we have another premise that enables us to detach our conclusion. That premise is that the condition is "inevitable." More precisely, it is that, no matter what Vincent does, the others will not go to aid of the child. Nothing he can do will make them do it. This fact, together with the conditional obligation to go to the aid of the child if no one else does, entails that Vincent absolutely ought to go to the aid of the child.[13]

12. For further discussion of conditional obligation, see Part Two of my *Doing the Best We Can*.
13. See also P. S. Greenspan, "Conditional Oughts and Hypothetical Imperatives," *The Journal of Philosophy*, LXXII, 10 (May 22, 1975): 259–276.

Corresponding arguments apply to each of the other adults. Therefore, the objection can be rebutted. If the adults have the conditional obligation the objectors allege them to have and it is stipulated that no one can make anyone else go to the aid of the child, then each of them absolutely ought to go to the aid of the child. Hence, I feel that my counterexample stands.

IV

By way of conclusion, I want to say a few words about what the failure of PMH may show. In the first place, I think we must view with skepticism any philosophical argument in which PMH appears as a premise. So, for example, if someone attacks egoism, appealing to the fact that egoism conflicts with some form of PMH, we will probably have to reject the argument. For we have no reason to suppose that any interesting form of PMH is true. Equally, if someone attempts to defend act utilitarianism by claiming that, of all normative theories, it alone is consistent with some form of PMH, we must reject this argument as well. For, in the first place, most forms of PMH are false. In the second place, I believe it has been shown that act utilitarianism is not consistent with the interesting forms of PMH. Similar comments apply to all other uses of PMH in arguments or theories. Insofar as any philosophical view depends upon PMH, that view is suspect.

But beyond this, I think that the failure of PMH may show us something of interest about the concept of morality itself. Some moral philosophers think of morality as a sort of social institution, designed to serve certain social purposes. For example, some suggest that morality is designed to harmonize conflicting interests. Others say it is designed to maximize social welfare.

I am convinced that this conception of morality is mistaken. Of course, I recognize that social groups adopt or establish various moral principles, and that frequently the selection of these principles is in some way guided by judgments of social utility. However, it seems clear to me that this sort of adoption or establishment of a moral principle cannot help to make the principle true, if in fact it is false. Beliefs about what's right and wrong, no matter how widespread, may be mistaken.

So let us distinguish between moralities – moral codes adopted by various social groups – and Morality – the truth about what we ought to do. I admit that moralities may be social instruments (although I suspect that no even remotely plausible morality would be consistent with any interesting form of PMH). My main thesis, and what I've attempted to

61

show here, is that Morality is not consistent with PMH. If I am right about this, then we should reconsider the doctrine that Morality is primarily designed to maximize some social goal, such as harmony or welfare. I have tried to show that, if Morality has this purpose, then it fails to do what it is supposed to do. My own view, for what it's worth, is that Morality doesn't have any purpose. Indeed, the suggestion that Morality has a purpose strikes me as being as odd as the suggestion that mathematics, or ornithology, has a purpose.

Essay 4

On the consistency of act- and motive-utilitarianism: A reply to Robert Adams

INTRODUCTORY COMMENTS

If we take our utilitarianism *narrowly*, we take it simply as a principle about the normative status of actions. If we take it *widely*, we take it as a family of principles about the normative status of all sorts of things – actions, motives, traits of character, and so on. Because of its more extensive application across the evaluative board, wide utilitarianism is more impressive.

However, it is not clear that one can consistently maintain a utilitarianism of acts and a utilitarianism of, for example, motives. In his important paper "Motive Utilitarianism," Robert Adams argued that these views are inconsistent in some cases. Thus, the prospects for wide utilitarianism are dim. Adams drew an even more sweeping conclusion: The moral point of view cannot be the utilitarian point of view.

My overt aim in Essay 4 is to show that Adams's argument does not succeed. If we formulate our act utilitarianism and our motive utilitarianism correctly, they are bound to be consistent. Along the way, I try to establish some other small points about Adams's formulation of the doctrines and arguments.

Adams made use of a traditional formulation of act utilitarianism. This is his "AU," and it is based on the standard concepts of act, alternative, and consequence. Although there is some confusion about this in the essay, it is reasonable to assume that he meant to make use of a similarly traditional formulation of motive utilitarianism. This is his "MU." He tried to show that the right motive according to MU may be incompatible with the right action according to AU.

Although Adams's paper is well known and often cited, I found it very hard to understand how the argument is supposed to work. When it finally became clear to me, I recognized that the central point of his argument has nothing to do with *acts* and *motives*. Surprisingly, it turns out that the core of Adams's argument is relevantly like the core of Castañeda's "problem for act utilitarianism"! A course of action that has greater utility than any time-identical alternative may contain as a component something that does not have greater utility than any time-identical alternative. I point this out in Section 4.

The implication of this point is this: Adams's argument really shows nothing peculiarly about act and motive utilitarianism. The inconsistency arises not because of the mixture of acts and motives, but from the fact that the chosen formulation of act utilitarianism is independently inconsistent (as Castañeda had shown in 1968). If we make use of forms of act and motive utilitarianism based on world utilitarianism, the conflict disappears.

The essay thus has a deeper and more constructive point. Discussion of logical features of act utilitarianism, as well as discussion of logical relations among forms of utilitarianism, may well be pointless if we start with defective formulations of the views. Such discussion might be more fruitful if we started with coherent formulations. I believe that world utilitarianism offers the best foundation for such discussions. In any case, as I show in the essay, the appeal to world utilitarianism seems to dissolve the alleged conflict between act and motive utilitarianism. For all Adams has shown, the moral point of view might be the point of view from which the principle of utility is applied directly to all objects of moral evaluation.

4

On the consistency of act- and motive-utilitarianism: A reply to Robert Adams

1. WIDE VS. NARROW UTILITARIANISM

Some take utilitarianism to be a theory exclusively about the normative status of acts. Others take it to be a family of theories concerning the normative status not only of acts, but of a whole range of objects, including such things as motives, rules, traits of character, social institutions, etc.[1] In virtue of its capacity to provide wider conceptual unification, it seems to me that the latter (or "wide") interpretation makes utilitarianism more impressive.

In an important and frequently cited paper published more than fifteen years ago, Robert Adams presented an argument that has been taken to show that utilitarianism cannot be construed in this wider way.[2] More precisely, Adams focussed on what happens when we try to combine act utilitarianism and motive utilitarianism. Adams argued that 'right action, by act-utilitarian standards, and right motivation, by motive-utilitarian standards, are incompatible in some cases.' [475] If Adams' argument succeeds, extensions of it would presumably show that we cannot combine act utilitarianism with "trait of character utilitarianism" or with "social institution utilitarianism". The implication would be that we cannot coherently think that utilitarianism applies across the board to all subjects of moral appraisal.

Near the end of his paper, Adams sums up what he thinks he has established: 'The moral point of view – the point of view from which moral judgments are made – cannot safely be defined as a point of view

---

1. A particularly interesting discussion of this issue can be found in Michael Slote's 'Utilitarianism: Pro and Con,' which was presented at the Rochester conference on consequentialism in May of 1992.
2. Robert Adams, 'Motive Utilitarianism,' *The Journal of Philosophy*, LXXIII, 14 (August 12, 1976), 467–481. Parenthetical page references that follow are to Adams' article.

in which the test of utility is applied directly to all objects of moral evaluation. For it is doubtful that the most useful motives, . . . are related to the most useful acts in the way that the motives, . . . regarded as right must be related to the acts regarded as right in anything that is to count as a morality.'[479]

I believe that a certain form of utilitarianism is true. This form of utilitarianism entails a form of act utilitarianism and a form of motive utilitarianism. I think each of them is true, and (obviously) that they are consistent. In this paper, I want to show that this form of utilitarianism is not cast into doubt by Adams' argument. Along the way, I want to establish several other critical points. But we should begin at the beginning. In order to understand Adams' claims, we must first understand act utilitarianism and motive utilitarianism.

2. AU & MU

Adams does not present an explicit statement of the sort of act utilitarianism he has in mind. But a number of remarks scattered through the paper make it quite clear that his form of act utilitarianism is nothing out of the ordinary. Let us first say that the *consequences* of a possible act are all the later events that would occur as a result of the act, if it were performed. I assume that in all interesting cases, some of these consequences have some sort of *value*, positive or negative. Let us say that the *utility* of a possible act is equal to the sum of the values of its consequences. The *alternatives* to an act are the other possible acts that the agent could have done on that occasion instead of the act. Now we can say that an act *maximizes utility* iff no alternative has higher utility. This enables us to state a very traditional form of act utilitarianism:

AU: An act is morally right iff it maximizes utility.

Adams does present an apparently official statement of motive utilitarianism:

> Accordingly, the theory that will be my principal subject here is that one pattern of motivation is morally better than another to the extent that the former has more utility than the latter. The morally perfect person, on this view, would have the most useful desires, and would have them in exactly the most useful strengths; he or she would have the most useful among the patterns of motivation that are causally possible for human beings. Let us call this doctrine *motive utilitarianism*.[470]

In light of the fact that Adams explicitly presents this as his official statement of motive utilitarianism, it might seem that there could be no reasonable doubt about how he intends that doctrine to be understood. However, a number of remarks made elsewhere in the paper convince me that the view actually under consideration in the paper is not the one stated in the official formulation.

Notice that the official formulation says something about which motives are *better*, but it says nothing about which motives we *ought to have*, or which motives it would be morally *right* for us to have. Thus, the doctrine stated in the official formulation is not analogous to AU. We might have expected that motive utilitarianism would provide a criterion of rightness and wrongness for various possible motives, just as act utilitarianism provides such a criterion for various possible acts. We find no such thing in the passage quoted above.

Adams' argument is based upon an example involving a person ("Jack") who visits the cathedral at Chartres. In his discussion of the example, Adams describes Jack's pattern of motivation. Adams says that this motivation ' . . . is *right* by motive utilitarian standards.' [471. Emphasis added] In the same context, he remarks that motive utilitarianism would rule out as *impermissible* a certain other pattern of motivation. [471–2] These remarks are in conflict with the official formulation, since it does not mention rightness or permissibility. In a later passage, Adams makes the real import of motive utilitarianism quite clear. He says that 'Motive utilitarianism is . . . about what motives one ought to *have*.' [474] Clearly, then, the doctrine Adams really had in mind is not the one stated in the passage quoted above. Rather, it is a normative theory about right, wrong, and obligatory motives, and it is intended to be analogous to AU.[3]

In light of all this, it seems appropriate to view what appears to be the official doctrine as somewhat misleading, and to suppose that motive utilitarianism is a normative theory about right motivation, much as act utilitarianism is a normative theory about right action.

3. In 'Utilitarianism and Welfarism,' *The Journal of Philosophy*, LXXVI, 9 (September, 1979), Amartya Sen notes (467–468) that Adams' official statement of motive utilitarianism does not have the implications about right and wrong motivation that Adams claims it has. He also points out that motive utilitarianism does not have any direct implications concerning the criterion of "good persons". See also Peter Railton, 'How Thinking about Character and Utilitarianism Might Lead to Rethinking the Character of Utilitarianism,' in Peter A. French et al., *Midwest Studies in Philosophy*, XIII (Notre Dame: University of Notre Dame Press, 1988), 398–416. Railton also notes with surprise [401] that Adams' official statement of motive utilitarianism does not have the implications about right and wrong motivation that Adams claims for it. Railton resolves the tension by taking the official formulation as accurate, and supposing that Adams' remarks about implications are mistaken. I have resolved the tension in the opposite way, primarily because Railton's resolution makes the alleged conflict between act- and motive-utilitarianism harder to grasp.

By analogy to what was said earlier in connection with action, let us say that the *alternatives* to a motive are the other motives that the person could have had instead; the *consequences* of a motive are the things that would happen as a result if the person had the motive. The *utility* of a motive is the sum of the values of the value-laden consequences of its being had. (I assume that when we evaluate the consequences of a motive for application of motive utilitarianism we use the same standard of evaluation that we use when we evaluate the consequences of actions for the application of AU.) A motive *maximizes utility* iff no alternative motive has greater utility. With this as background, we can state a form of motive utilitarianism that is genuinely analogous to AU – and a form that does have the implications that Adams mentions.

MU: A motive is morally right iff it maximizes utility.

In MU, the test of utility is applied directly to motives, just as this same test is applied directly to acts in AU. The point of the application of the test is, as in AU, to determine what is right. In this case, of course, MU determines which motives are right to have, just as AU determines in an analogous way which actions are right to perform.

In spite of the fact that I have departed from the official word of Adams' text, I feel confident that my formulations of AU and MU are quite close to the spirit of what he intended. These views embody the notion that the maximization of utility is the universal standard of moral rightness. Whether we are assessing acts or motives, these principles tell us that rightness invariably coincides with the maximization of utility.

3. JACK AND THE CATHEDRAL

Adams presents the case of Jack and the cathedral in order to show that ' . . . right action, by act-utilitarian standards, and right motivation, by motive-utilitarian standards, are incompatible in some cases.' [475] In particular, Adams' claim is that in this example Jack's 'motivation is right by motive-utilitarian standards, even though it causes him to do several things that are wrong by act-utilitarian standards.' [471] Because the example is both complex and important, I want to provide here a rather lengthy passage from Adams' paper. My interpretation follows.

> Jack is a lover of art who is visiting the cathedral at Chartres for the first time. . . . He is so excited that he is spending much more time at Chartres than he had planned . . . In fact, he is spending too much time there, from a utilitarian point of view. He had planned to spend only the morning, but

he is spending the whole day; and this is going to cause considerable inconvenience and unpleasantness. He will miss his dinner, do several hours of night driving, which he hates, and have trouble finding a place to sleep. On the whole, he will count the day well spent, but some of the time spent in the cathedral will not produce as much utility as would have been produced by departing that much earlier. At the moment, Jack is studying the sixteenth to eighteenth century stone choir screen. He is enjoying this less than other parts of the cathedral, and will not remember it very well. It is not completely unrewarding, but he would have more happiness on balance if he passed by these carvings and saved the time for an earlier departure . . . he is more strongly interested in seeing, as nearly as possible, everything in the cathedral than in maximizing utility. This action of his is therefore wrong by act-utilitarian standards . . .

On the other hand, Jack would not have omitted these things unless he had been less interested in seeing everything in the cathedral than in maximizing utility. And it is plausible to suppose that if his motivation had been different in that respect, he would have enjoyed the cathedral much less. It may very well be that his caring more about seeing the cathedral than about maximizing utility has augmented utility, through enhancing his enjoyment, by more than it has diminished utility through leading him to spend too much time at Chartres. In this case his motivation is right by motive-utilitarian standards even though it causes him to do several things that are wrong by act-utilitarian standards. [470–1]

In order to simplify and clarify the example, let us introduce some abbreviations, some utility ratings, and a diagram. First, some abbreviations:

Mmax: The motive of wanting to maximize utility.
Msee: The motive of wanting to see as much as possible at the cathedral.
A1: The act of studying the cathedral during the morning with motive Mmax.
A2: The act of studying the cathedral during the morning with motive Msee.
A3: The act of leaving early in the afternoon.
A4: The act of staying in the cathedral in the afternoon.

Now some utility ratings, and their explanations. Let's suppose A1 would produce +5 units of value, whereas A2 would produce +10. This captures the stipulation that caring about the cathedral augments utility, by enhancing Jack's enjoyment of his time there. Next, we must suppose that U(A3) is greater than U(A4), since A4 will lead to all the unpleasantness surrounding the drive in the dark, the missed dinner, and the trouble about finding a hotel. I propose that U(A3) $= +2$, whereas U(A4) $= -2$.

Let us furthermore assume that if Jack has Mmax, then he will perform A1 and A3. Although this is obviously artificial, let us also assume that his

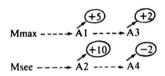

Figure 1

having Mmax will not have any other utility-affecting results. As a result, he will enjoy a total utility of +7 in virtue of having Mmax. Since no one else will be affected, U(Mmax) = +7. On the other hand, if Jack has Msee, he will perform A2 and A4, and will enjoy a total utility of +8. Assuming that no other motives are possible for Jack, and no one else will be affected, it then turns out that U(Msee) = +8, and MU implies that it would be right for Jack to have motive Msee.

Notice that Jack has two main options for action early in the afternoon – leaving early (A3) and staying late (A4). Since the utility of A4 is lower than that of A3, A4 is wrong by AU standards. But Adams has already told us that A4 – the AU-wrong act for early in the afternoon – is a consequence of Msee – the MU-right motive for the morning. This, I take it, is why Adams concludes by saying that Jack's ' . . . motivation is right by motive-utilitarian standards, even though it causes him to do several things that are wrong by act-utilitarian standards.' [471]

The example is complex. Perhaps Figure 1 will make it easier to grasp. Numbers in circles indicate amounts of pleasure; arrows represent causal connections.

The crucial facts about the case are these: Msee has better results than its alternative, and so is required by MU; one consequence of Msee is A4; A4 has worse results than its alternative, and so is prohibited by AU. A right motive seems to lead to a wrong act.

4. HAS ADAMS SHOWN TOO MUCH?

Adams introduced the example of Jack and the cathedral in order to show that the demands of AU sometimes conflict in a certain way with the demands of MU. I think the example succeeds: given a variety of natural assumptions about AU, MU, and the example, I agree that if Jack has the motive that is right according to MU, he will as a result perform an act that is wrong according to AU. The theories are in this way incompatible.

However, I believe that a trivial modification of the example will es-

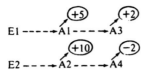

Figure 2

tablish that AU is self-incompatible in the very same way. As I see it, the conflict illustrated by Adams has nothing special to do with motives and acts – it is instead a result of certain features of the standard (and, as I see it, inadequate) formulation of utilitarianism. Here's the revised example. Suppose that Jack has a cold, and thinks it might be a good idea to (E1) take a long-lasting cold remedy before he sets out in the morning. On the other hand, he knows that the cold remedy will make him drowsy, and might therefore diminish his enjoyment of the cathedral. His other option, E2, is to refrain from taking the cold remedy (but carry a lot of extra tissues).

Suppose that if he performs E1, he will have a fairly good time at the cathedral but will indeed be rather drowsy. This will slightly diminish his enjoyment of the experience. Let us say that his time in the cathedral will be worth +5 points. Due to drowsiness, he will leave early and have a fully satisfactory evening (worth +2 points). On the other hand, if he performs E2, he will not be drowsy, and he will have a much better time in the cathedral (worth +10 points) but he will have such a good time that he will stay much too late and will end up missing dinner, getting lost in the dark, and sleeping in his car (altogether worth −2 points). Figure 2 illustrates the new example.

It should be fairly clear that, given natural assumptions similar to the ones made above in connection with Adams' example, the total utility of E1 is +7 whereas the total utility of E2 is +8. Since these acts are assumed to be alternatives for Jack in the morning, AU implies that he ought to perform E2 – he should avoid taking the cold remedy. On the other hand, it appears that in the afternoon, Jack will have his choice of (A3) leaving early and (A4) staying late. As before, A3 is the better choice, but if Jack did the right thing in the morning (namely, E2), he will thereby be caused to perform the less-good A4 in the afternoon. Thus, he will stay too late in the cathedral, miss his dinner, get lost in the dark, and sleep in his car. My conclusion is this: if the original example showed that the demands of AU are sometimes in conflict with those of MU, then the revised

71

example shows that the demands of AU are sometimes in conflict with each other.

5. A CONSISTENT PAIR OF VIEWS

I mentioned earlier that I believe a certain form of utilitarianism. I also said that this form of utilitarianism implies a form of act utilitarianism and a form of motive utilitarianism. Since I think each of these views is true, I also think that the whole package is consistent.

My form of utilitarianism starts with the assumption that at every moment of moral choice, there are many possible worlds *accessible* to the moral agent.[4] Consider some infant at the very moment when she begins to exist. There are various possible ways in which she might live out her life. For each of these total life histories, there is a possible world – the world that would exist if she were to live out her life in that way. Call these worlds the "original stock" for the person. As time goes by, the person filters out world after world. By acting in this way rather than in that, she bypasses, or rules out, many possible worlds. Once bypassed, a given world is never again accessible to a person. If we select a person, s, and a time, t, at which s exists, there will be a not-yet-ruled-out subset of s's original stock. Each member of this subset is a possible world that is, in an important sense, still possible for s. I say that each such world is "accessible" to s at t.

I also assume that our theory of value will generate a morally relevant ranking of these accessible worlds. For present purposes, it is not necessary to lay out the details of the theory of value. I merely assume that worlds are to be evaluated in accordance with the very same theory of value that Adams used when he evaluated actions and motives. If a world, w, is accessible to s at t, and no better world is also accessible to s at t, we can say that w is a "best" for s at t. This enables me to state the fundamental principle of my form of utilitarianism:

U: As of t, s morally ought to see to the occurrence of p iff p is true in all the bests for s at t.

U is formally different from traditional forms of utilitarianism in a few ways. For one thing, U purports to be a criterion for a *time-relativized* concept of moral obligation. Thus, according to U, I might have a moral

---

4. What follows is a simplified presentation of the view I defend in *Doing the Best We Can*, (Dordrecht: Reidel, 1986).

obligation *as of now* to see to p; but then, perhaps because I foolishly bypass all my p-worlds, I might have a moral obligation *as of some later time* to see to the negation of p.

Furthermore, there is no explicit reference to *actions* in U. Rather, U purports to state conditions under which a person morally ought to *see to the occurrence of a state of affairs*. Thus, according to U, it might be Jack's moral obligation as of some time to see to such things as *there being a map in the glove compartment; the car being parked in a legal parking space,* and *the guide getting a good tip*. None of these is in any natural sense an "act". On the other hand, according to U, it might also be Jack's moral obligation as of some time to see to such things as *Jack's placing a map in the glove compartment at 9:00 AM, Jack's parking the car in a legal parking space at 10:00 AM,* and *Jack's giving the guide a good tip at 3:00 PM*. States of affairs such as these play the role of actions in the theory.

Let us say that a state of affairs is "act-describing" provided that it is relevantly like the last three mentioned in the previous paragraph. Each such state of affairs mentioned some specific person (its "agent"), some type of behavior (putting a map in the glove compartment, parking the car, etc.), and some specific time. Since U purports to give necessary and sufficient conditions for the moral obligatoriness as of a time for any state of affairs, it follows that U also gives such conditions for act-describing states of affairs. As a result, U trivially entails a version of act utilitarianism:

Ua: If p is an act-describing state of affairs, and s is the agent of p, then, as of t, s morally ought to see to the occurrence of p iff p is true in all the bests for s at t.

Consider the state of affairs *As of 9:00 AM, Jack wants to maximize utility*. This state of affairs mentions a particular person, and says that he has a certain sort of motivation as of a particular time. Let us say that any such state of affairs is "motive-describing", and let us say that its "subject" is the person said in it to have the motive. This enables us to formulate a version of motive utilitarianism:

Um: If p is a motive-describing state of affairs, and s is the subject of p, then, as of t, s morally ought to see to the occurrence of p iff p is true in all the bests for s at t.

Um is also a direct implication of U.

Clearly, there cannot be a case in which the requirements for action imposed by Ua as of some time conflict with the requirements for motivation imposed by Um as of the same time. To say otherwise is to say

73

that the motives s has in all his bests as of some time are incompatible with the actions s performs in all his bests as of that same time. But since s's bests as of t are all accessible to s as of t, it is within s's power to do what he does in them. Hence, it must be within s's power as of t to have the motives he has in his bests while performing the acts he does in his bests. Therefore, there can be no causal conflict between the requirements imposed by Um upon an agent at a time and those imposed upon the same agent at the same time by Ua.

Let us look more closely at Adams' original case involving Jack and the cathedral. Let us first consider what my view says about the normative status of various acts and motives relative to some time early in the morning. At around 9:00 AM, several worlds are accessible to Jack. In the best of these he has Msee, has a fine time in the cathedral during the morning, but stays too late and suffers the consequences later in the day. So, U implies that as of 9:00 AM his motivation ought to be Msee, and his actions ought to be A2 and A4. It is important to notice that my view implies that Jack's moral obligation as of 9:00 AM is to stay late at the cathedral (A4). The fact that A4 has lower utility than A3 is, on U, irrelevant. What's relevant here is that A4 is part of a total sequence of actions that is better than any alternative total sequence. So U's normative implications are different from AU + MU's. Jack's case no longer is one in which right motivation causes later wrong action; it is one in which right motivation causes later *right* action.

The evaluation relative to later times of Jack's actions is a bit more complex. Suppose Jack adopts Msee, and has a delightful time in the cathedral all morning. As I understand Adams' story, the adoption of Msee in the morning precludes early departure in the afternoon. Thus, the choice of Msee in the morning rules out all possible worlds in which he leaves the cathedral early. Once bypassed a world never again becomes accessible. Accordingly, at 2:00 PM there is no world accessible to Jack in which he leaves the cathedral early. Hence, even in the best worlds accessible to him at 2:00 PM, he stays too late. Ua then (trivially) generates the result that A4 is permissible as of 2:00 PM. Once again, there is no conflict between right action and right motivation.

Perhaps I have misunderstood the story. Perhaps Adams intended that it would be possible at 2:00 PM for Jack to leave early even if he had already adopted Msee in the morning. In this case there must have been another world accessible to Jack in the morning. In this world, Jack starts the day by adopting Msee. He then enjoys the cathedral during the morning. However, in this world, Jack suddenly changes his motivation after lunch, decides to become a maximizer, and leaves the cathedral, thereby gaining all the advantages of an early departure. If such a world is accessible to Jack in the morning, and it is his best at that time, then his obligations as of that time are to be motivated and to behave as he does in that world. Again, there is no conflict, since in this case right motivation in the morning leads to right action later in the day.

6. CONCLUSIONS

Adams' example of Jack and the cathedral was originally intended to reveal that there can be conflict between the requirements of motive utilitarianism and act utilitarianism. If we take MU and AU as our formulations of these doctrines, then the example does indeed reveal a conflict. However, the conflict in question results from an inadequate formulation of the utilitarian doctrines; motives play no essential role in it. Precisely the same sort of conflict arises even when MU is left out of consideration and AU is applied by itself.

If we formulate act and motive utilitarianism as I suggest we should, no such conflict arises. The motives we should have, and the acts we should perform, are determined in exactly the same way: as of any time, we should be motivated as we are in the best worlds then accessible, and we should behave as we do in the best worlds accessible. In no case will these demands be causally inconsistent. Although I have not shown it here, my view is that U may be taken as a global theory of normative evaluation. It tells us what actions we should perform, what motives we should have, what traits of character we should develop, etc. In short, U is a consistent formulation of the sought-after "wide" utilitarianism.[5]

5. I am grateful to Shelly Kagan, Owen McLeod, Eric Moore, and Ted Sider for helpful critical comments on earlier drafts.

Part II

Hedonism

Essay 5

Two questions about pleasure

INTRODUCTORY COMMENTS

World utilitarianism, as presented in the papers in Part I of this book, is a view in normative ethics. It purports to tell us how we ought to behave. According to that view, at each moment, a person ought to bring about the states of affairs that occur in the best worlds then accessible to him or her. This is my reformulation of what I take to be the core insight of consequentialism. It is my interpretation of the idea that our moral obligation is always to do the best we can – to make the world as good as we can make it.

As stated, the theory is pretty abstract. It purports to tell us something of the *structure* of the concept of moral obligation, and it purports to tell us something about the connection between normative concepts (moral rightness, wrongness, and obligatoriness) and axiological concepts (good and evil). But it does not tell us what makes one world better than another.

There are many different axiological theories. These include simple hedonism, qualified hedonism, eudaimonism, pluralism, and many others. They generate different rankings of worlds. World utilitarianism might be linked to any of these axiologies – and, of course, we will get different normative results if we link it to one of them rather than to another.

Because hedonism is one of the oldest, most plausible, and simplest of axiological theories, it is reasonable to take it as our starting point. Perhaps we can combine world utilitarianism with a hedonistic ranking of worlds so as to produce a full-fledged normative theory with real "bite."

A glance at the literature on hedonism quickly reveals enormous confusion. There is great controversy about the nature of pleasure and pain; and there is great controversy about what the hedonist wants to say about them. The confusion and controversy are so great, it seems to me, that it would be a big mistake either to endorse hedonism or reject it. In either case, we would be succumbing to the temptations of Ramboism. Instead, I think it best to try to understand the ideas at the heart of hedonism.

79

Traditionally, hedonism has been expressed by such formulas as "Pleasure alone is intrinsically good," "Pleasure is the only thing worth seeking for its own sake," and "Pleasure is The Good." It is obvious that it is impossible to understand hedonism without first understanding pleasure. What is this thing called pleasure?

Philosophers are deeply divided about the nature of pleasure. A small group, including the early G. E. Moore, take pleasure to be a single, phenomenologically uniform, directly introspectable sensory property – the feeling of "pleasure itself." A much larger group are "hedonic pluralists." They think that feelings of many different sorts may correctly be called pleasures. The pluralists disagree among themselves about what makes a feeling be a pleasure. Some, including Sidgwick, think that the crucial fact is that the one who experiences the feeling "apprehends it as desirable." Others, including Brandt, think that the crucial fact is that the one who experiences the feeling *likes it for its own sake*. Still others have other views.

Some philosophers, perhaps tossing in the wake churned up by the passage of the later Wittgenstein, seemed to want to claim that pleasure is not a feeling at all. One thinks here of Gilbert Ryle.

In "Two Questions about Pleasure" I present my view about the nature of pleasure, as well as objections to some of the most prominent alternatives. My view about *sensory pleasure* is a form of pluralism. I think that many phenomenologically distinct feelings are correctly called pleasures. I call these "sensory pleasures." There is nothing novel about this aspect of my view. I believe that many others share it.

What's novel about my view is that I propose to explain the concept of *sensory pleasure* by appeal to the concept of *propositional pleasure*. That is, I propose to define "x is a sensory pleasure for S at t" by appeal to the concept expressed by "S is pleased at t that _____ is the case." Whereas some others have taken sensory pleasure as the fundamental hedonic phenomenon and have tried to explain propositional pleasure (often in causal terms) by appeal to it, I reverse the process. I take propositional pleasure to be the fundamental hedonic phenomenon, and I propose to define sensory pleasure by appeal to it.

I should point out that "Two Questions about Pleasure" is exclusively about the nature of pleasure. It does not contain any formulation of hedonism. It might seem, given what I here say about sensory pleasure, that I would want to go on to say that hedonism is the view that sensory pleasures are the fundamental intrinsic goods.

But that is not my view. In Essays 6 and 7, I go on to discuss several formulations of hedonism. I try to reveal some perplexities that we will encounter if we attempt to understand hedonism to be the view that sensory pleasures are intrinsically good. Rather, as I try to show in Essay 7, hedonism is better construed as a thesis about *propositional pleasure*.

5

Two questions about pleasure

1.

In this paper, I present my solutions to two closely related questions about pleasure. One of these questions is fairly well known. Quite a few philosophers have discussed it, and the literature contains many proposed answers. The second question seems to me to be at least as interesting as the first, but it apparently hasn't interested quite so many philosophers. I know of only a few proposed answers.

Before the questions can be presented, it will be necessary to draw a distinction. This is the distinction between what I call 'sensory pleasure' and what I call 'propositional pleasure'. Let's first consider sensory pleasure.

2.

We use a variety of ordinary language expressions to ascribe sensory pleasure. For example, we may say that a person is 'feeling pleasure', 'experiencing pleasurable sensations', 'having pleasurable feelings', etc. These expressions are true of a person if and only if he is experiencing sensory pleasure.

Certain rather fundamental biological processes are ordinarily accompanied by pleasurable feelings. These include nutritive, reproductive, and other such processes. Imagine that you are on a sunny tropical island. Imagine that the sky is clear and the sun bright. Imagine that the beach is clean and warm. Imagine that you are lying on the sand, delighting in the fresh air, sunshine, peacefulness, and warmth. You are experiencing many pleasurable sensations. These would include the pleasures associated with the feelings of warmth, the smell of the fresh salty air, and the tingling feeling produced by the caress of the gentle breeze. Each of these sensations is pleasurable or 'pleasure-giving'. Each is, in my terminology, a sensory pleasure.

Propositional pleasure is another matter. We ascribe propositional pleasure to a person when we say that he is pleased that something or other is the case; when we say that he takes pleasure in something or other's being the case; when we say that he is pleased about something or other's being the case, etc. Consider a man with smart children. Suppose he learns that his children have gotten report cards filled with 'A's. This is a source of pride and satisfaction for him. He is pleased that his children have gotten good report cards. In this case, the man's pleasure has an 'object', and the object is a proposition (the proposition that his children have gotten good report cards). Thus, he is experiencing propositional pleasure.

Much more could be said about the distinction between sensory and propositional pleasure. However, my present purpose is not to clarify or explain this distinction. It is merely to draw attention to the fact that the distinction exists. Furthermore, I fear that if I were to discuss the distinction much further at this point, I would enter controversial territory. For now, it will be sufficient to take note of the fact that some hedonic phenomena seem to be primarily sensory phenomena. Others seem to involve a propositional attitude. Later, I will attempt to sharpen the distinction.

3.

One thing to notice about sensory pleasure is its apparent heterogeneity. The man on the beach enjoys some pleasurable smells as well as some pleasurable feelings of warmth. Each of these sensations is pleasant, pleasurable, 'pleasure-giving'. Some would find nothing odd in saying that each of these sensations 'is a pleasure'. Nevertheless, from the strictly phenomenological perspective, they seem to have very little in common. One is an olfactory sensation – it is the smell of fresh, salty air. The other is an all-over bodily feeling of warmth. Aside from the fact that they are experienced simultaneously and by the same person in the example, they seem to be utterly unlike.

In order to see the heterogeneity of sensory pleasures even more clearly, consider the pleasurable sensations you get when you eat delicious, salty peanuts and drink sparkling, cold beer. The taste of the peanuts is a pleasure. The taste of the beer is a pleasure. Yet, unless your taste sensations are profoundly unlike mine, the taste of the peanuts has little in common with the taste of the beer. Indeed, it is reasonable to suppose that we who love to eat peanuts while we drink beer love this, at least in part, because of the remarkable contrast between the two leading sensations involved. (The phenomenological contrast between the taste of cold

83

beer and the feelings of warmth enjoyed while sunbathing is even more striking – yet each of these may be a sensory pleasure.)

Sensory pleasures, then, are a heterogeneous collection of sensations. Yet each member of the set is a pleasure. Why is this so? Is there some interesting feature common to all sensory pleasures? If so, what is it? These questions serve to identify the first question about pleasure. We can call it 'the heterogeneity question'. It is a question about sensory pleasures, and it can be stated succinctly: Is there some feature common to all sensory pleasures, in virtue of which they are pleasures? If so, what is it? The same question could be asked, perhaps in a more old-fashioned way, by asking 'what is the nature of sensory pleasure?'[1]

4.

The second question concerns certain relations between the concept of sensory pleasure and the concept of propositional pleasure.

We use the word 'pleasure' and various cognates to indicate what seems to be a fundamentally sensory phenomenon – sensory pleasure. We also use these words to indicate what seems to be a propositional attitude – propositional pleasure. This leads me to wonder whether there is some interesting semantical connection between the two uses, and whether there is some interesting necessary connection between the two phenomena. There are several main possibilities here.

It might turn out that the two styles of talk are directly intertranslatable. Perhaps each is a mere stylistic variant of the other. In this case, it would be misleading to say that sensory pleasure and propositional pleasure are two different hedonic phenomena. It would be more appropriate to say that there is a certain hedonic phenomenon that can be expressed either in the sensory mode or in the propositional mode. The choice of linguistic mode would be determined on stylistic, rather than ontological, grounds.

A second possibility is that the fundamental hedonic phenomenon is sensory pleasure. It might be the case that there is a certain phenomenological feature present in all and only cases of sensory pleasure, and that

1. In the *Philebus*, Socrates says, '[Pleasure] has one name, and therefore you would imagine that she is one; and yet surely she takes the most varied and even unlike forms. For do we not say that the intemperate has pleasure, and that the temperate has pleasure in his very temperance, – that the fool is pleased when he is full of foolish fancies and hopes, and that the wise man has pleasure in his wisdom? How foolish would any one be who affirmed that all these opposite pleasures are severally alike!' Plato, *Philebus* 12b.

when we say that someone is experiencing sensory pleasure, we are just saying that he is having a sensory experience with this feature. The concept of propositional pleasure, on the other hand, might be definable by appeal to the concept of sensory pleasure. For example, it might turn out that when we say that someone takes propositional pleasure in some state of affairs, we just mean that that state of affairs causes him to experience sensory pleasure. In this case, I would be inclined to say that sensory pleasure has a sort of conceptual primacy over propositional pleasure. The concept of sensory pleasure would, in this case, be the more fundamental of the two, and the concept of propositional pleasure would be definable in terms of it. A number of distinguished philosophers have defended various versions of this view.[2]

The third possibility is the reverse of the second. Perhaps the concept of propositional pleasure is the more fundamental, and the concept of sensory pleasure is to be analyzed by appeal to it. If we took this approach, we might say that the fundamental hedonic phenomenon is not a feeling, or a sensation. Rather, we would say that the fundamental hedonic phenomenon is a propositional attitude we can take toward a state of affairs – something in this respect like hope, or fear, or belief. If we adopted this approach we might go on to say that statements about sensory pleasure are analyzable by appeal to statements about propositional pleasure. For example, we might maintain that a statement to the effect that someone feels sensory pleasure just means that there are some feelings such that he takes propositional pleasure in the fact that he has them. In this case, we could say that propositional pleasure has conceptual primacy over sensory pleasure.

A final possibility should be mentioned. It might turn out that the concepts of sensory and propositional pleasure are independent – perhaps statements about sensory pleasure neither entail nor are entailed by statements about propositional pleasure. Perhaps it is just an accident that we use such similar forms of speech to indicate the two phenomena. Perhaps there are at best some analogies between the case in which a person feels sensory pleasure and the case in which someone takes propositional pleasure in some state of affairs.[3]

So we have our second question about pleasure. Are there any conceptual links between sensory and propositional pleasure? Is either concept

2. Several versions of this view are discussed below in Section 8.
3. Perhaps there are other possibilities. This should suffice.

definable by appeal to the other? Is either conceptually prior to the other? What is the nature of the conceptual linkage, if any, between sensory and propositional pleasure? We can call this 'the linkage question'.

In order to sharpen the questions, as well as to demonstrate their legitimacy, it may be worthwhile to consider some of the most attractive answers that have been proposed. I start with the heterogeneity question.

5.

We sometimes say that pleasurable sensations 'give us pleasure', or that we 'get' or 'derive' pleasure from them. If we take such locutions very seriously, we may arrive at one of the simplest proposed answers to the heterogeneity question.

We might say that the pleasurable feeling of warmth and the pleasurable smell of the fresh salty air in fact do have something in common. However, the common feature is not something that could be discovered by direct phenomenological scrutiny of these sensations. Rather, to discover what they have in common, we would have to reflect upon their causal consequences. It could be claimed that these pleasurable sensations are pleasurable in virtue of the fact that each of them causes a special feeling we might call 'the feeling of pleasure itself'.

When he wrote *Principia Ethica*, G. E. Moore apparently believed in some version of this view. He there suggested that a person feels sensory pleasure iff

> . . . his mind, a certain definite mind, distinguished by certain definite marks from all others, has at this moment a certain definite feeling called pleasure. . . .
> It is enough for us to know that 'pleased' does mean 'having the sensation of pleasure,' and though pleasure is absolutely indefinable, though pleasure is pleasure and nothing else whatever, yet we feel no difficulty in saying that we are pleased.[4]

This first, or Moorean, view seems to be based on the idea that there are really two different sorts of sensory pleasure. Some sensory experiences are sensory pleasures because they are feelings of this 'certain definite feeling called pleasure', or 'pleasure itself'. These would be the most fundamental hedonic phenomena. Other sensory experiences are sensory

4. Moore [1962], p. 12. I have no reason to suppose that Moore continued to hold this view as he matured.

pleasures of a derived sort. They are said to be pleasures because they are feelings that immediately cause feelings of the first sort.[5]

Whenever a person experiences pleasure itself, his experience has some determinate intensity. In other words, he feels some particular amount of pleasure itself. When a person has a derived sensory pleasure, his pleasure has two intensities. One is the intensity of the sensation that immediately causes the pleasure, and the other is the intensity of the pleasure it causes. When we say that one derived sensory pleasure is 'greater' than another, we mean that the one causes a more intense feeling of pleasure itself than the other. Pretty obviously, the two intensities may vary independently.

It must be admitted that the Moorean view is suggested by a number of ordinary language expressions, and that it would serve as a basis for a relatively straightforward hedonic calculus. In spite of the fact that it has these attractive features, the Moorean view is not popular. The central difficulty is straightforwardly phenomenological. The alleged sensation of pleasure itself has proven extremely elusive. No matter how carefully they scrutinize their feelings, phenomenological researchers fail to locate the indefinable feeling Moore attempted to indicate.

Another difficulty is epistemic. Suppose I am drinking beer and eating peanuts more or less simultaneously. Suppose each of the tastes is pleasurable. Suppose, however, that the taste of the peanuts is more pleasurable than the taste of the beer. According to the Moorean view, here's what's happening. I am experiencing the taste of beer and the taste of peanuts. Each taste sensation is causing the feeling of pleasure itself. However, the taste of the peanuts is causing a more intense feeling of pleasure itself than is the taste of the beer.

If the Moorean view were true, I would face a certain slight difficulty when I tried to determine which taste is the greater pleasure. For, according to this view, I would be having four simultaneous relevant sensory experiences: the taste of the peanuts, the taste of the beer, and two feelings of pleasure itself, one more intense than the other. While it would be reasonable for me to assume that the feelings of pleasure were being caused by the tastes, I might have to engage in some causal experimentation in

5. Examples such as the following show why it is important to include the 'immediately': suppose a person experiences some painful feeling, F_1. Sadistic bystanders start to laugh. The victim doesn't know what they are laughing about, and begins to laugh, too. He experiences a happy feeling, F_2. F_2 causes a feeling of pleasure itself. We might want to say that F_2 is a sensory pleasure. However, we don't want to say that F_1 was a sensory pleasure, even though it indirectly caused a feeling of pleasure itself. Hence the need for 'immediately'.

order to determine which taste was causing which feeling of pleasure itself. Perhaps I would put aside the beer and munch on peanuts alone for a while. I could then check to see which feeling of pleasure persists. Then I might put aside the peanuts for a while, and take my beer straight. Once again, I could check to see which feeling of pleasure persists. With luck, I might be able to determine which taste sensation was the greater sensory pleasure.

In fact, however, it seems to me that I never have to engage in this sort of causal experimentation in order to determine which of two simultaneous sensations is the more pleasurable. In a case such as the one imagined, I would be able to tell immediately that the taste of the peanuts was more pleasurable than the taste of the beer. Hence, there is something wrong with the epistemology generated by the Moorean view.[6]

6.

Recent writers on the topic generally maintain that what makes a feeling a sensory pleasure is not how it feels.[7] Rather, what makes it a sensory pleasure is the fact that the person who experiences that feeling has a certain attitude toward his having of it. A not-very-plausible version of the view is suggested by Derek Parfit:

6. In Kenny [1963], p. 129, Kenny presents an argument substantially like this one. Commenting on a view relevantly like the one here under consideration, he says, 'It would be possible to make exactly the same mistakes about what was giving one pleasure as it is possible to make about what has given one a stomach-ache. If, say, one had enjoyed listening to the first performance of a new overture, it would be a mere hypothesis that what one had enjoyed was listening to the overture and not, say, sitting in row G of the dress circle. This hypothesis would need to be verified in accordance with Mill's canons: . . . ' Kenny claims that the argument is a development of one used by Ryle in Ryle [1956]. In Ryle [1949] and [1954], Ryle presented several further arguments against this sort of view. Ryle's arguments have become the focus of much later discussion. See especially Alston [1967], Penelhum [1964], and Penelhum [1957].

7. Another once-popular view is the so-called 'hedonic tone theory' defended by Duncker in Duncker [1940]. According to this view, every sensory experience can be evaluated with respect to its position on the 'pleasure/pain dimension'. If an experience has a phenomenally given positive hedonic tone, then it belongs in the upper part of the pleasure/pain dimension, and is a sensory pleasure. If it has a phenomenally given negative hedonic tone, then it belongs in the lower part of the pleasure/pain dimension, and is a sensory pain. Otherwise, the experience rates a zero in the pleasure/pain dimension, and is neither a sensory pleasure nor a sensory pain. Other notable defenders of the hedonic tone theory include C. D. Broad and Moritz Schlick. See Perry [1967], pp. 193–194, for discussion and references. See Brandt [1959], p. 305, for criticism.

What pains and pleasures have in common are their relations to our desires. . . . all pains are when experienced unwanted, and a pain is worse the more it is unwanted. Similarly, all pleasures are when experienced wanted, and they are better or greater the more they are wanted. . . . one of two experiences is more pleasant if it is preferred.[8]

Parfit seems to be maintaining that a sensation of any phenomenological sort is a sensory pleasure iff at the time he has it, the person who has that sensation wants to be having it. Taken at face value, the view seems pretty obviously false. Suppose I am doing research for an introspective psychological study of the feeling of dizziness. I want to experience dizziness. I decide that I will spin around until I am dizzy, and then focus on the feeling. Suppose I spin and become dizzy. I might then feel dizzy while wanting to feel dizzy. In spite of all this, my feeling of dizziness would not be a pleasurable feeling. It would not be a sensory pleasure.

One thing to note about this example concerns a distinction between what we might call 'intrinsic desire' and what we might call 'extrinsic desire'. Let's say that a person has an intrinsic desire for a thing iff he desires that thing for itself, *per se*, independently of its consequences and accompaniments. Let's say that a person has an extrinsic desire for a thing iff he desires that thing for something else, such as its anticipated consequences or accompaniments. A miser might desire money intrinsically. The rest of us desire it only extrinsically.[9] In the dizziness example, it is most plausible to suppose that my desire to feel dizzy is purely extrinsic. I want to feel dizzy because I want to understand dizziness, and I think that I have to experience it in order to understand it. Were it not for my research interest in dizziness, I probably would not want to experience that feeling. This suggests a slight modification of Parfit's proposal. Perhaps a feeling is a sensory pleasure iff, at the time he has it, the person who has that feeling intrinsically desires to have it.[10]

This proposal is more plausible than its predecessor, but is still not right. Further consideration of misers reveals the problem. I suppose that misers

8. Parfit [1984], pp. 493–494.
9. I use 'intrinsic desire' and 'extrinsic desire' in such a way as to make it possible for a person to have both sorts of desire for a given thing at a given time. A person who is partially miserly might have this sort of mixed desire for money. I use 'purely intrinsic desire' and 'purely extrinsic desire' to indicate unmixed cases.
10. In Brandt [1959], Brandt discusses this sort of view. At one place, he considers the view that " 'x is pleasant' simply means, 'x is a part of my experience that I wish to continue on its own account' ". He offers some modifications, but eventually (307) accepts an analysis according to which pleasures are intrinsically desired parts of experience.

start out desiring money purely extrinsically. As time goes by, their desire for money gradually becomes at least partially intrinsic. The same phenomenon might occur in connection with some sensation. Suppose I have been doing research on dizziness for many years. In connection with my research, I have developed a strong extrinsic desire to feel dizzy. As time goes by, I begin to lose interest in my research, and I become more interested in the dizziness for its own sake. On some occasions I spin around to make myself dizzy even though I've long since given up my research project. Dizziness, which I formerly desired only extrinsically, is now something I desire at least partially intrinsically. Nevertheless, the feeling of dizziness, when I get it, may fail to be a sensory pleasure.

A thoroughly indoctrinated ascetic provides a counterexample in the other direction. He may be utterly convinced that pleasure is worthless. As a result of this conviction, he may lose all extrinsic desire for pleasure. Eventually, however, he may find that he has no desire for pleasure. When some sensory pleasure occurs, he has neither intrinsic nor extrinsic desire to be having that sensation. Thus, we cannot say that sensory pleasures are feelings that are intrinsically desired.

A final version of the propositional attitude view was suggested by Sidgwick. Sidgwick defines sensory pleasure as:

> ... feeling which the sentient individual at the time of feeling it implicitly or explicitly apprehends to be desirable; desirable, that is, when considered merely as feeling, and not in respect of its objective conditions or consequences ... [11]

Sidgwick's view is structurally quite like the views we have just considered. According to it, a feeling is a sensory pleasure in virtue of the fact that the person who experiences that feeling has a certain attitude toward it. The distinctive feature of Sidgwick's approach concerns the nature of the attitude. Whereas others appealed to such attitudes as preference, desire, and intrinsic desire, Sidgwick appeals to 'apprehension as intrinsically desirable'. This seems pretty implausible.

Any antihedonist who sincerely maintains that some sensory pleasures are intrinsically worthless or evil would apparently serve to refute Sidgwick's view. For any such person could experience a sensory pleasure without believing that feeling to be intrinsically good. I assume that such a person experiences sensory pleasure but does not 'apprehend it to be intrinsically desirable as feeling'. [12]

---

11. Sidgwick [1962], p. 131.
12. I am here overlooking some complexities in Sidgwick's view. Other passages (111)

It also seems to me that a person might apprehend some nonpleasurable sensory experience to be intrinsically desirable. For example, a person might observe a child suffering undeserved pain. The observation of this unjustified evil might produce a painful feeling of anger. G. E. Moore and others would say that this painful feeling of anger is intrinsically good.[13] While it is not entirely clear to me that this would count as a case of 'apprehending' a feeling to be intrinsically desirable, it certainly seems close. If it is, then it shows that it is possible for someone to apprehend a feeling to be intrinsically desirable, even though that feeling is not a sensory pleasure.

There are other proposed answers to the heterogeneity question, but I prefer not to canvass them here.[14] I hope this relatively brief survey suffices to show that there is a genuine question about the nature of sensory pleasure; that a number of distinguished and insightful philosophers have proposed or suggested answers; and that many of these answers are in one way or another unsatisfactory. Let us turn now to the second question about pleasure – what is the linkage (if any) between sensory and propositional pleasure?

7.

So far as I know, only a few philosophers have attempted to answer the linkage question. While they have given a few different answers, their answers are alike in several important respects. These philosophers seem to agree (a) that sensory pleasure is the more fundamental hedonic phenomenon, that (b) propositional pleasure is to be analyzed by appeal to sensory, and that (c) when we say that a person takes propositional pleasure in some state of affairs, we are saying something to the effect that there is some causal connection somehow involving that state of affairs and some experience of sensory pleasure.

One version of this approach has been suggested by a few philosophers. It's not clear to me that any of these philosophers would defend it in this

suggest that he wants to provide a sort of naturalistic analysis of the meaning of 'desirable'.

13. Moore [1962], p. 217 says, 'Yet pity for the undeserved sufferings of others, endurance of pain to ourselves, and a defiant hatred of evil dispositions in ourselves or in others, seem to be undoubtedly admirable in themselves; . . . '. Brentano maintained a similar view.

14. In Goldstein [1985], p. 54, Goldstein hints at a few possibilities. One of these is that sensory pleasures are feelings to which we are normally 'attracted'.

simple form.[15] We might say that a person is pleased that p iff p causes him to feel sensory pleasure. In other words, a person takes propositional pleasure in a state of affairs iff that state of affairs 'makes him pleased' – or causes him to experience sensory pleasure.

This view seems to me to be confused. Clearly, there is a difference between the case in which someone is pleased *as a result of* some state of affairs, and the case in which he is pleased *that* that state of affairs is occurring. As I see it, the proposed analysis runs these things together.[16] To highlight the difference, consider a case in which a sensory pleasure is being caused by factors of which the subject is unaware.[17] For example, suppose that suitable electrodes have been implanted in a man's brain, but he is unaware of their presence. When a slight current is passed through the electrodes, the man experiences a sensory pleasure – it feels like the pleasurable sensations one normally has while lying on a warm tropical beach. The cause of the man's sensory pleasure is the passage of current through the electrodes. In this case it would be correct to say that the man is pleased *as a result of* the passage of current through the electrodes in his brain, but it would be wrong to say that the subject of the experiment is pleased that a slight current has been passed through the electrodes in his brain.

This example suggests a slight alteration of the proposal. Perhaps we should say that a person takes propositional pleasure in a state of affairs, p, iff he is aware that p is the case, and p causes him to experience sensory pleasure.

Further reflection on the example shows, however, that this modification doesn't constitute any improvement. Suppose we tell the electrode-man that there are some electrodes in his brain, and that the passage of

15. This view is discussed in Penelhum [1964], p. 228: 'To say that someone took pleasure in something would therefore be to say that it caused him to experience this feeling.' It would also be interesting to compare this simple view to the far more sophisticated one defended by Wayne Davis in Davis [1981b]. There Davis says: 'A is pleased that p iff it makes A happy that p'. (p. 308).

16. Part of the difficulty here may be due to sloppy usage. Some of us use 'I am pleased because p' in such a way as to make it unclear whether we mean to say that p is the *cause* or whether we mean to say that p is the *object* of our pleasure. Perhaps this lends credibility to the view that p is the object of our pleasure iff it is the cause. B. A. O. Williams noted this confusion (Williams [1959], p. 57) and presented a neat argument to show that the view is confused. Suppose I erroneously believe that I have just inherited a large sum of money. That I inherited the money may be the *object* of my pleasure, but, since it hasn't occurred, it cannot be the *cause* of my pleasure.

17. This critical point probably would not apply to the view defended by Davis. I hope to discuss Davis's view in detail elsewhere.

92

current in them is causing him to feel sensory pleasure. Now he's aware of the cause of his sensory pleasure. Still, he might not be at all pleased that there are electrodes in his brain, and he might not be pleased that current is being passed through them. He might be an unwilling and unhappy participant in what seems to him to be a thoroughly ghoulish experiment.

A slightly different thesis about the linkage between sensory and propositional pleasure was apparently maintained by Brentano.[18] He held that *love* and *hate* are two utterly fundamental, unanalyzable attitudes. To love a state of affairs is to have some sort of 'pro-attitude' toward it. It is to favor it, to like it, to be 'for' it. Brentano maintained that a person's love of some state of affairs may cause him to experience sensory pleasure. When this happens, the sensory pleasure is said to 'redound from' the love of the state of affairs. In a remarkable passage, Brentano cites two alleged historical instances of this phenomenon:

> When Newton read that his astronomical hypotheses had been confirmed by new measurements, his joy became more and more intense and he was finally so overcome that he could no longer continue reading. He succumbed to the intensive sensuous pleasure which had redounded from his higher feelings. The same was true of Archimedes when he called out "Eureka!" as though intoxicated. Even those pleasures one may take in the awareness of virtue or vice may give rise to violent sensuous passions.[19]

Chisholm interprets Brentano as having held that a person takes propositional pleasure in a proposition just in case his love of that proposition causes him to experience some sensory pleasure.[20] Thus, in the example concerning Newton, this is what happened: Let 'C' indicate the proposition that Newton's hypotheses had been confirmed by new measurements. Newton loved C. His love of C caused Newton to experience some sensory pleasure. When we say that Newton took propositional pleasure in C, what we mean is that his love of C caused him to experience sensory pleasure. In general, we can say that when sensory pleasure redounds from someone's love of a state of affairs, he then takes proposi-

---

18. Brentano [1969], p. 155. Brentano goes on to suggest that Aristotle held a view much like his own, and suggests that it can be found in Book X of the *Nichomachean Ethics*. Brentano's theory is reformulated and defended by Chisholm [1986], Chapter 3, pp. 15–22.
19. Brentano [1969], p. 155.
20. Chisholm confirmed this interpretation in personal correspondence. A relevantly similar view is defended by Robert M. Gordon in Gordon [1974].

tional pleasure in that state of affairs. Let us formulate the Brentano–Chisholm version of the view in question as follows:

PP: s takes propositional pleasure in p at t = df. s's love of p at t causes s to experience sensory pleasure at t.

I assume that the intensity of a person's propositional pleasure in a state of affairs is equal to the intensity of the sensory pleasure he feels as a result of his love of that state of affairs.

In order to see how the Brentano–Chisholm proposal is supposed to work, consider again the man with smart children. Suppose the children come home from school, and present their report cards to their father. He sees that they have gotten good grades. He loves the fact that they have gotten good grades. His love of this fact causes him to experience some pleasurable sensations. Perhaps the pleasurable sensations are internal, bodily feelings. Maybe he feels a pleasurable 'glow of pride'. The precise nature of the sensory pleasure does not matter. So long as his love of the fact that they got good grades causes him to feel some sensory pleasure, it is correct to say that he is pleased that they got good grades.

The Brentano–Chisholm view does not generate incorrect results in the case of the electrode-man. Let E be the state of affairs of current being passed in the electrodes in the man's brain. E causes the man to feel sensory pleasure. On the Brentano–Chisholm view, this fact is irrelevant. The question here is whether the man's love of E causes him to feel sensory pleasure. If the electrode-man were like me, he wouldn't love E at all, and so his love of E wouldn't cause anything. Thus, we don't have to say that the electrode-man is pleased that current is being passed in the electrodes in his brain.

The Brentano–Chisholm view seems to me to face a number of difficulties. One problem is straightforwardly phenomenological. Sometimes when I take pleasure in some state of affairs, I do not experience any sensory pleasure. For example, there have been cases in which I was introduced to someone, and in which I was genuinely pleased that I was meeting that person, but in which I did not experience anything I would naturally call sensory pleasure. In one case that I recall pretty clearly, I was being introduced to a distinguished, elderly philosopher. There was nothing aesthetically pleasing about him, and so my visual experiences on that occasion were not sensory pleasures. His hand was somewhat limp and clammy, and so the tactual sensations associated with shaking his hand were not sensory pleasures. In spite of all this, I am certain that I was very pleased to be meeting him. It is therefore impossible to explain my propositional pleasure by claiming that my love of the fact that I was meeting this man caused me to feel some sensory pleasure. In the case described, I didn't feel any sensory pleasure, and so my love of the state of affairs of my meeting him evidently did not cause any sensory pleasure.

Another difficulty for any such view is this: we can surely imagine a person who has been so anesthetized that he temporarily cannot experience any sensory pleasure. For example, consider a man who has been in a motorcycle accident, and who has been shot full of a powerful anesthetic. Suppose this man can feel neither sensory pleasures nor sensory pains. He may nevertheless be pleased to find he's still alive. Clearly, then, we cannot maintain that his propositional pleasure is to be explained by saying that his love of the fact that he is alive causes him to feel sensory pleasure.

A final difficulty is epistemic. Suppose a man is pleased about two different things at once. For example, suppose he's pleased that his son got good grades (S) and he's also pleased that his daughter got good grades (D). Suppose, finally, that he's more pleased about D than he is about S. If the Brentano–Chisholm causal view were true, the man would be loving two states of affairs simultaneously, and each love would be causing a sensory pleasure. The sensory pleasure caused by the love of D would be greater than the sensory pleasure caused by S.

It seems to me that, if this were an accurate account of the man's circumstance, then the man would face a certain difficulty if he tried to figure out whether he was more pleased about S or D. For he would have to determine which love was the cause of which sensory pleasure. However, it seems to me that we generally don't face this sort of difficulty when we reflect on our propositional pleasures. I think that if I were in this man's situation, and I reflected on the question whether I was more pleased about S or D, I would not have to engage in any causal experimentation in order to reach a decision. Hence, it seems to me that the Brentano–Chisholm view generates the wrong epistemology for propositional pleasure.[21]

So it seems to me that the linkage question is legitimate, too. It is

21. In Gordon [1974], Gordon discusses this point in a section entitled 'How to Find Out What You Are Angry About: The Hard Way.' My impression is that Gordon thinks that you can find out what you're angry about by subjecting yourself to 'neurological studies'. My hunch is that such studies could at best reveal what is 'making you angry'. If I'm right, Gordon has confused *being made angry by p* with *being angry that p*. I formerly thought I understood some of the fundamentals of the epistemology of pleasure. Conversations with Jaegwon Kim convinced me that things are a bit less clear than I took them to be. I hope to return to this topic.

reasonable to suppose that there is some connection between the concept of sensory pleasure and the concept of propositional pleasure, but none of the suggestions considered here is fully adequate.

In the final sections of this paper, I will propose my own answer to the linkage question and my own answer to the heterogeneity question. Perhaps surprisingly, I give only one answer. I believe that this single answer suffices for both questions. I turn now to the presentation of that answer.

8.

My answer to the heterogeneity question is, roughly, this: all sensory pleasures are alike in virtue of the fact the individuals who have them take a certain sort of propositional pleasure in the fact that they have them when they have them. My answer to the linkage question is, roughly, this: when we say that a person experiences sensory pleasure, what we mean is that there is a sensation such that he then takes a certain sort of propositional pleasure in the fact that he has that sensation. Thus, both questions are answered by appeal to a special sort of propositional pleasure, which for present purposes I take as an unanalyzed conceptual primitive.

Since I take propositional pleasure as conceptually primary, it is incumbent upon me to attempt to make this concept reasonably clear before going on. I now turn to that project.

Propositional pleasure is a 'pro-attitude'. It belongs in the same family as wanting, and favorably evaluating. It is like these pro-attitudes in several respects. One of these concerns intensity. A person may be pleased that p is true, and pleased that q is true, but he may be *more pleased* about p than he is about q.

Propositional pleasure is different from these other propositional attitudes. I may want something to occur without being pleased that it is occurring. This happens most naturally when I am convinced that it isn't happening. Some have suggested that propositional pleasure can be identified with the conjunction of belief and desire.[22] The idea here is that someone is pleased that p is the case iff he believes that p is the case and wants p to be the case.

---

22. Davis [1981a], p. 113. 'Someone is happy that it is going to rain if he is certain that it will and wants it to.' Of course, Davis mentions happiness, not pleasure. However, if, as he suggests elsewhere, these are identical, we get the desired result. See Davis [1981b], pp. 306–307 where Davis says, 'I believe that *pleasure* can be identified with occurrent, nonrelational happiness. *A person experiences pleasure if, and only if, he experiences happiness.*'

While propositional pleasure is quite like belief plus desire, I think there are some subtle differences. One difference concerns what we might call 'non-hedonic sources of desire'. Suppose I think I deserve some punishment. I might be such a fanatic about justice that I actually want to get that punishment. Then, when I am getting the punishment, it might be correct to say that I want to be punished, and I believe that I am being punished, even though it would not be quite right to say that I am pleased that I am being punished. As I see it, to be pleased about a state of affairs, one must have a slightly different pro-attitude toward it – one must 'welcome' that state of affairs.

Another difference concerns the case in which I want a certain state of affairs to occur and think it will, but in which the state of affairs is far in the future, and my belief in it is thoroughly unjustified. Suppose for example that I want the weather to be fair next week, and, without good evidence, think it will be. It still seems wrong to say that I am pleased that next week's weather will be fair. Perhaps it would be better to say that I confidently hope that next week's weather will be fair.

It might be suggested that to take pleasure in some state of affairs is just to take that state of affairs to be good. Once again, however, it seems to me that there are some subtle differences. Suppose I love the taste of beer and peanuts and am right now drinking some beer and eating some especially good peanuts. Suppose I am aware of the fact that a certain neighbor is also drinking beer and eating peanuts right now. Let F be the proposition that I am drinking beer and eating peanuts now, and let N be the proposition that my neighbor is doing likewise. I might take more pleasure in F than I do in N, even though I recognize that F is not more valuable than N. My axiological intuitions tell me that F and N are equal in value. If I'm sufficiently fairminded, I might even fail to prefer F to N. For all that, I take more pleasure in F than I do in N. I am more pleased that F is occurring than I am that N is occurring. I believe that this case shows that taking pleasure in a state of affairs is different from believing it to be good.

More extreme examples can be imagined. A thoroughly malicious person might take pleasure in some state of affairs even though he was utterly convinced that it was quite bad. For example, a cruel-hearted and envious person might take pleasure in a rival's suffering without for a moment believing it to be good that his rival suffers.

Some propositional attitudes are 'truth-entailing' – if a person stands in such an attitude toward some proposition, then that proposition must be true. A good example here is knowledge. Some philosophers have suggested that propositional pleasure is in this way a truth-entailing attitude. According to this view, I cannot be pleased that my children have done well in school unless they have.

My own impression is that propositional pleasure is not truth-entailing. I am convinced by examples such as this: suppose some children are in fact not doing well in school, but have become expert counterfeiters. They produce remarkably realistic counterfeit report cards. The grades on the counterfeits are far superior to those on the genuine articles. They present the counterfeit report cards to their father, who is taken in by the hoax. He thinks they are doing very well in school, and is pleased about this. He says, 'I am pleased that my children are doing so well in school.'

I would say, in a case such as this, that the father's statement might be correct. As I see it, one can take propositional pleasure in a state of affairs even though that state of affairs is not occurring. Some philosophers seem to agree with me.[23] Others clearly disagree.[24] For present purposes, it may be best to settle for a compromise.

Imagine two fathers, as alike as possible. Each is joyfully studying his children's report cards. Each is noting an unbroken string of 'A's, and each is (as I would put it) pleased that his children are doing well in school. Imagine further that one of these fathers is studying a genuine report card that accurately reflects his children's academic successes. The other is studying a carefully contrived counterfeit that reflects his children's growing expertise in counterfeiting. Surely, the two fathers are alike in some important respect. I see nothing wrong with saying that each is pleased that his children are doing well in school. If this seems a violation of

---

23. Terence Penelhum seems to be a good example. 'We are often pleased by a supposed fact which is not a fact at all. . . . Pleasure at any agreeable piece of misinformation will fit into this category, as when I am pleased to hear the false report that the horse I bet on has won the race'. Penelhum [1964], p. 84. I understand Penelhum to be saying that it is possible for a person to be pleased that his horse has won, even though in fact his horse has not won.

   Chisholm seems to be another example. In Chisholm ([1986], Chapter 3, Section 7), he discusses the case of Charles Evans Hughes, who for a time thought he had been elected President of the United States. Chisholm suggests that as a matter of ordinary language, we would not say that Hughes was pleased that he won. However, Chisholm says, 'Surely the object of his pleasure was his winning the election – not his coming to believe that he had won the election.' Chisholm suggests that we should 'violate our ordinary language' and treat 'pleased that' as non-truth-entailing.

   Other examples include Irving Thalberg, who discusses (Thalberg [1962], p. 67) the case of a man who is mistakenly delighted that he won the Irish Sweepstakes; and B. A. O. Williams, who discusses (Williams [1959], p. 57) the case of a person who is pleased that he has inherited a fortune, when in fact he has inherited nothing.

24. Examples include Gordon ([1974], p. 34), and almost all of my friends and colleagues.

ordinary linguistic practice, we may introduce a notational convenience. Let us say that one father is pleased that his children are doing well. (This father is the one whose children are in fact doing well.) We can say that the other father is pleased* that his children are doing well. (This is the father of the counterfeiters.) From here on, when I speak of propositional pleasure, I mean to indicate the attitude expressed by the statement that someone is pleased* that something is the case.

Virtually all writers on the topic agree that propositional pleasure entails belief. If you are pleased that something is the case, then you believe it is the case. Some even go so far as to say that propositional pleasure entails knowledge.[25] Since I have stipulated that propositional pleasure is not truth-entailing, I am committed to denying this last thesis.

Having said these few words in an attempt to clarify the concept of propositional pleasure, I want to turn to the central projects: explaining the nature of sensory pleasure and describing the conceptual linkage between it and propositional pleasure.

8.1

Consider what happens when a happy sunbather enjoys the warmth of the sunshine on a tropical beach. He has a certain sensory property – the property of feeling warmth in a certain way. Let's call this property 'W'. Suppose a certain sunbather, s, is characterized by W at a time, t. Then a certain state of affairs occurs. It is [Ws,t]. While it involves a certain violation of ordinary English, we can say that this state of affairs is a 'sensation'. In general, we can say that if F is a sensory property, s a potential sensor, and t a time, then the state of affairs of s *having F at t* (or [Fs,t]) is a potential sensation. If s exemplifies F at t, then it is an actual sensation.

We might propose to explain sensory pleasure by saying that a sensation is a sensory pleasure iff the sensor takes propositional pleasure in it at the time of its occurrence. In other words:

SP1: [Fs,t] is a sensory pleasure iff [Fs,t] is a sensation, [Fs,t] occurs, and s takes propositional pleasure in [Fs,t] at t.

Unfortunately, this approach is too simple. There are obvious counterexamples. Suppose a man has been in a terrible motorcycle accident. Now he's recuperating in the hospital. He feels numb all over. The doctor

---

25. Wayne Davis says that propositional happiness presupposes knowledge. Davis [1981b], pp. 305–306. Robert Gordon says the same thing. Gordon [1974], p. 34.

tells him that he might be permanently paralyzed – but then again it might just be temporary. He tells the motorcyclist to concentrate on the feelings in his toes. If he feels an unpleasant stinging sensation in his toes, then he will surely recover completely. The motorcyclist focusses on his toes. Soon he begins to feel a stinging sensation. He is delighted. He takes propositional pleasure in the fact that he feels a stinging sensation in his toes. Contrary to what SP1 says, the sensation is not a sensory pleasure. It is painful.[26]

In order to improve upon SP1, it will be necessary to distinguish *intrinsic* propositional pleasure from *extrinsic* propositional pleasure. Sometimes a person takes propositional pleasure in a state of affairs purely for its own sake. For example, consider a person who loves the taste of peanuts. Suppose he is eating some peanuts and is savoring the taste. He may take pleasure in the fact that he is experiencing that taste. It may be that all of the pleasure he takes in this fact is 'intrinsic' – none of it is derived from anticipations or expectations of other things to which the tasting of the peanuts may lead. He takes pleasure in the tasting entirely 'for its own sake'.

Sometimes a person takes propositional pleasure in one thing because he takes propositional pleasure in another. A common example concerns money. An ordinary, non-miserly person may take pleasure in the fact that he has a lot of money. Of course, if he's non-miserly, he takes pleasure in having the money only because he recognizes that his possession of the money enables him to purchase various items that he wants to purchase. If he discovered that money had become worthless, he might no longer take propositional pleasure in the fact that he has so much of it.

In other cases, a person takes pleasure in one thing not because he thinks that thing will enable him to get another, but because the first thing somehow is an indicator, or sign, of the other thing. For example, consider again the man who takes pleasure in his children's good report cards. He takes pleasure in the fact that they got good grades, not because he thinks it will *enable* his children to become good students, and surely not because he thinks it will *cause* them to be good students, but because it serves as

---

26. The dizziness example discussed above in Section 6 would also serve to refute this thesis. In that example, a person wanted to experience dizziness and then did so. It would be reasonable to suppose that, when he experienced dizziness, he was pleased to be experiencing it. However, the feeling of dizziness was a not a sensory pleasure. According to my view, a feeling is a sensory pleasure only if the person who has it takes *intrinsic* pleasure in the fact that he has it. The man who wants to be dizzy takes only *extrinsic* pleasure in his dizziness.

good evidence for the belief that they already are good students. He takes pleasure in their being good students.

Whenever a person takes pleasure in any of these ways in one thing because of another we may say that his pleasure in the first is 'extrinsic propositional pleasure'. The second thing may be said to be the 'source' of the derived pleasure in the second.

For my purposes here, the central concept is the concept of intrinsic propositional pleasure. We must recognize that not all intrinsic pleasure is *pure* intrinsic pleasure. It is possible for a person to take some intrinsic pleasure in a state of affairs while also taking some extrinsic pleasure in that state of affairs. For example, my doctor might tell me that my health would be improved if I were to enjoy myself more. Then, when I experience some pleasurable sensation, I might take both intrinsic and extrinsic propositional pleasure in the fact that I am feeling that sensation.

8.2

A more plausible account of sensory pleasures is based on the concept of intrinsic propositional pleasure. According to this view, a sensation is a sensory pleasure iff its sensor takes intrinsic propositional pleasure in it at the time of its occurrence. In other words:

SP2: [Fs,t] is a sensory pleasure iff [Fs, t] is a sensation, [Fs,t] occurs, and s takes intrinsic propositional pleasure in [Fs,t] at t.

SP2 does not go astray in the case of the injured motorcyclist. Though he takes pleasure in the stinging sensation in his toes, he does not take intrinsic pleasure in that stinging. His pleasure is entirely derived. He takes pleasure in the stinging sensation because he believes that it is a sign that he will not be paralyzed, and he's pleased that he will not be paralyzed.

Nevertheless, SP2 is not quite right. A rather complicated case will reveal the difficulty. Suppose I am an unhappy old sadist. I am unhappy, let us suppose, because I have a miserable toothache. On my way to the dentist's office, I pass a large mirror. I mistake the mirror for a window. I look into the mirror and see an unhappy-looking old man, obviously suffering from a toothache. I take intrinsic propositional pleasure in the old man's sensation. Unbeknownst to me, the old man with the toothache is me.

In this sort of case, SP2 yields the result that the old sadist's toothache is a sensory pleasure. This seems wrong to me, in spite of the fact that the old sadist takes intrinsic pleasure in it. Thus, I want to introduce a modification into SP2.

8.3

We must distinguish between the case in which I take pleasure in s's having F, and s happens to be me, and the case in which I take pleasure in the fact that I myself have F. The former sort of case (illustrated by the sadist who sees himself in the mirror) is not relevant to my present purposes. For present purposes, it will be necessary to focus on the second sort of case.

Suppose that [Ws,t] is the state of affairs of s feeling warmth at t, and suppose that I am s. Even though [Ws,t] is directly about me, I might take pleasure in [Ws,t] without recognizing that it is I myself who is the feeler of the warmth in [Ws,t]. This would be a case of 'de re pleasure in a sensation that happens to be mine'. On the other hand, suppose that I take pleasure in the fact that I myself am feeling warmth now. Suppose I have no doubt or confusion about the identity of the person experiencing the warmth. I correctly take him to be me. This would be a straightforward case of 'de se pleasure'.

Another sort of de se pleasure involves much less self-awareness. Suppose I am enjoying the warmth on the tropical beach. Suppose I am drowsy and non-self-conscious. I am pleased to be feeling this lovely warmth, but I am not giving any thought to the identity of the feeler of the warmth. I am not consciously taking him to be me, and I am not consciously taking him to be anyone else. I'm just not thinking of him.

Some philosophers might hesitate to say, in a case such as this, that I am experiencing de se pleasure.[27] The problem, as they see it, is that one cannot have a de se attitude unless one has 'active self-awareness'. My own view is different. On my view, a person can have a de se attitude even though he is not aware of himself. As I see it, when a non-self-conscious person is pleased to be warm, he has a de se attitude. He is pleased that he himself is warm.

The proper analysis of de se attitudes is a matter of controversy. It isn't clear that de se attitudes are genuinely *propositional* attitudes, and so it is not clear that de se propositional pleasure takes a proposition as its object. It might be that there is no such proposition as the proposition that I

27. A particularly clear statement of this position can be found in Peter Markie [1984].

myself am feeling warmth. Perhaps it would be better to say that the object of a *de se* attitude is a property.[28] My proposal about pleasure can be stated in the propositional style as follows:

SP3: [Fs,t] is a sensory pleasure iff [Fs,t] is a sensation, [Fs,t] occurs, and s takes intrinsic *de se* propositional pleasure in [Fs,t] at t.

A variant of SP3 can be stated in a 'non-propositional' form as follows:

SP3': [Fs,t] is a sensory pleasure iff [Fs,t] is a sensation, [Fs,t] occurs, and s is intrinsically pleased at t that he himself is feeling F at t.

Yet another variant can be stated in a manner that may seem to some to be better suited to the case of non-self-conscious individuals:

SP3": [Fs,t] is a sensory pleasure iff [Fs,t] is a sensation, [Fs,t] occurs, and s is intrinsically pleased at t to be feeling F.

I believe that these three versions of my view are equivalent. Obviously, I will not be able to defend this view here.

According to my account, here's what happens when the happy sunbather experiences sensory pleasure on the beach: there is a certain sensory property, W, which characterizes people if and only if they are feeling warmth in a certain way. The sunbather, s, is characterized by W at t. The state of affairs, [Ws,t], is a sensation. At t, the sunbather is intrinsically pleased to be characterized by W.

In every case of sensory pleasure, there are two relevant 'amounts' or intensities. One is the intensity of the sensation, indicated by 'F' in SP3. The other is the intensity of the propositional pleasure that the sensor takes in F. These amounts vary independently. Thus, a certain feeling of warmth may be a sensory pleasure, and yet, as that feeling of warmth becomes more intense, it may become less of a pleasure. This explains the somewhat paradoxical fact that more intense pleasures are sometimes less pleasurable.

Now we can see how a single answer suffices for both questions. I propose to answer the heterogeneity question by saying this: all sensory pleasures are alike in virtue of the fact that the people who experience them take intrinsic *de se* propositional pleasure in the fact that they are having them. I propose to answer the linkage question by claiming that the concept of sensory pleasure is analyzable by appeal to the concept of propositional pleasure. More specifically, according to my suggestion,

28. David Lewis seems to prefer to put things in this way. See his [1979]. Chisholm, in [1981], seems to advocate a similar approach.

when we say that a person is experiencing sensory pleasure, what we mean is that there is some sensation he is having such that he is intrinsically pleased to be having that sensation. So, on my view, propositional pleasure is the more fundamental concept, and the concept of sensory pleasure can be analyzed by appeal to it.[29]

BIBLIOGRAPHY

Alston, William [1967], 'Pleasure', in Paul Edwards (ed.), *The Encyclopedia of Philosophy* (New York: Macmillan & Co), 6 341–347.

Brandt, Richard [1959], *Ethical Theory* (Englewood Cliffs: Prentice-Hall, Inc.).

Brandt, Richard [1979], *A Theory of the Good and the Right* (Oxford: The Clarendon Press).

Brentano, Franz [1969], 'Loving and Hating', appendix to *The Origin of our Knowledge of Right and Wrong*, translated by Roderick M. Chisholm and Elizabeth H. Schneewind (London: Routledge and Kegan Paul) 137–160.

Chisholm, Roderick M. [1981], *The First Person* (Minneapolis: University of Minnesota Press).

Chisholm, Roderick M. [1986], *Brentano and Intrinsic Value* (Cambridge: Cambridge University Press).

Davis, Wayne [1981a], 'A Theory of Happiness', *American Philosophical Quarterly*, **18** Number 2 (April) 111–120.

Davis, Wayne [1981b], 'Pleasure and Happiness,' *Philosophical Studies*, **39** 305–317.

Davis, Wayne [1982], 'A Causal Theory of Enjoyment,' *Mind*, **XCI** 240–256.

Duncker, Karl [1940], 'On Pleasure, Emotion, and Striving', *Philosophy and Phenomenological Research*, **I** 391–430.

Edwards, Rem B. [1979], *Pleasures and Pains: A Theory of Qualitative Hedonism* (Ithaca: Cornell University Press).

Freud, Sigmund, *Beyond the Pleasure Principle*.

Goldstein, Irwin [1985], 'Hedonic Pluralism', *Philosophical Studies*, **48** 49–55.

Gordon, Robert M. [1974], 'The Aboutness of Emotions', *American Philosophical Quarterly*, **11** Number 1 (January) 27–36.

29. A number of people read earlier drafts of this paper, and made useful suggestions. Among these are Mark Aronszajn, Tom Blackson, Eva Bodanszky, Michael Jubien, Jaegwon Kim, and Gareth Matthews. I have also benefitted enormously from discussions with Roderick Chisholm. I thank Professor Chisholm for permitting me to see prepublication draft of [1986].

An earlier version of this paper was presented at the October 1986 meeting of the Creighton Club. I am grateful to several members of the Club for the very useful suggestions they made on that pleasant occasion.

Gosling, J. C. B. [1969], *Pleasure and Desire* (Oxford: The Clarendon Press).

Kenny, Anthony [1963], *Action, Emotion and Will* (London: Routledge and Kegan Paul).

Lewis, David [1979], 'Attitudes De Dicto and De Se', *Philosophical Review*, **88** (October) 513–543.

Markie, Peter [1984], '*De Dicto* and *De Se'*, *Philosophical Studies*, **45** 231–237.

Moore, G. E. [1962], *Principia Ethica* (Cambridge: Cambridge University Press).

Parfit, Derek [1984], *Reasons and Persons* (Oxford: The Clarendon Press).

Penelhum, Terence [1957], 'The Logic of Pleasure', *Philosophy and Phenomenological Research*, **17** 488–503.

Penelhum, Terence [1964], 'Pleasure and Falsity', *American Philosophical Quarterly*, **I** 2 (April) 81–91.

Perry, David [1967], *The Concept of Pleasure* (The Hague: Mouton). Plato, *Philebus*.

Ryle, Gilbert [1949], *The Concept of Mind* (London: Hutchinson).

Ryle, Gilbert [1954], 'Pleasure', *Proceedings of the Aristotelian Society*, supplementary volume **28** 135–146.

Ryle, Gilbert [1956], *Dilemmas* (Cambridge: Cambridge University Press).

Sidgwick, Henry [1962], *The Methods of Ethics* (London: Macmillan & Co, Ltd.).

Thalberg, Irving [1962], 'False Pleasures', *The Journal of Philosophy*, **59** 65–74.

Von Wright, G. H. [1963], *The Varieties of Goodness* (London: Routledge and Kegan Paul).

Williams, B. A. O. [1959], 'Pleasure and Belief', *Proceedings of the Aristotelian Society*, supplementary volume **33** 57–72.

Essay 6

Mill, Moore, and the Consistency of Qualified Hedonism

INTRODUCTORY COMMENTS

The title of this essay suggests that it concerns the controversy about qualified hedonism. However, overt discussion of that controversy takes up just a tiny fraction of the paper. Most of the paper is devoted to a more fundamental issue – how to formulate an axiological theory, with a few versions of hedonism as the examples. I spend a lot of time trying to show that standard formulations of hedonism are so confused that it's pointless to consider whether they are consistent with each other, and so on.

The paper has some clearly "negative" aims. I want to show that typical formulations of hedonism are seriously defective. Thus, for example, I discuss the sort of formulation often encountered in the writings of Plato, Aristotle, Moore, and many others. These philosophers sometimes state the central thesis of hedonism by saying "Pleasure alone is intrinsically good." The problem here is that "pleasure" seems to be a singular noun – the name of some feeling or some property. But this can't possibly be right. Hedonists do not want to say that there is exactly one intrinsically good thing. They want to say that lots of things are intrinsically good (this life, that world, the other consequence, many different experiences), and they want to say that these things have different intrinsic values and they occur at different times. So, formulations such as the ones cited must have the *number* wrong. Maybe their authors meant to say that *pleasures* (plural) are intrinsically good. But what are these?

Some philosophers take "pleasures" to be "pleasant things." Thus, for example, both Brandt and Dahl say that hedonism is the view that "all and only pleasant things are intrinsically good." This again is an unacceptable way to state the central doctrine of hedonism. In a footnote I try to explain why this formulation fails. Roughly, the problem is that "pleasant things" are things that generally give us pleasure – things in which most of us typically take pleasure. Hedonists do not want to say in such a case that the pleasant thing itself (such as Crescent Beach on Block Island) is intrinsically good; they might instead want to say that the pleasures visitors get from experiencing Crescent Beach are intrinsically good.

Chisholm (following Brentano and others) has proposed a much more plausible approach. He takes pleasures to be "hedonic states" – states of affairs to the effect that someone feels some pleasure. We might then say that hedonism is the view that these hedonic states are the only intrinsic goods (and, correspondingly, that "doloric states" are the only intrinsic evils). Chisholm starts in this way and adds to this the claim that the intrinsic value of a complex state of affairs such as a possible world is the sum of the intrinsic values of the pleasures and pains contained.

My next negative aim is to show the terrible muddles we get into if we formulate hedonism in any such way. Formulations following the pattern of Chisholm's are self-contradictory. They say, first, that hedonic states are the only intrinsic goods; immediately thereafter, they go on to say that other states are also intrinsically good if they contain more pleasure than pain. You can't have it both ways. The problem can be avoided if we employ the notion of the "basic intrinsic value state." I take this to be a very important and almost universally overlooked axiological concept. I think failure to make use of this concept simply ruins a good deal of the literature in axiology. I first came across the idea in Gilbert Harman's "Toward a Theory of Intrinsic Value."

Making use of the concept of the basic intrinsic value state, I formulate a version of simple hedonism and a version of qualified hedonism. I point out that if we formulate qualified hedonism as I suggest, it is an internally consistent theory. It is also a form of hedonism. Thus, I claim, Moore was wrong.

I should perhaps mention that there is very little discussion of the nature of pleasure in this paper. My focus is entirely on "structural" aspects of the formulation of the hedonistic axiological theory. In Essay 7 I try to combine the conception of pleasure from Essay 5 with the conception of axiology from Essay 6.

6

Mill, Moore, and the consistency of qualified hedonism

1. INTRODUCTORY COMMENTS

Certain facts are pretty well known: Bentham said that quantity of pleasure being equal, pushpin is as good as poetry.[1] But this seemed implausible; surely a life devoted to pushpin is less valuable than a life devoted to poetry. Mill tried to straighten this out. He claimed that if it were a choice between pushpin and poetry, quantity of pleasure would not be equal, but (just in case that turns out to be a mistake) utilitarians can rise to higher ground – they can alter the axiology just to be sure. Mill said: 'it would be absurd that, while in estimating all other things quality is considered as well as quantity, the estimation of pleasure should be supposed to depend on quantity alone.'[2] Moore then came along and said that Mill thus contradicted himself.

> . . . if you say, as Mill does, that quality of pleasure is to be taken into account, then you are no longer holding that pleasure *alone* is good as an end, since you imply that something else, something which is *not* present in all pleasures, is *also* good as an end. . . . If we do really mean 'Pleasure alone is good as an end,' then we must agree with Bentham that 'Quantity of pleasure being equal, pushpin is as good as poetry.'[3]

Moore's point was that Mill's "qualified hedonism" is inconsistent because, as a form of hedonism, it includes the view that pleasure alone is intrinsically good, yet, because the hedonism is *qualified*, it also includes the view that something other than pleasure is intrinsically good.[4]

1. Jeremy Bentham, *The Rationale of Reward* in *The Works of Jeremy Bentham*, ed. John Bowring (New York: Russell and Russell, 1962), Vol. two, 253.
2. J. S. Mill, *Utilitarianism* (Indianapolis: Bobbs-Merrill, 1967): 12.
3. G. E. Moore, *Principia Ethica* (Cambridge: Cambridge University Press, 1962): 80.
4. Moore also attacks Mill on other grounds. He says that there is an incompatibility between Mill's qualified hedonism and his views about the preferences of experienced judges. I shall not discuss this line of argument here, since I think it would be a good idea for Millians simply to drop the so-called "judgment of preference". It is not an essential component of Mill's qualified hedonism.

Some commentators sided in this with Mill.[5] Others agreed with Moore.[6]

My own view is that the doctrines under consideration have been so incoherently formulated that discussion of their consistency is premature. If each doctrine is self-contradictory, then there's little point in struggling to see whether they are consistent with each other. Before we can profitably consider Moore's argument, we have to understand the doctrines in question. What is hedonism? What is qualified hedonism? When we know what these views are, we will be better positioned to evaluate the claim that qualified hedonism is inconsistent with hedonism.

I proceed as follows: first I review some typical formulations of hedonism. I point out several respects in which these typical formulations are incoherent. They fail to express the hedonistic intuition. Then I formulate a simple hedonistic doctrine, making use of the concept of the basic intrinsic value state. I try to show that the revised formulation succeeds in stating a possible hedonistic intuition. Then, after presenting some variant forms of hedonism, including my interpretation of Mill's qualified hedonism, I return to the main point: I try to show that Moore's objection evaporates once hedonism and qualified hedonism are properly stated.

2. TRADITIONAL FORMULATIONS OF HEDONISM

We can roughly sketch the fundamental insight behind hedonism by saying that it is the view that pleasure is The Good – it is ultimately pleasure that gives value to everything else that is valuable; a life filled with pleasure is the best life one can live. The more pleasure one enjoys, the better one's life, other things being equal. Pain, on the other hand, is The Bad. It functions as the mirror image of pleasure, making lives worse as they contain more of it, ceteris paribus.

That rough sketch is rough indeed. In order to serve a useful purpose in serious moral philosophy, the theory must be stated in greater detail,

5. In this article 'Is Mill's Hedonism Inconsistent?' *American Philosophical Quarterly Monograph Number 7* (Oxford: Basil Blackwell, 1973): 37–54, Norman Dahl cites William Frankena and Ernest Sosa as philosophers who side with Mill in this dispute. Dahl also defends Mill's position. See p. 40. Michael Zimmerman also defends Mill; see his 'Mill and the Consistency of Hedonism,' *Philosophia* 13 (1983): 317–335.
6. Dahl cites A. C. Ewing, Raziel Abelson, Richard Taylor and several others as examples of philosophers who side with Moore. See p. 40.

and with greater precision. Of course, many philosophers have proposed formulations. I want to show that typical formulations of the theory are unacceptable; they fail to express the hedonistic intuition.

In their classic discussions of hedonism, the "greats" tend to speak very loosely. Plato, Aristotle, Bentham, Mill, Sidgwick, Moore, et al. sometimes identify hedonism as the view that "pleasure alone is good as an end,"[7] or the view that "pleasure is the good,"[8] or the view that "pleasure is the only thing desirable as an end."[9] Norman Dahl says that hedonism is the view that 'pleasure and only pleasure is good.'[10] Richard Brandt says that hedonism is (in part) the view that 'only pleasure is intrinsically desirable.'[11] Let us record this element of hedonism as follows:

H1: Pleasure is intrinsically good; nothing other than pleasure is intrinsically good.[12]

7. 'By Hedonism then I mean the doctrine that pleasure alone is good as an end – 'good' in the sense which I have tried to point out is indefinable.' Moore, op. cit., 62.
8. Plato, *Philebus*, in *The Dialogues of Plato*, ed. by B. Jowett (New York: Random House, 1937): vol. II, p. 345.
9. Mill, op. cit., 10.
10. 'Hedonism is the theory of value according to which pleasure and only pleasure is good.' Norman Dahl, op. cit., 37; see also 41, 43.
11. Richard Brandt, 'Hedonism.' *The Encyclopedia of Philosophy*, ed. Paul Edwards (New York: Macmillan Publishing Co., 1967): vol. 3, p. 432.
12. There is a popular but importantly different conception of hedonism to be found in the literature. Richard Brandt often formulates the doctrine in this other way. In his *Ethical Theory*, he states the central doctrine of ethical hedonism as follows: 'A thing is intrinsically desirable (undesirable) if and only if and to the degree that it is pleasant (unpleasant).' (300; 315) He expands his presentation by formulating four allegedly hedonistic principles. The first of these is '(a) Everything that is pleasant is intrinsically desirable.' (315) Brandt says relevantly similar things in his article "Hedonism" in the *Encyclopedia of Philosophy*, cited above in fn. 11. A similar view is expressed by Norman Dahl in his 'Is Mill's Hedonism Inconsistent?', cited above in fn. 5. I assume that when Dahl says 'good' he means 'intrinsically good'. On p. 43 Dahl says: "(A) An object is good if and only if it is pleasant. (B) An object is better than another if and only if there are differences in the pleasures associated with the two objects that determine their difference in value. (C) An object is better than another if and only if (all things considered) it is more pleasant."

Brandt and Dahl say in these passages that hedonism is the view that *pleasant things (or "objects") are intrinsically good*. This seems to me to be a huge mistake. Consider Crescent Beach on Block Island. It is one of the most pleasant things I have ever experienced. Yet no careful hedonist would want to say that Crescent Beach is intrinsically good. Why not? Because Crescent Beach does not have its value solely in virtue of its intrinsic nature; because Crescent Beach does not have its value of necessity; because the value of Crescent Beach changes through time. (These tests for intrinsic value all derive from Moore, and are defended and explained by Chisholm. I take them to be uncontroversial.)

110

Although (as the cited passages demonstrate) some who have written on hedonism write as if they think that H1 states the whole of the doctrine, this cannot possibly be true.[13] Surely, the doctrine contains a corresponding element about the badness of pain:

H2: Pain is intrinsically bad; nothing other than pain is intrinsically bad.

Consider H1. It seems to imply that there is exactly one thing that has positive intrinsic value – something called 'pleasure'. According to H2 there is exactly one thing that has negative intrinsic value – something called 'pain'. What sort of objects are these? What is their ontological category? Presumably, they are properties, or characteristics – the former is the property one has when one is (as they say) "feeling pleasure", the latter is the property one has when one is "feeling pain". Although one could write books on the details of this alleged property of feeling pleasure,[14] I prefer to carry on here as if there were no problem about these properties. It is a problem for another day.

H1 and H2 seem to me to get the ontology of intrinsic value wrong. They say that the sole bearers of intrinsic value are two properties – pleasure and pain. Yet we say that good things *happen*; and we say that *several* different good things may happen at the same time; and we say that some intrinsically good things involve me, and others involve you. If there were only one good thing, and if that thing were a property, then all these common sayings would be erroneous. (Similarly for pain.)

It might be thought that when Brandt and Dahl speak of "pleasant things" or "pleasant objects", they really mean *pleasant experiences* or *pleasant states of affairs*. Even if so understood, the proposed interpretation of hedonism is utterly wrong. Consider the state of affairs *Fred's lolling about on Crescent Beach on a hot summer afternoon*. It is an extremely pleasant state of affairs. Yet no careful hedonist would want to say that it is intrinsically good. Why not? Because it has different values on different occurrences; because it does not have its value in virtue of its intrinsic nature; because it does not have its value of necessity. Such states of affairs, if they are valuable at all, are at best extrinsically valuable.

Consider the experiences I have while on Crescent Beach. They are marvelously pleasant experiences. Yet no careful hedonist would want to say that they are intrinsically good. Why not? Because none of those experiences has its value in virtue of its intrinsic nature; because none has its value of necessity. The hedonist might want to say that the pleasure arising from those pleasant experiences is intrinsically good.

13. Dahl, op. cit., for example, gives an extended and detailed formulation of hedonism, but never mentions pain!
14. I presented my own account of the nature of pleasure in my 'Two Questions about Pleasure,' in *Philosophical Analysis*, ed. by David Austin (Dordrecht: Kluwer Academic Publishers, 1988): 59–81.

4. A CHISHOLMIAN APPROACH

In *Brentano and Intrinsic Value*, Roderick Chisholm presents a more attractive approach to the ontology of hedonism.[15] He formulates a very simple sort of hedonism in this way:

> States of pleasure are the only things that are intrinsically good and states of pain are the only things that are intrinsically bad. . . . of two pleasures, the one that is the more intense one is of greater value and . . . of two displeasures, the one that is the more intense is of lesser value. . . . We can say of a pleasure or displeasure that it has a value of *n* if and only if it has an intensity of *n*.[16]

When Chisholm here speaks of 'states of pleasure', he means to indicate a certain class of *states of affairs*. These are propositional entities such as, for example, the state of affairs of *Chisholm's feeling pleasure of intensity + 8 at Noon on July 19, 1994*.

Following Chisholm's suggestion, we can replace H1 and H2 with formulas that say that the only intrinsic goods are "hedonic" states of affairs; the only intrinsic bads are "doloric" state of affairs. We can say that a hedonic state of affairs is one in which some person feels pleasure of some intensity at some time. The crucial feature of a hedonic state of affairs may be brought out by consideration of a grammatical feature of the English sentence that is used to express it. The feature is: the verb is '_____ feels pleasure to _____ at _____', and the blanks are filled in with terms that indicate a person, a number, and a time. Doloric states of affairs are to be treated in a corresponding way.

Following up on these Chisholmian suggestions, we may restate our hedonistic doctrines as follows:

H1c: Hedonic states of affairs are intrinsically good; states of affairs that are not hedonic are not intrinsically good.

H2c: Doloric states of affairs are intrinsically bad; states of affairs that are not doloric are not intrinsically bad.

Now we can say that intrinsically good things happen; that they involve people; that several different ones can happen at the same time; etc. So

---

15. Roderick M. Chisholm, *Brentano and Intrinsic Value* (Cambridge: Cambridge University Press, 1986): 74. Chisholm does not accept this form of hedonism. He presents it as a "pretense" for the purpose of illustrating various abstract principles about axiological theories.

16. Ibid.

this seems to be an improvement over the earlier view according to which the bearers of intrinsic value are properties.

But H1c and H2c do not constitute a full statement of the hedonistic view. As Chisholm suggests, the hedonist wants also to say something about how good or bad such states of affairs are. In the quoted passage, Chisholm suggests that the intrinsic value of such a thing is equal to the n-value, where the n-value is the number indicating the intensity.[17] Let us assume that the n-values of hedonic and doloric states of affairs have been assigned so that the n-values of hedonic and doloric states of affairs properly reflect the amounts of pleasure and pain they contain, and add this to the package:

H3: The intrinsic value of a hedonic or doloric state of affairs is equal to its n-value.

One of the fundamental aims of an axiological theory is to provide rankings of outcomes, lives, and worlds. It is important that the theory do this, so that e.g. God will be able to use the axiology to decide which world is best; consequentialists will be able to use the theory to decide which outcome is best; life-evaluators will be able to use the theory to decide which life is best; etc. So far, our hedonism does not do this. How are we to add it?

In a passage immediately following the one just quoted, Chisholm says:

Now we may consider a number of wholes that would be "mere sums" if our hedonistic assumptions were true. The value of each such whole would be "merely a sum of the values of its parts".[18]

Clearly, the suggestion here is that if we want to find the intrinsic value of a complex thing such as the total consequence of some action, or a life, or a possible world, then (provided that we are not dealing with an organic unity) we should find the sum of the intrinsic values of the hedonic and doloric states contained therein. In light of this, we should add further components to our hedonistic theory.

H4. The intrinsic value of a possible world is the sum of the intrinsic values of the hedonic and doloric states of affairs true there;

17. It might appear that Chisholm has erred in leaving out all mention of *duration*. However, if the times in the states of affairs are all instants, and never intervals, then the question of duration does not arise.
18. Chisholm, op. cit., 74. The internal quotations presumably are intended to recall Moore's terminology in *Principia Ethica* about "mere sums".

H5. The intrinsic value of a consequence is the sum of the intrinsic values of the hedonic and doloric states of affairs contained in that consequence;

H6. The intrinsic value of the life of a person, s, at a world, w, is the sum of the intrinsic values of the hedonic and doloric states of affairs true in w, and with s as subject.

If n-values were assigned correctly in the first place, then it should turn out that any mere sum that is good according to hedonism will have a positive intrinsic value, and any mere sum that is bad according to hedonism will have a negative intrinsic value.

I take it that (at the time of *Brentano and Intrinsic Value*) Chisholm would offer the conjunction of H1c, H2c, H3, H4, H5, and H6 as his formulation of a certain simple sort of hedonism. Let us call this theory 'CH'.

5. DIFFICULTIES FOR CH

CH confronts a variety of serious difficulties. First of all, it is internally inconsistent. In H1c and H2c, Chisholm tells us that nothing is intrinsically good or intrinsically bad other than hedonic and doloric states of affairs. Yet in H4, H5, and H6, he commits himself to the view that "mere sums" such as total consequences of actions, whole human lives, and possible worlds may also be intrinsically good or intrinsically bad. Yet none of these is itself a hedonic state or a doloric state. Each of them may be understood to be a larger state of affairs that may contain hedonic and doloric states as parts.

On the same page of *Brentano and Intrinsic Value* on which he asserts that 'states of pleasure are the only things that are intrinsically good', Chisholm presents a little chart illustrating several sorts of mere sum. Several of these are "mixed wholes" having both good parts and bad parts. An example of such a state of affairs would be:

1. Smith feeling pleasure of intensity $+2$ at noon & Jones feeling pain of intensity -1 at midnight.

Chisholm's chart indicates that the intrinsic value of (1) is $+1$, and this seems reasonable. Hedonists would want to say that (1) is an intrinsically good state of affairs. Yet according to H1c, nothing other than hedonic states of affairs is intrinsically good. Obviously, (1) is not a hedonic state of affairs, as we have defined that concept. One could revise the concept of a hedonic state, saying that a hedonic state is one that entails that

114

someone feels pleasure of some intensity at some time, and go on to claim that (1) is a hedonic state, since it entails that someone feels pleasure. But then one would run into trouble with states such as this:

2. Smith feeling pleasure of intensity +1 at noon & Jones feeling pain of intensity −2 at midnight.

On the new account of hedonic states, (2) would be counted as hedonic, since it entails that someone feels pleasure. In this case, H1c would be mistaken, since according to H1c all hedonic states are supposed to be intrinsically good. This one (if it is one) is not intrinsically good. (Corresponding difficulties arise for H2c and the concept of doloric state.)

One could resolve these problems by returning to the original concepts of hedonic and doloric states and deleting the second conjunct from H1c and H2c. However, it is questionable whether the resulting theory is a form of hedonism, since it seems to be compatible with the idea that e.g. "epistemic" and "aesthetic" states of affairs that have nothing to do with pleasure are also intrinsically good.

I want next to focus on a problem concerning principles H4–H6. Suppose a certain person in fact experiences just one short pleasure at a certain world. Suppose no one ever experiences any other pleasure or pain there. Intuitively, the hedonist would want to say that "just one intrinsically good thing" takes place at this world. However, infinitely many hedonic states of affairs are true at the world:

3. The man standing ten feet from a big oak tree feels pleasure to +10 at noon.
4. The man standing fourteen feet due north of a greenish rock feels pleasure to +10 at noon.
5. The man standing 96 yards due east of a yellow flower feels pleasure to +10 at noon.

Principle H3 implies that each of these has an intrinsic value of +10. Since there are infinitely many states of affairs relevantly like these three, differing only in the definite description to be used to pick out the man, principle H4 implies that the intrinsic value of the world is infinitely large. Similarly for principle H6 and the intrinsic value of the man's life. This is surely wrong. Let us call this "the problem of double counting".

There are other difficulties. Consider a slightly more complex case:

6. The man who yesterday felt −500 units of pain feels pleasure to +5 at the time right before he will feel another −500 units of pain.

Principle H3 implies that (6) has intrinsic value of +5, but you can see that (6) guarantees almost a thousand units of intrinsic badness. Any world where it is true will get, as a result of its truth there, −995 units of intrinsic badness. Surely, the hedonist does not want to say that (6) is intrinsically good; that a world is made five units better by the truth of (6) in that world. Let us call this "the problem of stray hedons".

6. A NEW FORM OF HEDONISM

Principles like H4– H6 purport to determine the intrinsic value of complex things by summing the intrinsic values of their parts. So long as a hedonistic theory makes use of such principles of aggregation, it will have to isolate some special group of hedonic and doloric states of affairs. These will be the "basic hedonic and doloric states".[19] The basics will be chosen in such a way as to express just the essential hedonic or doloric information. Every time a person enjoys some pleasure, there will be just one basic. This will avoid the problem of double counting. The basics will also be selected in such a way as to insure that no excess information is contained. This will avoid the problem of stray hedons.

More exactly, if we are hedonists of the simplest sort, we will want our basic hedonic states to be states of affairs such as the ones expressed by sentences such as these: 'I now feel pleasure to +25', 'she now feels pleasure to +5', 'he then felt pleasure to −50'. The sentences contain no descriptions of the people, no descriptions of the times, no descriptions of the numbers. They are *de re* with respect to persons, numbers and times. Each such sentence expresses a state of affairs about some person, number, and time, and says, with respect to that person, that he or she feels pleasure to the extent indicated by the number at the time.

Let us call states of affairs such as these "basic hedonic states". Let us use the term "basic doloric state" for a state of affairs relevantly like a basic hedonic state, except that it attributes *pain* of some intensity to some person at some time. Following Chisholm, let us use negative numbers in the standard way to indicate the intensities of pain in the basic doloric states.

We are now prepared to state the first component of our hedonistic theory. This component identifies what the theory takes to be the basic intrinsic value states.

---

19. Following up on a suggestion of Gilbert Harman, in his 'Toward a Theory of Intrinsic Value', *The Journal of Philosophy* LXIV, 23 (December 7, 1967): 792–804.

H1f. Every basic hedonic state is a basic intrinsic value state; every basic doloric state is a basic intrinsic value state; nothing else is a basic intrinsic value state.

The second component of the theory tells the intrinsic value of each basic intrinsic value state:

H2f. If p is a basic intrinsic value state, then the intrinsic value of p = the n-value of p.

In light of the way n-values were assigned, it should be clear that hedonic states will have positive intrinsic values, with more intense states getting higher values. Doloric states will have negative intrinsic values, with more intense states getting lower values.

The remaining components of the theory are "aggregative" – they purport to explicate the intrinsic values of complex things such as worlds, lives, and consequences in terms of the intrinsic values of basic intrinsic value states true in them. In this simplest of hedonistic theories, the aggregative principles are "summative". They say that the value of the complex is in every case the sum of the intrinsic values of the relevant basics.[20]

H3f. The intrinsic value of a possible world is the sum of the intrinsic values of the basic intrinsic value states true there.
H4f. The intrinsic value of a consequence is the sum of the intrinsic values of the basic intrinsic value states contained in that consequence.
H5f. The intrinsic value of a life of a person, s, at a world, w, is the sum of the intrinsic values of the basic intrinsic value states true at w with s as subject.

Although I shall not include it as a part of the theory, I assume that if a state of affairs has a positive (negative) intrinsic value, then it is intrinsically good (bad); one state of affairs is intrinsically better than another iff it has a higher intrinsic value. The resulting theory than consists of H1f–H5f together with the stated definitions and assumptions. I take this to be an extremely simple (and utterly implausible) sort of hedonism, one that adequately expresses the rough idea that "pleasure is the only good; pain the only bad; more intense pleasures are better; more intense pains are

---

20. I assume here that the number of basic intrinsic value states true at a world is always finite. If it were infinite, the summative principles would fail. In that case, we would have to make use of more sophisticated mathematics in our aggregative principles.

worse". I shall not devote any space here to showing that the proposed hedonistic theory avoids the difficulties encountered by the theories discussed earlier.

7. SOME PROBLEMATIC CASES

Consider the states of affairs expressed by the following sentences:

e. Eudoxus felt +10 at t & Mrs. Eudoxus felt +11 at t'.
f. The woman in blue felt +57 once last week.
g. Eudoxus felt +25 on two occasions.

None of these is a basic intrinsic value state according to H1f. None of them is a world, a life, or a total consequence of an action. Thus, none of the principles stated here provides any intrinsic value for these things. Yet it may seem that hedonists are obliged to say that each of them is intrinsically good. So it would be nice to have some further principles that tell us how to calculate the intrinsic values of non-basics, presumably by appeal to logically connected basics.

We might suppose that the intrinsic value of a non-basic is the sum of the intrinsic values of the basics it entails. In the case of (e) this suggestion seems to work, since (e) entails two basics, and their intrinsic values are +10 and +11, and there surely can be no objection to the conclusion that the intrinsic value of (e) is +21. But in general the suggestion does not work, as reflection on (f) and (g) shows. Neither of these entails any basics, and so the proposed principle fails to supply any intrinsic value for them. Hedonists may be disappointed.

Another principle would be based on such considerations as these: consider possible worlds in which (g) is true. At each such world, some basics about Eudoxus must also be true. Of course, different ones will be true at different worlds. But (g) entails that basics with intrinsic values summing to +50 must be true. (f) entails that some basic with intrinsic value +57 must be true. (e) entails that basics with intrinsic values summing to +21 must be true. We might then suppose that where p is a non-basic, p's intrinsic value is n iff p entails that basics with intrinsic values summing to n must be true.

But this suggestion does not have universal application. Consider these:

h. Someone feels pain, but someone else feels twice as much pleasure.
i. Someone is feeling pleasure now.
j. Eudoxus is feeling more than 25 units of pleasure.

The hedonist may want to say that (h) is intrinsically good. Yet there is no number, *n*, such that (h) entails that basics with intrinsic values summing to *n* is true. The same is true of (i) and (j).

The upshot is that there seems to be no way to assign intrinsic values to some things that are neither basics nor lives, nor consequences nor worlds. One proposal then would be simply to ignore these things. We can call them "don't cares", and allow their intrinsic values to remain undefined.[21] Since the theory does assign an intrinsic value to each total consequence, each life, and each possible world, perhaps we can make do with a theory that leaves some states of affairs without any determinate intrinsic value.[22]

8. MORE HEDONISTIC THEORIES

In the passage I cited at the outset, Mill replies to some familiar objections to the hedonistic element in his utilitarianism. Mill says:

> It is quite compatible with the principle of utility to recognize the fact that some kinds of pleasure are more desirable and more valuable than others. It would be absurd that, while in estimating all other things quality is considered as well as quantity, the estimation of pleasure should be supposed to depend on quantity alone.[23]

He goes on to say that pleasures arising from the "higher faculties" are worth more than those arising from the "lower". And he also makes some dubious claims about the preferences of experienced judges.[24]

Part of Mill's view is the claim that pleasure comes in several different forms. He might agree to a distinction among sensual, aesthetic, intellectual, and moral pleasures.[25] A sensual pleasure would be one arising from eating or drinking, sexual activity, sunbathing, having your back rubbed, etc. An aesthetic pleasure would be one arising from an experience of

21. If we say this, we ally ourselves with Michael Zimmerman, who has spoken of "evaluatively incomplete" states of affairs. See, for example, Zimmerman's 'Evaluatively Incomplete States of Affairs,' *Philosophical Studies* 43 (1983): 211–224.
22. Earl Conee has pointed out (in correspondence) that there are some axiological projects for which it might be important to have determinate intrinsic values for disjunctive and other so-far indeterminate states of affairs. He mentions calculations of expected utility.
23. Mill, op. cit., 12.
24. I allude here to Mill's view that experienced judges in suitable choice situations will always prefer the higher pleasure to the lower. As I see it, this so-called "judgment of preference" is not an essential component of Mill's qualified hedonism.
25. Although the passages seem to support just a two-way distinction between "higher" and "lower", where the higher pleasures are mental and the lower are bodily. The details are not important here. I am just trying to show that the fundamental idea of qualified hedonism is coherent.

something beautiful, such as a painting or a piece of music. An intellectual pleasure is a pleasure arising from learning something, and a moral pleasure is a pleasure arising from behaving nobly.

Mill says that pleasures of these different sorts are of different "qualities". Some are "higher" than others. We can understand his view to be that moral pleasures are of the greatest quality; they are the "highest" of pleasures. Intellectual pleasures are next in quality, with aesthetic pleasures in third place and finally sensual pleasures being the lowest. In order to make presentation of the theory simple, let us suppose that each of these sorts of pleasure has a "q value", or numerical indicator of its quality. They are specified as follows:

sensual pleasure   1
aesthetic pleasure   2
intellectual pleasure   3
moral pleasure   4

A simple modification to the hedonistic theory presented in Section 7 will yield a formulation of Mill's Qualified Hedonism. The modification concerns the basics. According to one possible interpretation of Mill, we should start by identifying what we may call "basic qualified hedonic states". These are states of affairs relevantly like the basic hedonic states of the earlier theory. However, in the present case, the basics are all of this form: *S feeling pleasure of intensity n and quality m at t.* In any actual basic hedonic state, s will be some person, *n* and *m* will be numbers indicating respectively the intensity and the quality-level of the pleasure experienced by s, and t will be an instant of time.

The first component of Millian Qualified Hedonism is this:

H1m: Every basic qualified hedonic state is a basic intrinsic value state; every basic qualified doloric state is a basic intrinsic value state;[26] nothing else is a basic intrinsic value state.

The second component of the theory tells the intrinsic value of each basic intrinsic value state:

H2m: If p is a basic intrinsic value state, then the intrinsic value of p = the product of the *n*-value of p and the *q*-value of p.

So much for the basics on this form of qualified hedonism. The rest of

---

26. The careful reader may have noticed that I never introduced or explained "qualified doloric states". Neither did Mill. I am not sure how this should go.

the theory consists in aggregative principles specifying the intrinsic values of worlds, lives, and consequences. On the simplest interpretation, we could take these to be the same as the ones already at hand. Thus, we could understand Millian qualified hedonism to be the conjunction of H1m, H2m, H3f, H4f, and H5f, together with the associated definitions and explanations.

If I were a hedonist, I would defend a more complicated form of hedonism. I think that pleasures are intrinsically better when they are deserved; intrinsically worse when they are not deserved. I think that pains are intrinsically worse when they are undeserved; less intrinsically bad when they are deserved. Accordingly, I would think that some of the basic intrinsic value states are what we may call "desert qualified hedonic states", roughly of this form: *s feels pleasure of intensity n and quality m at t when s deserves to be feeling pleasure of intensity n' and quality m' at t*. Others are "desert qualified doloric states", which are structurally like desert qualified hedonic states, but attribute pain to the recipient.

If I were a hedonist, I would go on to claim that the intrinsic value of a basic intrinsic value state is a function of the intensity and quality received and the intensity and quality deserved. Thus, for each basic intrinsic value state, there are four numbers, representing respectively the intensity of pleasure received; the quality of pleasure received; the intensity of pleasure deserved; and the quality of pleasure deserved by the recipient on the occasion of the basic. The intrinsic value of the basic is a mathematical function of these four values. This is not the place to lay out the details of the function. The remaining components of my form of desert qualified hedonism would follow the pattern already introduced.[27]

I leave it to the interested reader to cook up further forms of hedonism. The pattern should be clear: first tell us what are the basic intrinsic value states according to the theory; then tell us the intrinsic values of the basics; then give us principles of aggregation that specify the intrinsic values of worlds, lives, consequences, and perhaps other things as necessary.

9. FORMS OF HEDONISM

The forms of hedonism so far discussed have several things in common: each starts with an account of what it takes to be a basic intrinsic value

27. I presented a sketch of this theory in "Adjusting Utility for Justice: A Consequentialist Reply to the Objection from Justice," *Philosophy and Phenomenological Research* LV, 3 (September 1995), 567–585.

state; each specifies a precise intrinsic value for each basic; each goes on to present aggregative principles purporting to determine the intrinsic values of consequences, lives, and possible worlds by appeal to the intrinsic values of the basics true in those consequences, lives, and worlds.

A non-hedonistic axiology could have all of these features. Consider, for example, a theory according to which the basic intrinsic value states are all like this: *Otto having a Good Will to degree +26 at Noon today.* Such a theory (perhaps a Kantian axiology?) could then go on to say that each basic has an intrinsic value equal to its *n*-value, and that lives, consequences, and worlds are to be evaluated summatively in accordance with principles like H4f, H5f, and H6f.

So what makes a theory be a form of hedonism? It seems to me that the crucial fact is that according to every form of hedonism, the intrinsically good basics are attributions of some sort of pleasure to someone (or something). In some cases, it is simply the property of *feeling pleasure of some intensity*; in other cases it is the property of *feeling pleasure of some intensity and quality*. And in yet another case it is *feeling pleasure of some intensity and quality at a time when pleasure of some other intensity and quality is deserved.*

A theory might say that some, but not all, intrinsically good basic intrinsic value states are attributions of some form of pleasure. Perhaps the theory says that there are also intrinsically good basics that are attributions of knowledge, or virtue, or the Good Will. We can say that a theory is a form of *pure hedonism* iff it says that all intrinsically good basics are attributions of pleasure of some sort; and we can say that a theory is a form of *impure hedonism* iff it says that some but not all intrinsically good basics are attributions of pleasure of some sort.

Notice that every form of hedonism so far discussed has a view about the nature of the basic hedonic states, and every such view implies that every state recognized by it as a basic hedonic state is intrinsically good. This need not be the case. A hedonist might say that some forms of pleasure are so base and disgusting that basic hedonic states attributing these forms are intrinsically worthless or perhaps even intrinsically bad; or a hedonist might say that when a person deserves not to be having pleasure, his receipt of it is worthless. This introduces another distinction among hedonistic theories. Some are *universally hedonistic,* saying that every basic hedonic state is intrinsically good. Others are *non-universally hedonistic*; they say that some, but not all basic hedonic states are intrinsically good.

Further distinctions among possible forms of hedonism could be drawn, but, in the interest of conserving space, I will forbear from drawing them.[28]

10. MOORE'S ARGUMENT

Moore claimed that Mill's qualified hedonism is not a form of hedonism. He defended this claim by saying that qualified hedonism implies that 'something else, something which is not present in all pleasures, is also good as an end.' Moore was wrong. Mill's theory (or more properly, my revised formulation of it) is a form of hedonism. This follows from the fact that intrinsically good basic intrinsic value states according to Mill's theory are attributions of pleasure. The theory does not imply that there is some other sort of intrinsically good basic intrinsic value state; it does not imply, for example, that we must count as basic such things as *this experience being of quality n*.

It may be interesting to note that, as I have formulated it, Mill's theory is a form of *pure hedonism* because it implies that all of the intrinsically good basics are attributions of pleasure. It is also a form of *universal hedonism*, since it implies that all basic qualified hedonic states are intrinsically good.

I of course acknowledge that Millian qualified hedonism is inconsistent with Benthamic simple hedonism. They differ in what they take to be basic intrinsic value states. But this is no defect in the Millian view; it was

---

28. In 'Higher Goods and the Myth of Tithonus' (*The Journal of Philosophy* XC, 9 (September, 1993): 482–496), Noah Lemos has pointed out that certain passages in Mill strongly suggest that he did not think of the connection between higher and lower pleasures in the way I have sketched. Rather, Mill apparently thought that no amount of lower pleasure is equal in value to even the smallest amount of higher pleasure. Lemos points out that an axiology based on such "higher pleasures" cannot make use of aggregative principles such as H3f, H4f, and H5f.

However, I think it is possible to formulate the needed principles. Such principles would differ from the principles discussed in the body of the paper primarily in that they would not assign the same sort of numerical intrinsic values to higher and lower intrinsic goods. Instead, the theory would have to make use of two sorts of intrinsic value – "higher" and "lower". These would be assigned to basics in the expected way, and summative principles would yield both a higher and a lower value for every life, consequence, and world. Worlds, for example, would then be ranked as follows: if they have different amounts of higher intrinsic value, then the one with more higher intrinsic value is intrinsically better; if they are tied in terms of higher intrinsic value, but differ with respect to lower intrinsic value, then the one with more lower intrinsic value is intrinsically better.

intended to be different from the Benthamic view. I also grant that the Millian qualified hedonism is false.[29] My aim here has been to show that it is a consistent axiological view, and that it is a form of hedonism. I have not been trying to show that it is true.[30]

29. An argument against Millian QH: consider two possible worlds, w1 and w2. Suppose that these worlds are alike with respect to basic hedonic and doloric states. Suppose each world contains many basic hedonic states, and many basic doloric states. Suppose the worlds differ in that in w1 pain and pleasure are received by those who deserve them, in precisely the amounts they deserve, whereas in w2 pain and pleasure are received by those who do not deserve them – those who deserve pleasure receive pain, and those who deserve pain receive pleasure. Millian qualified hedonism implies that w1 is equal in intrinsic value to w2. However, it is obvious that w1 is much better than w2.

30. I am grateful to many teachers, students, colleagues, and friends for critical suggestions. Roderick Chisholm's work originally provoked me into thinking about these matters. I am extremely grateful to him for help and encouragement on this and other projects. Earl Conee, Eva Bodanszky, Michael Zimmerman, Ish Haji, Noah Lemos, Ned Markosian, and David Cowles also provided extensive and useful comments and suggestions.

Essay 7

On the intrinsic value of pleasures

INTRODUCTORY COMMENTS

Essay 7 has a "negative" aim and a "positive" aim.

In the first several sections of the essay, I explain one of the most influential current views about the nature of pleasure. This is the view of Sidgwick, Brandt, Alston, and others, according to which a feeling is correctly said to be a pleasure if the person who has that feeling likes it for its own sake, or enjoys it, or wants it to continue, or (in Sidgwick's words) "apprehends it as desirable in itself." In general, according to this view, any sort of feeling might be a pleasure – it doesn't matter how it "feels." A feeling is a pleasure if the one who feels it has an appropriate attitude toward it when he or she has it.

My negative aim in the essay is to show that it is impossible to combine any such "Sidgwickian" conception of pleasure with the classic Moorean conception of intrinsic value. The problem, in the abstract, is simple: On the Moorean conception of intrinsic value, intrinsically good things are supposed to have their values in virtue of their own intrinsic natures – because of the way they are "in themselves." Yet on the Sidgwickian conception of pleasure, no feeling is "intrinsically a pleasure." If a feeling happens to be a pleasure, it is so because of an extrinsic feature – the one who experiences it has the appropriate attitude toward it.

As a result, Sidgwickian hedonists are in a bind. They want to say that pleasures are intrinsically good – good in virtue of their own natures. Yet they also want to say that the feelings that happen to be pleasures are not pleasures in virtue of their own natures. They are pleasures in virtue of the fact that someone happens to have a certain attitude toward them. Thus, the feelings that are supposed to be *intrinsically* good turn out not to be good in virtue of their own natures.

For those of us who reject the early Moorean notion that there is a distinctive feeling of pleasure itself, this raises a deep puzzle: We cannot understand hedonism to be the view that experiences of the distinctive

125

feeling of pleasure itself are intrinsically good – for there is no such feeling. We cannot understand hedonism to be the view that *liked feelings* are intrinsically good – because this conflicts with elements of the classic conception of intrinsic value. So how are we to understand the main thesis of hedonism?

My positive aim in the essay is to show how we can answer this question. I appeal to the concept of propositional pleasure first introduced in "Two Questions about Pleasure." Making use of this concept, I give an account of basic hedonic states. A basic hedonic state is one such as this, where 'F' stands for some sensory feeling:

H: Jeremy taking immediate propositional pleasure at t in the fact that he himself is feeling F at t.

I then claim, in effect, that when hedonists say that pleasures are intrinsically good, they are (or ought to be) talking about these basic hedonic states. I try to show that it is reasonable to say that these things have their intrinsic values in virtue of their intrinsic natures. In this way, I demonstrate that we can formulate a version of the central doctrine of hedonism that makes use of the classic Moorean conception of intrinsic value.

I should mention that the Hedonic Thesis (which is discussed at length in the essay) is not intended to be the whole of hedonism. It is merely the core thesis of a possible hedonic view. I found that the essay became too long and cumbersome if I tried to formulate all of hedonism à la Sidgwick. I became embroiled in extraneous issues such as, for example, all the trouble involving failure to make use of basic intrinsic value states. Thus, in order to focus on the role of propositional pleasure in the formulation of hedonism, I narrowed the topic. I don't mention basics; I don't talk about principles of aggregation; I stick to what I here call the "Hedonic Thesis" – the view that pleasures are intrinsically good. This is not *all* of hedonism, but it is surely a central element.

7

On the intrinsic value of pleasures

1. INTRODUCTORY COMMENTS

A great many moral philosophers find themselves called upon to say something about the "Hedonic Thesis" – the view that "pleasure is intrinsically good". Hedonists typically want to defend the Hedonic Thesis, since it lies at the heart of their theory of value. Some pluralists want to affirm the Thesis; others want to deny it. Others may want neither to affirm nor deny the Thesis, but find it necessary to state and discuss it as they pursue some other project in moral philosophy.

In spite of the prominence of the Hedonic Thesis in moral philosophies of all sorts, there is disagreement about what it means. Some of this disagreement turns on yet more fundamental disagreement about the nature of pleasure. As a result of such disagreement, different philosophers have provided different and non-equivalent interpretations of the Hedonic Thesis.

In this paper I focus on a certain way of understanding the claim that "pleasure is intrinsically good". The problematic feature of this interpretation is not the concept of intrinsic goodness – that is understood in the classic Moorean way. Rather, it is the distinctive concept of pleasure presupposed.

This way of understanding the concept of pleasure apparently derives from some things Henry Sidgwick said in *The Methods of Ethics*.[1] It gained currency in recent years in America. A number of prominent philosophers construe pleasure in this Sidgwickian way. Among them are Richard

I am grateful to many friends for generous critical comments and suggestions. I am especially grateful to David Copp, Earl Conee, and three anonymous Editors of this journal for extensive and insightful criticism of an earlier draft; to Owen McLeod for criticism and bibliographic assistance; to Ingmar Persson, Irwin Goldstein, Michael Zimmerman, Ted Sider, Richard Feldman, and Chris Deaton and other students who took Philosophy 760 with me during the spring of 1996.
1. Sidgwick discusses the concept of pleasure in various places in *The Methods of Ethics* 7th Edition (London: Macmillan & Co., 1962). Some especially interesting and relevant passages occur in Book I, Chapter IV, Section 2; Book II, Chapters II – IV.

Brandt, William Alston and William Frankena. Brandt wrote a major ethics text, as well as books, journal articles, and an encyclopedia article in which the concept of pleasure was interpreted in this way.[2] Alston contributed an article on 'Pleasure' to *The Encyclopedia of Philosophy* in which he understood the concept in the same style.[3] Frankena wrote a very widely used introductory text in moral philosophy, as well as another article in the *Encyclopedia of Philosophy*.[4] His formulation is relevantly like Brandt's.

A generation of philosophy students grew up understanding 'pleasure' in the Hedonic Thesis in the Sidgwickian way. Of course, not everyone thinks the Thesis is true, but very many philosophers nowadays seem to assume that the Sidgwickian interpretation provides a conception of pleasure that can be used in the statement of the hedonic view. I think this is a mistake. My central aim in this paper is to show that when we combine Sidgwick's conception of pleasure with the classic Moorean conception of intrinsic value, we get an interpretation of the Hedonic Thesis that is incoherent. If we are to understand the Thesis, we must find some other way to interpret the concept of pleasure.

In this paper I first (Sections 2 and 3) present the Sidgwickian conception of pleasure. I then (Section 4) present the resulting formulation of the Hedonic Thesis. Next (Sections 5 and 6) I turn to arguments. I try to reveal the conceptual conflict at the heart of the Thesis, so interpreted. In a final section (Section 7) I sketch a more promising approach. I begin with some thoughts about the nature of pleasure.

2. THE HETEROGENEITY OF PLEASURES AND PAINS.

Think of an array of typical sensory pleasures: the taste of sparkling cold beer; the smell of roses; the feeling in your nether parts when reaching

2. I refer here to Brandt's *Ethical Theory: The Problems of Normative and Critical Ethics* (Englewood Cliffs: Prentice-Hall, Inc., 1959), 'Hedonism', in Paul Edwards (ed.) *The Encyclopedia of Philosophy* (New York: Macmillan Publishing Co. & The Free Press, 1967), vol. 4, pp. 432–435, *A Theory of the Good and the Right* (Oxford: The Clarendon Press, 1979), and 'Two Concepts of Utility', originally published in Harlan B. Miller and William H. Williams (eds.) *The Limits of Utilitarianism* (Minneapolis: University of Minnesota Press, 1982); reprinted in Brandt's *Morality, Utilitarianism, and Rights* (Cambridge: Cambridge University Press, 1992), pp. 158–175.
3. William Alston, 'Pleasure', in Paul Edwards (ed.) *The Encyclopedia of Philosophy* (New York: Macmillan Publishing Co. & The Free Press, 1967), vol. 6, pp. 341–347.
4. William Frankena, *Ethics* (Englewood Cliffs: Prentice-Hall, Inc., 1973) and 'Value and Valuation', in Paul Edwards (ed.) *The Encyclopedia of Philosophy* (New York: Macmillan Publishing Co. & The Free Press, 1967), vol. 8, pp. 229–232.

fruition in happy sex. Many philosophers recognize that pleasures such as these might not "feel alike". They might have no common phenomenologically given element.[5]

This raises a question: if these feelings do not feel alike, then why are they all called pleasures? In a typically thoughtful and perceptive passage, Sidgwick discusses this issue. He remarks that some writers seem to think that 'pleasure' expresses an indefinable quality of experience; that this feeling comes in various degrees; that it is in these ways analogous to the quality of feeling expressed by 'sweet'. But Sidgwick demurs:

> This seems to be the view of some writers: but, for my own part, when I reflect on the notion of pleasure . . . the only common quality that I can find in the feelings so designated seems to be that relation to desire and volition expressed by the general term "desirable". . . . I propose therefore to define Pleasure . . . as a feeling which, when experienced by intelligent beings, is at least implicitly apprehended as desirable or – in cases of comparison – preferable.[6]

Thus Sidgwick apparently held that a feeling is properly said to be a pleasure because the person who experiences that feeling "apprehends it as desirable". In subsequent passages the view is refined and developed.[7] Many other philosophers have agreed with Sidgwick's claim that pleasures do not "feel alike".[8] They have also agreed that what pleasures have in common is the fact that the "intelligent being" who experiences them has some favorable attitude toward them. There is some difference of opinion about the precise nature of the attitude.

Over a period of many years Richard Brandt consistently maintained a broadly Sidgwickian conception of pleasure. In his 1959 book *Ethical Theory*, Brandt said:

5. This is a consistent theme in Brandt's work. He makes the point in many passages. See, for example, *Ethical Theory* pp. 303–307; *A Theory of the Good and the Right* pp. 35–38; 'Hedonism' p. 433. I endorsed the view in my 'Two Questions about Pleasure' in David Austin (ed.) *Philosophical Analysis* (Dordrecht: Kluwer Academic Publishers, 1988), pp. 59–81. An interesting discussion of the view and some of its alleged implications can be found in Irwin Goldstein's 'Hedonic Pluralism', *Philosophical Studies* 48 (1985), pp. 49–55.
6. Sidgwick, *The Methods of Ethics*, p. 127.
7. Remarks similar to the one quoted from p. 127 can be found on pp. 42, 131 and elsewhere.
8. For further discussion of hedonic pluralism, see Cowan, J. L., *Pleasure and Pain: A Study in Philosophical Psychology* (London: Macmillan, 1968), Edwards, Rem B., *Pleasures and Pains: A Theory of Qualitative Hedonism* (Ithaca: Cornell University Press, 1979), and Gosling, J. C. B., *Pleasure and Desire: The Case for Hedonism Reviewed* (Oxford: The Clarendon Press, 1969). For further references, see fn. 1 in Goldstein's 'Hedonic Pluralism', p. 54.

"is pleasant" is to have the same sense as "is a part of an experience, containing a subjective element, which one wishes at the time to prolong (or in which one is absorbed without effort) for itself ".[9]

According to this formulation, a feeling is a pleasure because the person who experiences it *wishes to prolong it for itself*. Thus, Brandt substitutes a purely psychological concept ("wants to prolong") for Sidgwick's apparently partially value-theoretical concept ("desirable").

Almost a decade later, in his article "Hedonism" in the *Encyclopedia of Philosophy*, Brandt presented a very similar view. He there said:

> . . . it is plausible to say that a person is enjoying himself (that is, his state of mind is pleasant) if and only if at the time he likes his experience or activity *for itself*, in the sense that, aside from moral considerations or considerations of consequences or of the possibility that something he likes even better could be substituted, he does not wish to change it and in fact would wish to avoid changing it if such a change impended.[10]

This statement differs from the previous one only in details. The relevant attitude here is *liking it for itself* in the specified sense, rather than *wishing to prolong it for itself*.[11]

In his *Encyclopedia of Philosophy* article "Pleasure" William Alston presented a number of views about the nature of pleasure. The last of these – and the one to which he seems most sympathetic – is in important ways similar to Brandt's view. Alston explicitly mentions Sidgwick, and states the view in this passage:

> (E) To get pleasure is to have an experience which, as of the moment, one would rather have than not have, on the basis of its felt quality, apart from any further considerations regarding consequences.[12]

Alston's view is only trivially different from Brandt's. He says that what makes an experience a pleasure is that the one who has it *would rather have it than not, on the basis of its felt quality*.

If one thought that there is an attitude of "taking pleasure in", one might attempt to identify sensory pleasures by appeal to it.[13] One could

9. Brandt, *Ethical Theory*, pp. 306–307.
10. Brandt, 'Hedonism', p. 433.
11. Brandt says essentially the same thing in 'Two Concepts of Utility', pp. 164–165. A similar, but slightly more complex view is defended in his *A Theory of the Good and the Right*, pp. 38–42. According to the latter view, an experience is pleasant 'if and only if it makes its continuation more wanted.' (p. 40) The added complexity is that there must be a causal connection between the experience and the increased desire for continuation.
12. Alston, 'Pleasure', p. 345.
13. This is how I tried to explain "sensory pleasure" in my 'Two Questions about Pleasure'.

try to distinguish this attitude from the attitude of *wanting it to continue* as well as from *preferring to have it rather than not have it*. One could then say that when a person takes immediate pleasure in some feeling he is experiencing, then that feeling is called a pleasure; it is said to be a pleasant feeling.[14]

Let us generalize, so as to collect together a bunch of similar theories about the nature of pleasure. Each of these theories focusses on some special attitude. Different versions focus on different attitudes. It might be *apprehending as desirable*; it might be *enjoying for its own sake*; it might be *wanting it to continue for its own sake*; it might be *taking immediate pleasure in it*; it might be *finding it intrinsically enjoyable*.[15] The theories have this in common: each of them selects a certain attitude, A, and then maintains that a particular feeling is a pleasure (or is pleasant) on some occasion iff the person who experiences it takes up attitude A toward it on that occasion. We can call such feelings "Sidgwickian Pleasures". Philosophers in the Sidgwickian tradition maintain that the "pleasures" mentioned in the Hedonic Thesis should be understood to be Sidgwickian Pleasures.

3. A CRUCIAL DISTINCTION

It is important in this context to take note of a crucial distinction.

Some philosophers and psychologists apparently believe that there is a certain special feeling of "pleasure itself". They think that this feeling comes in various intensities and durations (and perhaps also in different "qualities") but that it is nevertheless phenomenologically uniform. When he wrote *Principia Ethica*, G. E. Moore held such a view. He said that when a person experiences pleasure,

> . . . his mind, a certain definite mind, distinguished by certain definite marks from all others, has at this moment a certain definite feeling called pleasure. . . . and though we may be more pleased or less pleased, and even, we may admit for the present, have one or another kind of pleasure; yet in so far as it is pleasure we have, whether there be more or less of it, and whether it be of one kind or another, what we have is one definite thing, absolutely indefinable, some one thing that is the same in all the various degrees and in all the various kinds of it that there may be.[16]

14. I return to this issue below in Section 7. See also my 'Two Questions about Pleasure'.
15. It should be clear that I am here glossing over differences among these definitions. For present purposes, the differences are unimportant. What's important is that on each of the cited views, there is some attitude, such that when we say that a feeling is a pleasure what we mean is that the person who has the feeling takes the attitude toward it.
16. See Moore, *Principia Ethica*, pp. 12–13. In the Preface to the Second Edition of *Principia*

Let us use the term "the Distinctive Feeling View" (or 'DFV') to indicate this Moorean conception of pleasure. According to DFV, there is a certain distinctive feeling, P, such that whenever a person is feeling pleasure, he or she is feeling P.

I can imagine a philosopher struggling to pinpoint this distinctive feeling. Since he has experienced it himself, he knows how it feels. However, he finds it impossible to define the feeling by appeal to its "feel". He agrees with Moore's 1903 view. The feeling itself is "absolutely indefinable".

However, such a philosopher might think he has found another way to identify the relevant feeling. He might think that as a matter of contingent psychological fact we always have a certain attitude toward this feeling. Perhaps he thinks that whenever we experience this feeling, we like it for its own sake, or want it to continue, or take a certain sort of enjoyment in it. He might also think that there is no other feeling that we like or enjoy in quite the same way. Such a philosopher might want to make use of this feature of pleasure in his attempt to pick it out. He thinks that the cited feature is a surefire (though contingent) mark of pleasure. He could go on to offer a sort of "definition" of pleasure. He might say that a person is experiencing pleasure if and only if she is experiencing something she likes for its own sake, or wants to continue for its own sake.

As a result of all this, a philosopher who adopts DFV might end up saying something very similar to the things that Sidgwick, Brandt and Alston have said. We might confuse this Moorean view with the Sidgwickian view. But there are crucial differences.

Sidgwickians reject DFV. They deny that there is some special feeling of pleasure itself. Brandt has consistently emphasized this point. For example, in *Ethical Theory* he said,

> There is virtual unanimity today that pleasantness is not an element of experience like a color patch or a sound. Just try to examine pleasantness by itself, in the way you can inspect a red patch by itself. It cannot be done. Pleasantness always seems to be the pleasantness *of* something, of an activity,

Ethica Moore says that he no longer thinks that pleasure is indefinable. I have not been able to find his alleged definition.

A more recent advocate of the Distinctive Feeling View seems to be David Brink, who describes hedonism as the view that 'The one and only intrinsic good is pleasure, which is understood as a simple, qualitative mental state; . . . '. *Moral Realism and the Foundations of Ethics* (Cambridge: Cambridge University Press, 1989), p. 221.

or some other elements of experience. . . . it is not a distinct element of experience (like a red patch). . . . [17]

In his *Encyclopedia of Philosophy* article "Pleasure", Alston said virtually the same thing, and even made use of the same contrasting example: 'When we reflect on a wide variety of cases of getting pleasure . . . we are unable to isolate a felt quality which they all share, in the way in which we can easily isolate a quality of redness which a number of different visual sensations share . . . '[18]

Consider a Sidgwickian who says that a feeling is a pleasure if and only if the one who experiences it wants it to continue for its own sake. Such a philosopher is *not* supposing that there is a certain distinctive feeling that as a matter of contingent fact we always want to continue for its own sake; such a philosopher is *not* merely trying to pick out this distinctive feeling by pointing out that it is the unique one towards which we happen to have this special attitude. Rather, the Sidgwickian is supposing that there are many different feelings, any of which might be a pleasure for some person on some occasion. The Sidgwickian is proposing to tell us what we mean when we say that a feeling someone feels on some occasion "is a pleasure" for that person on that occasion. According to the present version of the view, we are saying that the person who feels it on that occasion wants it to continue for its own sake. A person might in principle have this attitude toward virtually any feeling.

So we must be sensitive to a fundamental distinction. Some philosophers think that 'pleasure' picks out a certain distinctive feeling – that all pleasures are phenomenologically alike. Sidgwickians deny this. They think that 'pleasure' picks out feelings of various sorts, linked only by the fact that they are all liked for their own sakes by the people who experience them. A Sidgwickian could consistently maintain that any feeling could in principle be a pleasure. Even the feeling caused by overstimulated nerves in a rotting tooth could be a pleasure for someone on some occasion; and it would be a pleasure if the one who experienced it wanted it to continue for its own sake.

In any case, we are now ready to state the first components of the Sidgwickian conception of pleasure. They are:

17. Brandt, *Ethical Theory*, p. 305.
18. Alston, 'Pleasure', p. 344.

SH1: There is no such thing as "the feeling of pleasure itself"; pleasures are phenomenologically heterogeneous.

SH2: To say that a feeling is a pleasure (or a pleasant experience) is to say that the person who experiences it enjoys it for its own sake (or wants to prolong it for itself, or reacts in some other specified favorable way toward it).

4. THE HEDONIC THESIS

If we understand pleasure in the Sidgwickian way, then we will understand the Hedonic Thesis to be the view that these Sidgwickian pleasures are intrinsically good. Many philosophers have so construed the Hedonic Thesis. Brandt, for example, states the view in these words:

> . . . something is intrinsically desirable (undesirable) if and only if and to the degree that it is an experience with a subjective element that the person at the time wants to prolong (terminate or avoid) for itself . . . In brief, the intrinsically good consists of *liked* experiences containing a subjective or feeling element.[19]

In other writings, Brandt has formulated the Hedonic Thesis in a variety of ways, but he consistently maintained approximately the same fundamental conception throughout a long period of time.[20]

William Frankena apparently understood the Hedonic Thesis in a similar way. In his *Encyclopedia of Philosophy* article on 'Value and Valuation', Frankena said:

> More accurately, [hedonists] say that only experiences are intrinsically good, that all experiences which are intrinsically good are pleasant and vice versa, and that they are intrinsically good because and only because they are pleasant. These are the hedonistic theories of value . . . [21]

I have certain quibbles with certain features of this formulation of hedonism. Those are topics for another day.[22] Here I want to focus on the Sidgwickian aspect of the Hedonic Thesis. We may now state the central element:

---

19. Brandt, *Ethical Theory*, p. 307.
20. For example, in 'Hedonism', Brandt says that ethical hedonism ' . . . is the thesis that only pleasant states of mind are desirable in themselves; . . . ' (p. 432)
21. Frankena, 'Value and Valuation', p. 231. See also a similar passage in Frankena's *Ethics*, p. 84.
22. I have in mind here especially the failure to take account of the role of *basic intrinsic value states*. For a discussion of basics, see Harman, Gilbert H., 'Toward a Theory of Intrinsic Value', *The Journal of Philosophy* LXIV, 23 (December 7, 1967), pp. 792–804.

SH3: When we say that pleasures are intrinsically good, what we mean is that *Sidgwickian pleasures*, as defined in SH2, are intrinsically good.

Another component of the interpretation is a principle that specifies the degree of goodness of a pleasure. In *Ethical Theory* Brandt formulated a view according to which the intrinsic goodness of a pleasure is directly proportional to the extent to which the experiencer wants the pleasure to continue for its own sake.[23] Thus, if I am experiencing two feelings, and I want each to continue for its own sake, but I want more for the first to continue, then the first feeling is the greater pleasure and the intrinsically better feeling. The intensities of the feelings themselves are not directly relevant here.

We can state this as follows:

SH4: The intrinsic value of a Sidgwickian pleasure, as defined in SH2, is directly proportional to the intensity of the experiencer's desire for the experience to continue for its own sake.

I think it is fair to say that the core of the Sidgwickian view is embodied in SH1–SH4. A Sidgwickian maintains that the Hedonic Thesis ("pleasures are intrinsically good") means that *those feelings that we like, and wish to prolong for their own sakes, have positive intrinsic value.* Sidgwickians also hold that the amount of intrinsic value in an experience is determined by the intensity of the desire for the experience to continue (mutatis mutandis for those who specify some other attitude toward experiences).

5. WHY THE SIDGWICKIAN INTERPRETATION CANNOT BE TRUE

I think the Sidgwickian interpretation is unsatisfactory. It can't possibly provide an accurate account of the Hedonic Thesis.

The fundamental difficulty may be described abstractly: according to the first elements of the Sidgwickian interpretation, SH1 and SH2, the feelings that are pleasures are not intrinsically alike. Something is a Sidgwickian pleasure in virtue of the fact that someone happens to have a certain attitude toward it. This is a *contingent, extrinsic, relational* fact about any such feeling. Yet according to the third element of the Sidgwickian interpretation, SH3, such feelings are supposed to be "good in themselves". They are supposed to have their value "in virtue of their own nature". However, if their pleasantness is purely extrinsic and contingent,

23. Brandt, *Ethical Theory*, p. 307.

and their value supervenes upon their pleasantness, then they do not have their value "in virtue of their own natures"; they have it in virtue of the fact that they are liked.

The problem reveals itself in a variety of ways. Let us consider some of the most obvious.

5a. An argument based on Moore's principle of universality

In *Principa Ethica* (and also in "The Conception of Intrinsic Value") Moore enunciated a very plausible principle about intrinsic value.[24] He pointed out that judgments of intrinsic value have a sort of "universality" not shared by judgments of extrinsic value. His view was that if something has a certain intrinsic value, then anything intrinsically just like it must have the same intrinsic value. This is roughly equivalent to the claim that intrinsic values supervene upon intrinsic natures. A corresponding principle about extrinsic value does not hold. Since a thing has its extrinsic value in virtue of its relations to other things, two things might be exactly alike intrinsically, but differ in extrinsic value.[25]

Moore's principle is deeply rooted in the classic concept of intrinsic value. Since the time of Plato and Aristotle, philosophers have understood this concept in such a way that to say that a thing is intrinsically good is to say that it is good "in itself " – that it has its value in virtue of what it is, rather than in virtue of how it is connected to other things. If we understand the concept of intrinsic value in this way, we seem to have no choice: we must agree to this:

SUP: If something, x, has an intrinsic value of n, then anything intrinsically like x must also have an intrinsic value of n.

24. G. E. Moore, *Principia Ethica* (Cambridge: Cambridge University Press, 1903), pp. 23, 27; 'The Conception of Intrinsic Value' in his *Philosophical Studies* (London: Routledge & Kegan Paul, 1960), pp. 253–275, p. 265.
25. Moore struggled with the Principle of Universality in 'The Conception of Intrinsic Value'. There is good reason to be troubled by the principle. It is based upon a somewhat elusive conception of "intrinsic nature". We may say that a thing's intrinsic nature is the combination of all its intrinsic properties. However, if a thing's identity (e.g., in the case of Moore, the property of *being identical to G. E. Moore*) is one of its intrinsic properties, then no two things share an intrinsic nature. In this case, the principle has no application. If a thing's intrinsic value is an intrinsic property of that thing, then the principle is utterly trivial.

An interesting version of the principle would say this: if two things are exactly alike with respect to *non-evaluative purely general intrinsic properties*, then they must be alike with respect to intrinsic value. Of course, to complete the task, one would have to explain the technical terminology.

Now consider two typical Sidgwickian pleasures – the pleasures my brother and I recently experienced while drinking cold beer together. I enjoyed the taste of that beer, and fervently wished for the taste experience to continue. My brother, on the other hand, enjoyed the taste far less. He wanted his taste experience to continue, but his desire for continuation was less strong. This happened in spite of the fact that my brother's taste experience was intrinsically just like mine. The difference in reaction was due entirely to the fact that my brother does not share my taste in beer.

SH4 implies that my experience of the taste of beer was intrinsically good to a fairly high degree (because my desire for continuation was strong), but that my brother's experience of the taste of beer was intrinsically good to a much lower degree (because his desire for continuation was much less strong). But the experiences are stipulated to be intrinsically alike – my brother's taste experience was intrinsically just like mine; only his attitude toward his experience was different from my attitude toward mine. Hence, the Sidgwickian interpretation of the Hedonic Thesis conflicts with Moore's supervenience principle, SUP. If Sidgwickian pleasures are intrinsically good, then it is possible for there to be two intrinsically indiscernible experiences that differ in intrinsic value.

Reflection on more extreme examples of a similar sort should make it clear that the Sidgwickian approach allows for the possibility of two intrinsically indiscernible experiences one of which is a pleasure and the other of which is a pain. Given natural assumptions, the implication is that the pleasure is intrinsically good and the pain intrinsically bad – this in spite of the fact that they are in themselves exactly alike. This points to even deeper conflict with the supervenience principle.

5b. An argument based on the foundation of intrinsic value

Of course, there is no way to prove that my brother's sensory experience was intrinsically identical to my sensory experience. Maybe beer tastes different to him. Nevertheless, further reflections in this area will secure my point. Consider a Sidgwickian pleasure such as my experience of the pleasant taste of a cold beer. It is pleasant (according to the Sidgwickian view) because I want to prolong it for its own sake. If I had different likes and dislikes, or if my brain had been wired differently, or if I were bored with the taste of beer, or if I were suffering from depression, I might not have wanted to prolong it for its own sake. Thus, that very taste experience could have failed to be a pleasure. It was a pleasure not in virtue of

137

its own nature, but in virtue of the fact that I took up a certain attitude toward it.

If the Sidgwickian view were true, my taste experience would have been intrinsically good but *not in virtue of its own nature*. Instead, it would have been intrinsically good in virtue of the extrinsic, relational fact that I reacted to it in the way I did. But this seems impossible. Surely, if something is intrinsically good, it must be good in virtue of the way it is in itself, not merely because of some extrinsic relation it happens to bear to some other thing.

So we see that the Sidgwickian view violates another deep and plausible principle about intrinsic value. This principle says that if a thing is intrinsically good, then it is good in virtue of its own nature.[26] While the meaning of this principle is not entirely clear, it is sufficiently clear for present purposes. If an experience is good entirely in virtue of the fact that the one who has that experience wants to prolong it, then it is not good in virtue of its own nature. It is good in virtue of the fact that it bears some extrinsic relation to some other thing – a person who experiences it.

Perhaps it will appear that I am here appealing to a principle that Sidgwickians would not accept. Perhaps Brandt and the others would just reject the view that intrinsic values depend on intrinsic natures. Perhaps they would say that things get their intrinsic values from their extrinsic relations. In this case Sidgwickians could try to evade my objection by rejecting this element of the classic conception of intrinsic value.

I think it is interesting to note that Brandt and Frankena both explicitly endorsed the principle. Brandt first tried to identify a thing's intrinsic properties: he said that these are properties of a thing that

> do not involve anything beyond the thing or event or state of affairs . . .
> They are what they are independently of the remainder of the world, in
> the sense that it would be logically possible for the rest of the world to be
> different, but for them to remain the same. . . . Such properties we can call
> intrinsic, and we can say that something – an event, state of affairs, or thing
> – is intrinsically desirable if it is desirable in view of its intrinsic properties
> alone.[27]

26. In 'The Conception of Intrinsic Value' Moore goes so far as to suggest that this is a "definition" of intrinsic value. 'We can, in fact, set up the following definition. *To say that a kind of value is "intrinsic" means merely that the question whether a thing possesses it, and in what degree it possesses it, depends solely on the intrinsic nature of thing in question.*' (p. 260)

27. Brandt, *Ethical Theory*, pp. 302–303.

Thus Brandt himself explicitly endorsed the view that intrinsic values depend entirely upon intrinsic natures.

Although Frankena's discussion of this point is not very extensive, he clearly commits himself to the principle when he presents his "official" characterization of intrinsic value. He says:

D. Intrinsic values = things that are good in themselves or *good because of their own intrinsic properties.*[28]

Surprisingly, just a few pages after saying that intrinsic values depend entirely upon intrinsic properties, Brandt formulated hedonism as the view that Sidgwickian pleasures are the sole intrinsic goods; and on his view these are intrinsically good because they are pleasures, and they are pleasures in virtue of the fact that they stand in a certain external relation to some person. Hence, he seems to have formulated hedonism in such a way as to insure that it violates his own version of the principle.

This is a subtle and perhaps confusing point. Didn't Brandt stipulate that the experiencer must react in the specified way to a pleasure *for its own sake,* or *intrinsically?* And isn't that sufficient to show that the thus-created value is intrinsic?

This question is based upon a confusion. The classic conception of intrinsic value involves the notion that if some experience has an intrinsic value, then it has that value in virtue of its own intrinsic nature. So if an experience is intrinsically good, it is good because of the way *it* is. But if Sidgwickian pleasures are intrinsically good, they have their intrinsic values in virtue of the fact that their experiencers like them intrinsically. Consider the property of *being intrinsically liked.* This is *not* an intrinsic property of anything. If anything has that property, it has it in virtue of the fact that the thing stands in certain relations to certain other things. Thus *being intrinsically liked* is an extrinsic property of anything that has it. The fact that someone intrinsically likes a certain experience is an extrinsic fact about that experience. Since this is what (according to SH3) makes something intrinsically good, the Sidgwickian approach implies that intrinsic values are determined by extrinsic properties.

5c. An argument based on a principle about necessity

A closely related point concerns the necessity of intrinsic values. Since intrinsic values depend upon intrinsic natures, and intrinsic natures are

28. Frankena, *Ethics*, p. 82

thought to be essential to the things that have them, each thing is thought to have its intrinsic value of necessity. In other words, this is thought to be true:

NIV: If something, x, has an intrinsic value of n, then it is necessary that x has an intrinsic value of n.[29]

The Sidgwickian view is inconsistent with NIV. For if SH3 were true, my experience of the taste of beer would be intrinsically good in one possible world, but intrinsically worthless in another. It all depends upon whether I want to prolong it for its own sake; and this of course varies from situation to situation.

6. FURTHER PROBLEMS FOR THE SIDGWICKIANS

Imagine a person enjoying the taste of a cold beer. Suppose the sensory experience remains intrinsically unchanged over a period of time. Suppose that at the outset, the person enjoys the taste, and wants it to continue for its own sake. Imagine that his desire for continuation is quite strong – we may arbitrarily rate this desire as a +7. Suppose that as time passes the person gradually becomes tired of the taste of beer. Now his desire has diminished. It is rated at +3. Eventually, though the taste has not changed, the drinker is sated. He no longer wants the taste experience to continue. His desire for continuation is rated at 0.

Recall that Brandt maintained that the degree of intrinsic value of an experience is determined by the degree to which the experiencer wants to prolong the experience. One experience is intrinsically better than another if and only if the experiencer wants more to prolong the one than he does the other.[30] Thus the relevant intensity here is *not* the intensity of the experience itself. It is the intensity of the desire to prolong that

---

29. Chisholm endorses the principle in *Brentano and Intrinsic Value* (Cambridge: Cambridge University Press, 1986). 'For attributions of intrinsic value are necessary. If pleasure is intrinsically good in this world, then it would be intrinsically good in any world in which it might be found.' (p. 95)

   I think a suitably restricted version of the principle is true. I think it does not follow from the principle of universality, since I do not think that each thing has its intrinsic nature of necessity. (My current height is one of my intrinsic properties; I might have been taller.) However, if we take the fundamental bearers of intrinsic value to be states of affairs, and we assume that states of affairs do have their intrinsic natures of necessity, then we will think that the principle of necessity must be true.

30. Brandt, *Ethical Theory*, p. 307.

experience. '[O]f course, "to the degree that" can refer only to the strength of the desire to prolong or terminate.'[31] This component of the Sidgwickian view is formulated in SH4.

If SH4 were true, the drinker's original taste experience would have an intrinsic value of +7. His intermediate taste experience would have an intrinsic value of +3. And at the end his taste experience would have no intrinsic value. In other words, while the experience itself remained intrinsically unchanged, its intrinsic value would gradually decline and eventually fade away.

This example focusses attention on a curious fact about the view under consideration here. According to this view, each intrinsically good experience can be rated on two intensity scales. One scale rates the intensity of the pleasure itself – how "strong" is the pleasant feeling? The second scale rates the strength of the desire to prolong the pleasant feeling – how much does the experiencer want that feeling to continue? The curious fact is that according to SH4, the intrinsic value of an experience varies in proportion to variations in the *second* scale, not the first. This seems strange, since the first scale measures an intrinsic feature of the feeling and the second measures an extrinsic feature.

In classic forms of hedonism – such as Bentham's – it was assumed that there is such a thing as the distinctive feeling of "pleasure itself". It was furthermore assumed that the intensity of the pleasure itself is relevant to the intrinsic value of the pleasure. Other things being equal, the more intense pleasure is intrinsically better. This makes sense, since if it is the pleasure that is good in itself, it would be better in itself (other things being equal) if it were "greater in itself". But SH4 conflicts with this natural view about measurement. Note that SH4 presupposes that there is no such thing as the feeling of "pleasure itself". Rather, there are "pleasant feelings", which are just feelings that we want to prolong. Though the pleasant feeling is alleged to be the bearer of intrinsic value, its amount of value varies in proportion to the strength of some other thing – the experiencer's desire for the pleasant feeling to continue.

7. ANOTHER WAY TO FORMULATE THE HEDONIC THESIS

I think the Sidgwickians were right when they rejected the Distinctive Feeling View. There is no such thing as the alleged "feeling of pleasure

31. Ibid., p. 307.

itself ". Thus it would be a poor idea to understand the Hedonic Thesis as the claim that experiences of this alleged feeling are fundamental bearers of positive intrinsic value.

The Sidgwickian solution involves saying that certain other feelings are bearers of intrinsic value. These are the various and heterogeneous feelings we like, or wish to prolong, or enjoy for their own sakes. I have shown that this approach conflicts with several plausible axioms about intrinsic value. It might appear, then, that so long as we wish to stick with anything like the classic conception of intrinsic value, there is no satisfactory way to understand the Hedonic Thesis.

I think we can make some headway toward understanding the Thesis if we are willing to embrace a novel conception of pleasure. I turn now to a sketch of this conception and a discussion of its consistency with the classic conception of intrinsic value.

On my view, hedonic phenomena may be identified by appeal to a crucially important propositional attitude. This is the attitude we indicate when we say that someone "takes pleasure in" or "is pleased about" some state of affairs. Although I cannot define this attitude, I can say a few words about it. I think that when we take pleasure in a state of affairs, we "welcome" it in a certain way; we are "glad that it is happening"; we like it in a certain familiar way. In typical cases, if we take pleasure in some state of affairs, we may want it to continue, although this is not universally true.[32] I call this attitude "propositional pleasure" since it is a propositional attitude.

We may draw a number of distinctions involving this sort of propositional pleasure. For present purposes the most important is the distinction between *intrinsic* and *extrinsic* propositional pleasure. Sometimes we take pleasure in a state of affairs for its own sake, simply for itself. In these cases, our pleasure is focussed entirely on the state of affairs itself, and not upon its causes, accompaniments, or effects. In such cases, I say we take *intrinsic pleasure* in the state of affairs.

In other cases, a person may take pleasure in a state of affairs in virtue of its cause, or its expected consequences, or in virtue of what it signifies for the person, or in virtue of some other feature not intrinsic to the state

---

32. When joyfully reminiscing, one may take pleasure in various states of affairs that occurred long ago, and are now over. In such cases, one typically does not want to "prolong" the object of his pleasure. The "prolongation thesis" is more plausible when restricted to cases in which one takes intrinsic pleasure in some current feeling. It is somewhat more plausible to suppose that in such cases one always wants to prolong that feeling.

of affairs. In such cases, I say that the person is taking *extrinsic pleasure* in the state of affairs. Various combinations of intrinsic and extrinsic pleasure and displeasure are possible.

Suppose a person, O, is experiencing a delightful, pleasurable feeling, B. However, perhaps due to some moral or religious conviction, O is dismayed to find himself having that feeling, and even more dismayed to find himself taking pleasure in it. Then, in order to record the fact that the feeling is a pleasure for O, we can say that O is intrinsically pleased to be feeling B. In order to record the fact that O is dismayed to be feeling B we can say that O is extrinsically displeased to be feeling B. If his extrinsic displeasure is great enough, we may say that O is overall displeased to be feeling B. In the case described, we might also want to say that O is overall displeased about the fact that he is intrinsically pleased to be feeling B. One of the strengths of my proposal is that it is well suited to making these important distinctions, and expressing complex situations such as the one imagined.[33]

Although all these sorts of pleasure and displeasure are important, for present purposes the most important is *intrinsic propositional pleasure*.

Propositional pleasure is not a feeling. To take pleasure in a fact is not necessarily to have any sensory feelings. A person could take pleasure in various facts even if he were anesthetized. I may, for example, take pleasure in the fact that the war in Bosnia has at least temporarily stopped. I might do this even though I am not feeling any sensory pleasure. I might be feeling no sensations at all. So, from the fact that someone is taking propositional pleasure in some fact, it does not follow that he is experiencing any pleasant feelings.

When a person takes pleasure in some state of affairs, she does so for some stretch of time. For example, I might start being pleased about P when I wake up in the morning, and I might continue being pleased about P until lunchtime. In that case, this particular episode of proposi-

33. Another interesting sort of case was suggested by an editor for *Ethics*. This editor suggested that my view might go wrong because it is possible to be pleased to be experiencing a certain feeling even though the feeling itself is not pleasurable. But I believe that my theory is adequate to such cases. Suppose a certain chef is trying to make some food taste a certain way. Suppose that the chef himself does not find this taste (which we may call 'T') pleasant, but he knows that others will enjoy it. When he finally gets the taste just right, and samples the food, it may be true that he takes *extrinsic* pleasure in the fact that he himself is then experiencing T. His pleasure is extrinsic because he takes this pleasure in the taste in virtue of the fact that it signifies that others will enjoy the food he has prepared. He does not take *intrinsic* pleasure in the fact that he is then experiencing T. That is, his experience of T is not a sensual pleasure for him.

tional pleasure would have lasted for several hours. Every episode of propositional pleasure is like this. Each has a *duration*.

When a person takes pleasure in some state of affairs, he takes pleasure of some *intensity*. I may be very pleased that I survived the accident; I may be even more pleased that I was not injured at all; I may be much less pleased about the condition of my motorcycle. For simplicity in exposition, we may assume that we can assign numbers to episodes of propositional pleasure, so that there will be a convenient way to represent relative intensities of such episodes.

I am now prepared to identify the items that serve as "pleasures" on my view. Suppose that Jeremy is enjoying a cold beer. Suppose that what he likes about the beer is its distinctive taste, which we may call "B". Now consider the state of affairs of

J1: Jeremy taking intrinsic pleasure to degree +3 at t in the fact that he himself is experiencing B at t.

J1 is a *basic hedonic state of affairs*. We should take note of some crucial features of J1. First, notice that J1 involves some specific individual (in this case, Jeremy), some specific intensity of intrinsic propositional pleasure (in this case, +3), some specific time (in this case, t), and some specific "object" (in this case *Jeremy's experiencing B at t*). Notice that J1 as a whole says that the specified individual is taking intrinsic propositional pleasure of the specified intensity at the specified time in the specified state of affairs. Notice also that the object of Jeremy's pleasure is a contemporaneous fact about Jeremy's sensory experience – it says that he himself is just then experiencing a certain taste. Notice that Jeremy, the time, the intensity, and the taste are all introduced by *names* (rather than by descriptive phrases). States of affairs like J1 in these respects are basic hedonic states of affairs.

On my view, the Hedonic Thesis should be interpreted as the claim that these basic hedonic states are intrinsically good.

The proposed view is like Sidgwick's in this respect: like Sidgwick's view, my view is based on a rejection of the Distinctive Feeling View. Like Sidgwick, Brandt, Alston and the others, I think there is no such thing as "the feeling of pleasure itself". So I accept:

FH1: There is no such thing as "the feeling of pleasure itself"; a person can take pleasure in a state of affairs no matter what sensory feelings he is experiencing.

But the view is different from Sidgwick's in other important respects. On Sidgwick's view, when Jeremy enjoys the taste of a beer, the pleasure is *the taste of the beer*. It is a pleasure, according to Sidgwick, because Jeremy apprehends it as desirable. Thus, Sidgwick takes the pleasure to be the *object* of a certain attitude. Brandt's version of the view is relevantly similar. My view is different. On my view, the pleasure is the whole state of affairs that consists in Jeremy's taking intrinsic pleasure in the fact that he himself is experiencing this taste (rather than just the object of this attitude).

The second element in my view is an account of these basic hedonic states. They occupy a central place in the theory.

FH2: A state of affairs is a *basic hedonic state* iff there is an individual, S, a time, t, a positive number, n, and a sensory property, P, such that the state of affairs consists in S's taking intrinsic propositional pleasure at t to degree n in the fact that he himself is experiencing P at t.

I am proposing that we understand the Hedonic Thesis to be the claim that basic hedonic states such as J1 itself are bearers of positive intrinsic value. These are the "pleasures" to which we refer when we say that pleasures are intrinsically good. Thus I accept:

FH3: When we say that pleasures are intrinsically good, what we mean is that basic hedonic states, as defined in FH2, are intrinsically good.

Furthermore, although other more complex options are available, we can illustrate a simple sort of hedonistic view by saying that the intrinsic value of such a state is a function of its duration (indicated by the extent of "t") and its intensity (in the sample case, this is $+3$). Other things being equal, more intense and longer lasting basic hedonic states are intrinsically better.

So the final component of my view is:

FH4: The intrinsic value of a basic hedonic state, as defined in FH2, is a function of the intensity of its intrinsic propositional pleasure and its duration.

In order to determine whether the proposed conception of pleasures is compatible with the classic conception of intrinsic value, we have to identify the intrinsic properties of things like J1. As I see it, the following properties of J1 are intrinsic to it: *being about Jeremy, being a case of someone taking intrinsic pleasure to degree $+3$, having the fact that Jeremy is tasting B as its object*, etc. Any state of affairs that did not have these features would not be intrinsically like J1. (Extrinsic features of J1 include such prop-

145

erties as: *being expressed in English by the sentence 'Jeremy taking intrinsic plea-*
sure . . . ', being an example used in a discussion of hedonism, being deplored
by J. S. Mill, etc.)

It is reasonable to say that an item such as J1 bears its intrinsic value in
virtue of its own nature. A hedonist would say that it is intrinsically good
because it is a case of someone taking intrinsic pleasure in a certain feeling
he is then experiencing. Its intrinsic value is $+3$ because it is a case of
someone taking intrinsic pleasure of degree $+3$. The fact that J. S. Mill
deplored this state of affairs has no bearing on its intrinsic value. That is
an extrinsic fact about it.

It is also reasonable to say that J1 has its intrinsic value of necessity,
since it is reasonable to say that J1 has each of the cited intrinsic properties
of necessity. That is, J1 is essentially the state of affairs of *Jeremy taking*
intrinsic pleasure to degree $+3$ in the fact that Jeremy is experiencing B. If we go
to some other possible world, and find someone else drinking some beer,
or someone taking more or less than 3 units of pleasure in the taste of
beer, or someone taking pleasure in some other experience, then we
haven't found J1. We have found some other state of affairs. But if we
find this very state of affairs – J1 itself – at some possible world, we
may be sure that it will have the same intrinsic value there that it has
here. Those who believe the Hedonic Thesis will say that this value is
positive.

Suppose that Jeremy drinks beer for a long time, and gradually gets
bored with it. Several relevant states of affairs have taken place. Among
these, let us suppose, are J1 and these:

J2: Jeremy taking intrinsic pleasure to degree $+2$ at t2 in the fact that he himself
is experiencing B at t2.
J3: Jeremy taking intrinsic pleasure to degree $+1$ at t3 in the fact that he himself
is experiencing B at t3.

Someone who believes that "pleasures are intrinsically good" might want
to say that each of these states of affairs is intrinsically good. And he might
want to say that J1 is intrinsically better than J2, which in turn is intrinsically better than J3. This seems reasonable. On my proposal, such differences in intrinsic value depend entirely upon differences in intrinsic
natures, since the differences in amounts of propositional pleasure taken
are here *intrinsic* to the states of affairs. This, of course, is consistent with
the assumption that the taste of the beer, indicated by 'B', remains exactly
the same in the three states of affairs.

146

Thus, my interpretation of the Hedonic Thesis is consistent with the classic conception of intrinsic value according to which intrinsic values supervene on intrinsic natures, and are necessary to the things that have them.[34]

34. In his doctoral dissertation *Pleasure and Intrinsic Value* (Amherst: University of Massachusetts, 1980) Earl Conee briefly discusses the central point of the present paper. He says, 'For many persons, tasting an ice-cream sundae is a pleasant experience. Yet hedonists do not attribute intrinsic value to events of tasting. They hold that the pleasure of the taste is the intrinsic good in the experience, not the taste that is its object.' (p. 63) I think Conee here is too generous. Hedonists in the style of Sidgwick hold precisely the thing he says no hedonist holds. Of course, my aim in this paper has been to show that the view is incoherent; they should not hold this view.

Part III

Desert

Essay 8

Adjusting utility for justice: A consequentialist reply to the objection from justice

INTRODUCTORY COMMENTS

In Essay 8, I confront the most profound moral objection to act utilitarianism – the objection from justice. It may be useful here to present a particularly stark version of the objection. Suppose there are two sorts of people in the world, the Haves and the Have Nots. Suppose that the Haves have always enjoyed large amounts of pleasure; suppose that they never worked for the goods that provide the pleasure but simply stole them from the Have Nots; suppose, finally, that the Haves are nasty and cruel to the long-suffering Have Nots.

On the other hand, suppose that the Have Nots have struggled and suffered all their lives; they have not enjoyed any pleasures even though they are the rightful owners of the means to pleasure; suppose, finally, that the Have Nots are kind-hearted and decent – they treat each other and the nasty Haves with respect.

Suppose that it is now in your power to distribute some extra goods. You can give the new goods either to the Haves or to the Have Nots – but no other option is available. We stipulate that the amount of pleasure that will result will be exactly the same no matter which you do. The only difference is that if you give the goods to the Haves, they will experience the pleasure and the Have Nots will experience the disappointment of getting the short end of the stick again. If you give the goods to the Have Nots, *they* will experience the pleasure and the Haves will experience the disappointment.

Hedonism seems to imply that because the amounts of pleasure and pain are the same in both cases, the two outcomes are equal in value. Consequentialism seems to imply that each course of action on your part would be morally right – neither obligatory, neither forbidden. Surely, something has gone wrong here. Right-thinking people judge that it would be better to give the goods to the Have Nots. Surely, if such a case were to arise, your obligation would be to give the goods to the more deserving Have Nots.

My aim in "Adjusting Utility for Justice" is to show that there is a simple way to modify hedonistic utilitarianism so that it will not be open to this sort of objection. The modification leaves the *consequentialism* entirely intact. We still say that your moral obligation is to make the world as good as it can be. The modification occurs entirely within the axiology.

I propose to modify the axiology by adjusting the values of the various pleasures and pains. I claim that a pleasure is more valuable if it is deserved and less valuable if it is not deserved. I claim that a pain is less disvaluable if it is deserved and more disvaluable if it is undeserved. I present some graphs and principles designed to make these ideas clear. I call this "adjusting utility for justice." The aim is to make the value of a pleasure or a pain reflect not only the "raw amount" of pleasure or pain, but also the extent to which the recipient deserves that pleasure or pain.

The central point of "Adjusting Utility for Justice" is that we can in this way retain the fundamental utilitarian insight ("we ought to make the world as good as we can make it") and we can retain the fundamental hedonistic insight ("pleasure is The Good"), and yet we can at the same time also recognize and give due prominence to the role of justice in moral appraisal. We do this by adjusting the values of pleasures and pains so as to reflect the extent to which their recipients deserve them.

Two features of Essay 8 may strike the careful reader as being rather odd. First, such a reader will soon discover that world utilitarianism has been placed far in the background. It emerges briefly in a footnote. The discussion proceeds almost entirely with traditional act utilitarianism as the presupposed normative doctrine. This is especially clear in Section 2, where I present a form of consequentialism based on acts, alternatives, and consequences.

Second, the reader will soon discover that there is little mention of my propositional theory of pleasure in this essay. The discussion of hedonism in this essay seems to presuppose that pleasure is something that occurs in "episodes" – something that people "feel."

I argued strenuously against these traditional conceptions in the papers in Parts I and II of this book. I presented my own novel conceptions of consequentialism and hedonism. Thus the careful reader may be perplexed: If I reject both of these approaches and have defended allegedly superior alternatives, why do I make use of traditional act utilitarianism and traditional hedonism in this essay?

The answer is as simple as it is sad. When I wrote "Adjusting Utility for Justice," I believed that the vast majority of moral philosophers had taken no notice of world utilitarianism and propositional pleasure. The traditional conceptions still occupied center stage in the literature. Thus, because I wanted the results of "Adjusting Utility for Justice" to be of interest to my colleagues in the profession, I thought it would be best to present my arguments in the ways they seem to find familiar and congenial. My own views on the formulation of utilitarianism and hedonism therefore were hidden from view in this essay.

I am confident, however, that anyone who has studied the essays in Parts I and II (and who cares to take the trouble) will have little difficulty in seeing how to recast the discussion entirely in terms of world utilitarianism and propositional pleasure. That is how I think it *really* should go.

The central idea of "Adjusting Utility for Justice" is subjected to some searching criticism in Ingmar Persson's "Feldman's Justicized Act Utilitarianism," *Ratio* ix (1996), 39–46, and his "Ambiguities in Feldman's Desert-Adjusted Values," *Utilitas* (forthcoming).

8

Adjusting utility for justice: A consequentialist reply to the objection from justice

1. INTRODUCTION

In a famous passage near the beginning of *A Theory of Justice*, John Rawls discusses utilitarianism's notorious difficulties with justice. According to classic forms of utilitarianism, a certain course of action is morally right if it produces the greatest sum of satisfactions. And, as Rawls points out, the perplexing implication is ". . . that it does not matter, except indirectly, how this sum of satisfactions is distributed among individuals any more than it matters, except indirectly, how one man distributes his satisfactions over time."[1] He concludes the passage by saying that "[u]tilitarianism does not take seriously the distinction between persons."[2]

As I understand him, Rawls is here alluding to a very well known problem. It has been illustrated by appeal to a host of remarkably striking and ingenious examples. Among these are the Organ Harvest,[3] the Small Southern Town,[4] and the Colosseum.[5] One of the most

1. John Rawls, *A Theory of Justice* (Cambridge: Harvard University Press, 1971): 26.
2. Op. cit., 27.
3. The Organ Harvest is discussed in Judith Thompson's "Killing, Letting Die, and the Trolley Problem," *The Monist* 59 (1976): 204–217. Philippa Foot discusses essentially the same case in her "Abortion and the Doctrine of the Double Effect," *Oxford Review* 5 (1966).
4. Most of the elements of the case of the Small Southern Town can be found in E. F. Carritt's *Ethical and Political Thinking* (Oxford: Oxford University Press, 1947), in a passage that is cited in John Rawls, "Two Concepts of Rules," *The Philosophical Review*, 64 (1955): 3–32. Rawls' own "telishment" case is again quite similar. Kai Nielsen's case of the Magistrate and the Threatening Mob, described in his "Against Moral Conservatism" *Ethics* 82 (1972): 113–124, makes the same point. Nielsen's essay is reprinted in Louis Pojman, *Ethical Theory* (Wadsworth: Belmont, California, 1989): 181–188. The example appears on p. 183.
5. The case of the Christians in the Colosseum is briefly sketched by Amartya Sen in "Rights and Agency," *Philosophy and Public Affairs*, 11, 1 (Winter, 1982); reprinted in Samuel Scheffler, *Consequentialism and Its Critics* (Oxford: Oxford University Press, 1988): 191.

straightforwardly relevant examples is given by Ross in *The Right and the Good*. Ross sketches a case in which someone has the choice of either (a) giving 1000 units of value to a very good man, or else (b) giving 1001 units of value to a very bad man.[6] Ross points out that utilitarianism implies (given the standard set of provisoes) that it is morally obligatory that the value be given to the bad man, since the total value then enjoyed would be slightly greater. Ross believes that the implications of utilitarianism are mistaken.

Reflection on this case may clarify what Rawls must have had in mind when he said that "utilitarianism does not take seriously the distinction between persons." In Ross's example, some benefits must be distributed. One way of distributing the benefits would be on balance best, but that distribution gives all the benefits to the less deserving man. Utilitarianism pays no attention to facts about past behavior and meritorious character. It requires that the benefit be given in whatever way will be best, regardless of the history and character of the recipients. In this way, it may be said to fail to take seriously the distinction between people.[7]

Certain traditional forms of consequentialism are refuted by this sort of objection. However, I am convinced that the objection does not reveal any defect in the basic consequentialist insight – that we ought to behave in such a way as to make the world as good as we can make it. As I see it, what the objection reveals is that there are defects in the axiologies traditionally associated with consequentialism. I want to show that it is possible to construct an axiology that is sensitive to matters of justice. If we combine consequentialism with such an axiology, we can maintain the core insight of consequentialism while rebutting the objection from justice.

In this paper, I first present a fairly typical form of consequentialism and I show in somewhat greater detail how it goes wrong with respect to justice. I then sketch a novel value theory that takes explicit account of justice. I attempt to show that when we combine consequentialism with the new value theory, we get more palatable results in the problem cases. In a final section, I discuss some objections.

6. *The Right and the Good* (Oxford: Oxford University Press, 1930); reprinted in Pojman, op. cit., p. 258.
7. Although it is not clear that it was originally presented in order to establish this point, Williams' case of Jim and the Indians could be used to illustrate the problem about justice. See Bernard Williams, *Utilitarianism: For and Against* (Cambridge: Cambridge University Press, 1973); 77–150. Parfit's notorious population puzzles might also be viewed from this perspective. See Part Four of Derek Parfit, *Reasons and Persons* (Oxford: Oxford University Press, 1984).

2. CONSEQUENTIALISM: A PRELIMINARY STATEMENT

Typical forms of consequentialism are based on the idea that on each occasion of moral choice, there are several possible acts available to the agent. These are his "alternatives" on that occasion. For each alternative, there is a "total consequence." This is the combination of all the things that would happen as a result if the alternative were performed.[8]

In order to state the bare bones of a typical consequentialist theory, we need a ranking of total consequences in terms of intrinsic value.[9] Let us assume for a moment that this has been given: for each possible total consequence, there is a number indicating the total intrinsic value of that consequence. Let the numbers be assigned in the standard way with higher numbers representing better outcomes, and say that an act "maximizes intrinsic value" if and only if no alternative has a total consequence with greater intrinsic value.

We can now formulate the central principle of this form of consequentialism:

C: An act is morally right if and only if it maximizes intrinsic value.[10]

In order to give real substance to the theory, we must add an axiology, or theory of value. This will specify what it is about a total consequence that gives it its intrinsic value.

In virtue of its simplicity and familiarity, let us provisionally make use of a traditional form of hedonism.

According to this view, the fundamental bearers of intrinsic value are

8. For present purposes, I presuppose a traditional conception of alternatives and consequences. A particularly clear presentation of this sort of view can be found in Lars Bergstrom, "Utilitarianism and Alternative Actions," *Noûs* 5 (1971): 237–252. In my *Doing the Best We Can* (Dordrecht: Reidel, 1986) I tried to show why this approach to actions and alternatives leads to difficulties. A more refined version of the view presented here would follow the pattern of MO in *Doing the Best We Can*.

9. I am not proposing an account of the "essence of consequentialism." Very many normative theories that I would classify as consequentialist do not make use of rankings of total consequences in terms of intrinsic value. For example, consider the form of utilitarianism that says that we ought to maximize preference satisfaction. One could maintain this view and insist that nothing has intrinsic value. Another case is supplied by egoism. A typical form of egoism tells me to maximize my own welfare – it says nothing about intrinsic value. Finally, expected utility utilitarianism tells us that our moral obligation is to maximize expected utility, not intrinsic value.

10. For a more rigorous formulation of the central consequentialist doctrine, see the discussion of MO in *Doing the Best We Can*. It would be interesting to compare C to Moore's "ideal utilitarianism" as presented in *Principia Ethica*.

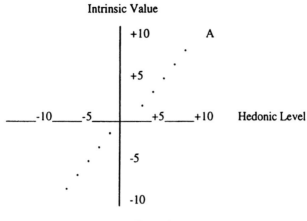

Intrinsic Value

+10   A

+5

-10____-5____ | ____+5____+10   Hedonic Level

-5

-10

Figure 1

episodes of pleasure and pain, where an episode is an event that consists in someone's feeling some amount of pleasure (or pain) for some stretch of time. Let us also assume that for each episode of pleasure or pain there is a number indicating the amount of pleasure or pain contained in the episode. We assign the numbers in the standard way, so that we can evaluate any episode of pleasure or pain in terms of its "hedonic level" – a measure of the amount of pleasure or pain in that episode.

According to this simple form of hedonism, the intrinsic value of an episode of pleasure or pain is a function of its hedonic level. We can display the function in a simple graph, Figure 1. The North–South axis of the graph indicates amounts of intrinsic value, with positive numbers representing intrinsic goodness and negative numbers indicating intrinsic evil. The East–West axis indicates hedonic level, with amounts of pleasure (increasing to the East) and pain (increasing to the West). The import of the graph is this: the intrinsic value of an episode of pleasure or pain is equal to the hedonic level of that episode.

Now we can state a principle concerning the intrinsic value of a whole consequence. According to this view, the intrinsic value of a consequence is the sum of the intrinsic values of the episodes of pleasure and pain that occur in that consequence. Let us call this axiology 'H' (for 'hedonism'). When we combine H with principle C we get perhaps the most familiar form of consequentialism – hedonic act utilitarianism.

157

Table 1

Actions	Value for A	Value for B	Total value
Give ticket to A	+10	−1	+9
Give ticket to B	−2	+10	+8

3. THREE CLEAN CASES

Some of the examples discussed in the literature involve puzzling and controversial combinations of extraneous moral issues, and so their impact is not entirely clear. For purposes of illustration it would be better to have "cleaner," less complicated cases. Let us attempt to construct some simple cases of this sort.

Suppose I am required to give away a ticket that will entitle its bearer to a free lunch. Suppose I can give this ticket either to A or to B. Each of them would enjoy a free lunch, getting (let us say) ten units of pleasure from the experience. Suppose, furthermore, that B would be slightly disappointed if A were to get the ticket. A, on the other hand, would be somewhat more disappointed if B were to get the ticket. Suppose that A and B are in all relevant respects quite similar, except that A has already enjoyed hundreds of free lunches, whereas B has never gotten even one. Suppose, finally, that no third party would be affected by my choice of A or B.

In this case, which we may call the *First Free Lunch*, C + H implies that the ticket should go to A. Table 1 is a chart that helps to explain why.

Provided that A would be slightly more disappointed than B by failure to receive the ticket, and A and B would be equally pleased to receive the ticket, and no one else would be affected by the distribution of the ticket, total intrinsic value is maximized by giving the ticket to A, even though he has already enjoyed far more free lunches than B. C + H then yields the result that it is my moral obligation to give the ticket to A. But this result is counterintuitive. Surely it would be more just to let B enjoy at least one free lunch – after all, B is in all relevant respects just like A except that he has so far had no free lunches, and A has had hundreds of them. Utilitarianism seems to ignore an important difference between people.

The *Second Free Lunch* is very similar to the first. Again I am required to give out a lunch ticket. Again I have my choice of giving it to A or giving it to B. Again each would enjoy the lunch, and each would be disappointed to fail to get the lunch – A a bit more than B. Let us imagine this time that A and B are alike with respect to past receipt of tickets for free lunches. However, in this case let us imagine that A has stolen and destroyed hundreds of lunches. Hundreds of decent people have gone hungry as a result of A's malicious thievery. B on the other hand is a decent fellow who has never stolen anyone's lunch.

We may assume that the numbers in Table 1 apply again in this case. Again, C + H implies that it is my moral obligation to give the ticket to A. And again the implications of the theory conflict with my moral intuitions. In light of A's miserable past behavior, it seems to me that the ticket should go to B in spite of the fact that utility would not thereby be maximized. There is a "distributional impropriety" in giving the free lunch to A when he has so wantonly destroyed the lunches of others. Therefore, as I see it, the *Second Free Lunch* reveals another way in which C + H fails to take account of differences between people.[11]

Let us now imagine a third example. Suppose this time that B is the legal owner of a ticket for a free lunch. Now A comes along and steals the ticket. He justifies his theft by appeal to a set of facts much like those illustrated in Table 1. Since he (A) would be more disappointed by failure to get the free lunch, utility is maximized by his getting it. Thus, he claims, when he stole the ticket he was doing the right thing.

Given the expected set of background assumptions, C + H implies in the *Third Free Lunch* that it was morally right for A to steal the ticket and that it would be right for him to get the lunch. And again it seems perfectly clear to me that the implications are false. If such a case were to occur, it would be unjust for the ticket and the free lunch to go to A. This injustice is sufficient, it seems to me, to make it morally wrong for A to steal the ticket. In this case the relevant difference between A and B is that B owns the ticket. C + H seems to ignore this fact.

I mentioned a number of examples at the outset. These include the Small Southern Town, the Colosseum, and the Organ Harvest. Although these cases are vastly more complex, each of them is in certain ways similar to the cases I have described. In every case, harms and benefits must be

11. The *Second Free Lunch* is in some important ways quite similar to Ross' example involving the good man and the bad man. It is also quite like an example Rescher presents on p. 47 of his *Distributive Justice*. Rescher's example involves a case in which someone has the choice of conferring a certain benefit on a man who is "the very personification of virtue" or else conferring a slightly larger benefit on someone who is "the embodiment of vice."

distributed in one of several ways. One distribution is stipulated to maximize utility. Unfortunately, that distribution also seems to involve substantial injustice. If the injustice is great enough, C + H yields the wrong moral judgment.

4. A NEW PROPOSAL

Reflection on such examples leads some philosophers to say that consequentialism is false. As they see it, the examples reveal that sometimes, because of its injustice, the best outcome is not the one we ought to produce. But there is another way to interpret these cases. Following Brentano and others, we might take them to show that there is something wrong with the axiologies traditionally associated with consequentialism.[12] A different axiology – one sensitive to justice and injustice – might imply that the acts that seem to be morally right in these examples have consequences that are in fact better than the consequences that would have been produced by their alternatives. And the greater value might arise, on the new axiology, from the amount of justice in the consequence.

In an attempt to develop these intuitions about the place of justice in axiology, I want to formulate an axiology that starts with hedonism, but incorporates the idea that the value of a pleasure or pain may be increased or decreased depending upon whether it is justly or unjustly experienced.[13] When we combine the new axiology with C, we will get a consequentialist normative theory that deals more successfully with the problems about justice.

12. In his essay "Loving and Hating," Franz Brentano presents a complex axiology, designed to accommodate a variety of moral intuitions, including intuitions about the value of justice. In one passage, he indicates that he thinks that the world is not made better when people receive goods they don't deserve. In this respect, my view is like Brentano's. See Franz Brentano, *The Origin of Our Knowledge of Right and Wrong*, ed. by Oskar Kraus, English edition ed. by Roderick Chisholm and Elizabeth Schneewind (London: Routledge and Kegan Paul, 1969): 149. In his "Rights and Agency," *Philosophy and Public Affairs* 11, No. 1 (Winter, 1982), reprinted in *Consequentialism and Its Critics*, ed. by Samuel Scheffler (Oxford: Oxford University Press, 1988): 187–223, Amartya Sen discusses "goal rights systems" of consequentialism. Such systems are in important ways similar to the sort of system I present here. More recently, David Sosa defended a similar view in "Consequences of Consequentialism," *Mind* 102, 405 (January, 1993): 101–122.
13. In Chapter 11 of *Confrontations with the Reaper* (Oxford: Oxford University Press, 1992) I sketched an axiology that is similar to this one. There, however, in an attempt to find a consequentialist account of the morality of killing, I considered the idea that life itself might be an intrinsic good, and that each person deserves not only some measure of pleasure, but some measure of life.

My conception of justice is based on the ancient and plausible idea that justice is done when people receive goods and evils according to *desert*.[14] The closer the fit between desert and receipt, the more just the outcome. Other things being equal, the more just outcome is the better. Before turning to the formulation of the axiology, I should say a few words about desert.

I will not be able to provide any analysis of the concept of desert.[15] It functions here as a conceptual primitive. However, the idea should be familiar. We often hear people say that a particularly vicious criminal "deserves to have the book thrown at him," or that a sick child "does not deserve to suffer in this way," or that those who have labored in the background "deserve their day in the sun." Roughly, to say that a person deserves some good is to say that it would be "distributionally appropriate" for him to get it. I assume that desert is a matter of degree, so that it makes sense to say that a certain person deserves a certain pleasure or pain *to a certain extent*. I will represent the various extents with numbers, in the usual way.

It is important to note that desert is not defined here in terms of moral obligation. The statement that a person deserves some good is not equivalent to the statement that she ought to get it, or to the statement that someone else ought to provide it. In some cases, although someone deserves some good, no one is in position to provide it; in other cases, for various reasons, some other considerations override the demands of justice. So the statement that someone deserves something does not entail the statement that she morally ought to get it. Equally, the statement that someone ought to get a certain good does not entail that she deserves it. If the results would be good enough, there could be a case in which someone morally ought to give a certain good to a certain recipient, even though the recipient does not deserve it.

Many different factors influence the extent to which a given person deserves a certain pleasure or pain. One of these is *excessive or deficient past*

---

14. Aristotle claims that one central sort of justice is "a species of the proportionate." His idea seems to be that distributions of goods and evils are just provided that they are proportional to the merits of the recipients. See *Nichomachean Ethics* V.3. In *Distributive Justice* (Bobbs-Merrill: New York, 1966), Nicholas Rescher defends a similar view, and cites supporting passages from Plato, various Roman jurists, Sidgwick, John Hospers, and others. Although there are important differences between Rescher's approach and mine, I have benefitted enormously from his work – especially his very extensive bibliography on utilitarianism and justice.

15. For an extensive discussion of the concept of desert, see *Desert*, by George Scher (Princeton University Press: Princeton, 1987).

receipt. Excessive past receipt lowers your desert level for a good; deficient past receipt increases it. To see how this works, imagine a case in which there are two possible recipients for some good. Suppose the potential recipients are alike in all relevant respects except that one of them has already received far more of that good than the other. Then, since other things are equal, the one who has so far been short-changed has greater desert. His desert level for the good is greater than the desert level of others who have already received more.

A recipient's *moral worthiness* may have an impact on his desert level, too. Suppose two potential recipients of good are alike in all other relevant respects, except that one of them has been good, whereas the other has been bad. Then the one who has been good has greater desert. If no other factors complicate the case, it would be more just for the good to be given to him.

A third factor is based on rights and claims. Other things being equal, someone with a *legitimate claim* on some good has greater desert relative to that good than does someone with less claim on it. Thus, if two recipients are in other respects similar, but one legally owns the means to a certain pleasure and the other does not, then the owner deserves more to have the pleasures arising from ownership of that object.

There are undoubtedly other factors that may influence the extent to which a person deserves some pleasure or pain, and in a full exposition of the theory of desert, each of them would be described in detail.[16] Furthermore, in real-life cases several of the factors may be jointly operative. The ways in which the factors clash and harmonize so as to yield an overall desert-level must also be investigated. However, since my aim here is primarily to show that it is possible to formulate an axiology that takes account of justice, and to show how such a theory can be combined with consequentialism to rebut the objection from justice, I shall not pursue these lines of inquiry here.

According to the axiology I want to defend, the intrinsic value of an episode of pleasure or pain is a function of two variables: (i) the amount

16. In *Confrontations with the Reaper*, I discussed the idea that a person's desert level relative to a certain good might be influenced by the amount of time and effort she has invested in acquiring that good. Thus, if two people are similar in other respects, but one of them has worked hard to cultivate a garden, whereas the other has done nothing in the garden, then the hard-working gardener has greater investment. She deserves more to enjoy the benefits deriving from the garden.

In *Distributive Justice* (Bobbs-Merrill: New York, 1966), Nicholas Rescher discusses seven "canons" of distributive justice. Each of these canons corresponds to a possible source of desert. See pp. 73–83.

of pleasure or pain the recipient *receives* in that episode, and (ii) the amount of pleasure or pain the recipient *deserves* in that episode. Roughly, the theory maintains that pleasure is generally intrinsically good; but it is better if it is fully deserved, and it is less good if it is not deserved. In extreme cases, if it is undeserved, it may be worth much less – indeed, it may be worthless or even bad. Pain, on the other hand, is generally intrinsically bad. However, it is even worse when the person who suffers it does not deserve it. It is less bad – and may even be good – if the person who suffers it fully deserves it.

Part of the content of the axiology may be expressed by some principles about desert and receipt. Each principle governs a class of cases involving a range of receipt and desert levels. One principle governs cases in which a person experiences some pleasure when she deserves it. It seems to me that it is especially good if someone who has "positive desert" gets to experience precisely the pleasure she deserves. Following Chisholm and Moore, I use the term "enhancement" to indicate this axiological phenomenon.[17] This is the first principle of "just deserts":

P1: Positive desert enhances the intrinsic goodness of pleasure.

Part of the import of P1 is illustrated in Figure 2. In Figure 2, we focus on the case of someone who deserves exactly 10 units of pleasure. The figure displays the outputs of intrinsic value generated by the function for various inputs of pleasure. However, this figure applies only to the case of a person who deserves to be getting 10 units of pleasure and so gives only a suggestion about cases involving people with other desert levels.

Point A on the figure indicates that when a person deserves 10 units of pleasure and gets 10 units of pleasure, then the episode as a whole has an intrinsic value of +20. Since justice is done when the deserving get what they deserve, intrinsic value is enhanced. Notice that the curve begins to flatten out as it moves northeast. This shows that as a person begins to receive more than she deserves, additional increments of pleasure have decreasing marginal intrinsic value. Again, this is a matter of justice. Point B is of interest, too. It indicates that it is intrinsically bad for a person who deserves 10 units of pleasure to get nothing instead.

The second principle concerns what happens when someone who deserves pain gets pleasure instead. If a person with negative desert enjoys

17. See *Brentano and Intrinsic Value*, pp. 85–87. Moore speaks of enhancement a few times in Chapter VI of *Principia Ethica*. See, for example, pp. 211 and 213.

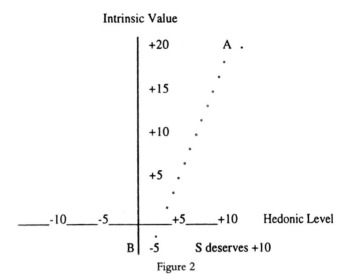

Intrinsic Value

+20   A .

+15

+10

+5 .

____-10____-5____|____+5____+10   Hedonic Level

B| -5   S deserves +10

Figure 2

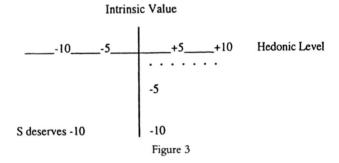

Intrinsic Value

____-10____-5____|____+5____+10   Hedonic Level

-5

S deserves -10   -10

Figure 3

pleasure, justice is not done, and the value of that pleasure is diminished, or "mitigated."[18] The general principle here is:

P2: Negative desert mitigates the intrinsic goodness of pleasure.

Figure 3 illustrates one possible view about how negative desert might mitigate the value of pleasure. Again, we consider only one class of cases:

18. Chisholm calls this phenomenon "defeat." See, for example, *Brentano and Intrinsic Value*, p. 83.

164

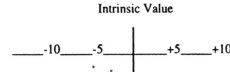

Figure 4

the cases in which the recipient deserves exactly 10 units of pain. Figure 3 shows outputs of intrinsic value for various inputs of pleasure.

The significance of the figure is this: when a person has negative desert, positive receipt is worthless. In such cases, pleasures – of any intensity – have no intrinsic value.

According to a somewhat more extreme view, when a person on the whole deserves pain, but receives pleasure instead, then the injustice of the situation is so great as to make it intrinsically bad.[19] If we accept this view, we will want to go beyond saying merely that negative desert *mitigates* the intrinsic goodness of pleasure. We will want to say that in some cases, negative desert "transvaluates" the goodness of pleasure. By this I mean to indicate that if a person's desert level is negative enough, positive receipt becomes intrinsically bad.[20] We can illustrate one version of this view as Figure 4.

We have so far considered two sorts of cases: those in which a person with positive desert receives pleasure, and those in which a person with negative desert receives pleasure. What about the case in which a person has "neutral" desert – he neither deserves pleasure nor deserves pain? In such cases the value of the pleasure is neither enhanced nor mitigated.

19. In *The Origin of Our Knowledge of Right and Wrong*, p. 23, Brentano says, "Pleasure in the misfortunes of others (Schadenfreude) is bad because [it is not a correct emotion]." In *Brentano and Intrinsic Value*, p. 76, Chisholm says that Meinong also used the term "schadenfreude" to indicate joy in another's pain. Following Brentano and Meinong, Chisholm maintains that joy is good, but joy in another's pain is neutral in value. In *Principia Ethica*, pp. 208–209, Moore says that "The first class [of great positive evils] consists of those evils which seem always to include an enjoyment or admiring contemplation of things which are themselves either evil or ugly." He goes on to cite cruelty and lasciviousness as examples.
20. Chisholm, *Brentano and Intrinsic Value*, p. 83.

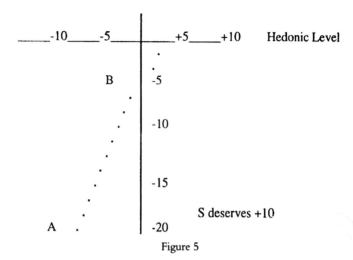

Intrinsic Value

_____-10_____-5_____|_____+5_____+10   Hedonic Level

B   -5

-10

-15

S deserves +10

A   -20

Figure 5

Hence, the intrinsic value of an episode of pleasure of this sort is directly proportional to the amount of pleasure it contains. The principle here is:

P3: Neutral desert neither enhances nor mitigates the intrinsic goodness of pleasure.

The fourth principle concerns the case in which someone deserves pleasure, but gets pain instead. As I see it, pain is bad enough; but when someone who deserves pleasure gets pain instead, the evil of that pain is made even worse, or (to use another Chisholmian term) "aggravated," by its injustice:

P4: Positive desert aggravates the intrinsic badness of pain.

P4 is the principle that stands behind the axiological intuition that it is worse for bad things to happen to good people than it is for bad things to happen to bad people. Figure 5 illustrates one view about how positive desert might aggravate the evil of pain.

Figure 5 applies only to cases in which someone deserves 10 units of pleasure. It illustrates a view about how this positive desert makes it especially bad for such a deserving person to get pain. Note, for example, Point A. This indicates that when a person deserves +10, but gets −10 instead, the whole episode is so unfair that it has an intrinsic value of −20.

166

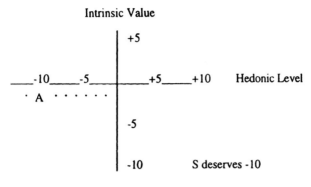

Intrinsic Value

+5

___-10___-5___|___+5___+10   Hedonic Level
· A · · · · ·

-5

-10   S deserves -10

Figure 6

The fifth principle concerns the case in which someone who deserves pain gets pain. Pain is generally bad; but it is not so bad for it to be experienced by someone who deserves it. In this case, since justice is done, the badness of the episode has been mitigated.

P5: Negative desert mitigates the intrinsic badness of pain.

Figure 6 illustrates one possible interpretation of P5.

Point A indicates what happens when ten units of pain are received by a person who deserves exactly ten units of pain. Since in this case the person gets exactly what he deserves, justice is done. The evil of the pain is mitigated by the negative desert of the recipient. Although he suffers some pain, the world is not made worse. The intrinsic value of the episode is zero.

Some philosophers seem to believe that the world is made *better* when the guilty suffer precisely the harm they deserve.[21] This phenomenon may be called the "transvaluation of the evil of pain by negative desert." One interpretation of this view is illustrated in Figure 7.

Point A on Figure 7 serves to illustrate the idea that it is slightly good

21. In *The Metaphysical Elements of Justice*, Kant describes a case in which some isolated society is about to disband. One murderer is still in prison, yet to be executed. Kant seems to want to say that even though in a case like this there is no utilitarian justification for carrying out the sentence, still the criminal ought to be executed. If we approach the case from the perspective of the principle of the transvaluation of the evil of pain by negative desert, we might claim that the world is made better by the infliction of deserved pain on the murderer. Thus, though traditional forms of utilitarianism might not be able to explain it, a version of C + JH might be able to explain why retributive punishment is justified.

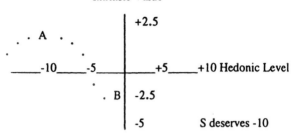

Intrinsic Value

+2.5

. A . .
.
____-10____-5____|____+5____+10 Hedonic Level
.
. B -2.5

-5   S deserves -10

Figure 7

(+2.5) for a person to receive ten units of pain when this is precisely what he deserves. This expresses the retributivist axiological intuition that sometimes it is good for bad people to be punished. The curve slopes downward in both directions from Point A in order to illustrate the idea that it is not so good for a person who deserves pain to get either more or less pain than he deserves. This corresponds to the intuition that punishment must be proportional to the crime.

The views expressed in Figures 6 and 7 are reminiscent of views endorsed by Meinong, Brentano, Chisholm, and Moore. Brentano, for example, discussed the case in which someone takes sorrow in someone else's sorrow. Since sorrow is precisely the right reaction in such a case, Brentano declared the whole state of affairs to be good.[22] Moore's views about hatred of evil and ugliness are again similar.[23] In my view, each of these cases illustrates the same general thesis: the evil of pain is mitigated (and in some cases perhaps transvaluated) by negative desert.

The final principle concerns the case in which a person with neutral desert receives pain. As I see it, the intrinsic value of any such episode of pain is directly proportional to the amount of pain it contains. Thus the principle is:

P6: Neutral desert neither enhances nor mitigates the evil of pain.

22. Brentano discusses this sort of case in "Two Unique Cases of Preferability," which is in the "Supplementary Notes" to *The Origin of Our Knowledge of Right and Wrong*, English edition edited by Roderick Chisholm; pp. 90–91.
23. Moore claims (PE, 217) that while the specific emotion of hatred is not intrinsically good, it is nevertheless intrinsically good for a person to hate what is evil or ugly. This is at least analogous to the idea that it is good to take pain in another's pain.

168

According to "justice adjusted hedonism" (or "JH"), the fundamental bearers of intrinsic value are episodes of pleasure and pain. In each case, the intrinsic value of the episode of pleasure or pain is not a simple function of hedonic level. Desert plays an essential role, too. As a result, some pleasures are not good (as shown in Figure 3) and some pains are not bad (as shown in Figure 7). In every case, the justice-adjusted intrinsic value of the whole episode is a function of the receipt level and the desert level of the recipient. The intrinsic value of a whole consequence is the sum of the justice-adjusted intrinsic values of the episodes of pleasure and pain that occur in that consequence.[24]

If we combine C with our new axiology, the resulting normative theory ("C + JH") is sensitive to matters of justice. It takes account of the enhancing, aggravating, mitigating, and perhaps transvaluating factor of desert. My claim is that the resulting theory generates correct results in the problem cases.

5. REEVALUATION OF PUZZLE CASES

In Section 3 I presented three cases in which C + H generated incorrect normative judgments. In order to apply C + JH to these cases, we have to recalculate the intrinsic values of the relevant consequences according to JH.

In the *First Free Lunch*, there were two potential recipients of a ticket for a free lunch. One recipient, A, had already received hundreds of such tickets. The other, B, had received none. But it was stipulated that A would suffer slightly greater disappointment if he failed to get the ticket. C + H implied that it was my obligation to give the ticket to A, and this seemed mistaken. Now let us consider what C + JH implies for the *First Free Lunch*.

Table 2 contains some numbers illustrating the application of the new axiology to the example:

24. In a number of places, Sen has argued that "sum ranking" is an important (and problematic) component of traditional utilitarianism. Roughly, the idea is that the total utility of an outcome is the sum of the utilities of the individuals in that outcome. See, for example, his Dewey Lecture, "Moral Information," *The Journal of Philosophy*, LXXXII, 4 (April, 1985) 175. My summation principle goes further: the total utility of an outcome is the sum of the utilities of the *basic utility-bearing states of affairs* in that outcome. A number of philosophers, influenced perhaps by Rawls and Bernard Williams, have claimed that this is the crucial element that obliterates the distinctions between people. I have attempted to retain an extreme form of sum ranking, while at the same time formulating the axiology in such a way as to respect the morally important distinctions between people.

Table 2

Actions	Value for A	Value for B	Total value
Give ticket to A	+8	−2	+6
Give ticket to B	−2	+20	+18

If A gets the ticket, he will experience ten units of pleasure. But in virtue of his excessive past receipt of tickets, his desert level is low – perhaps even negative. He doesn't deserve the pleasures derivable from more free lunches. As a result, the intrinsic value of his pleasure is mitigated. This is the import of principle P2. I have accordingly reduced the value of A's pleasure from +10 to +8.

If the ticket goes to A, then B will be disappointed again. He will suffer one unit of pain. But B does not deserve this pain. In virtue of his deficient past receipt, he deserves the pleasures of a free lunch. In accordance with Principle P4, it follows that the evil of B's pain is aggravated by his positive desert. I have therefore represented the value of B's pain as −2 rather than as −1. The justice-adjusted intrinsic value of giving the ticket to A is +6 (rather than +9 as before).

Now let's consider the results of giving the ticket to B. If B gets the ticket, A will suffer 2 units of pain. The happiness of B, if he gets the ticket, is fully deserved. After all, he has had far less than his fair share of free lunches, and has suffered far more than his fair share of disappointment. According to Principle P1, the value of his happiness is enhanced by his positive desert. Following the suggestion of Figure 2, I have assigned it a value of +20.

So the act that intuitively seems to be morally right – giving the ticket to B – also has better results according to JH. Thus, an example that refuted C + H does not refute C + JH.

The treatment of the *Second Free Lunch* and the *Third Free Lunch* according to JH is similar. In each of these cases JH implies that the best outcome is the one in which the ticket goes to the more deserving B. In the *Second Free Lunch*, this follows from the stipulated fact that A has behaved miserably, and has thereby lowered his desert level. In the *Third*, it follows from the fact that B is the legitimate owner of the ticket: he deserves the pleasures arising from ticket ownership; A does not.

I noted earlier that Rawls claimed that "utilitarianism does not take seriously the distinction between persons."[25] As I understand it, the point of this remark is that utilitarianism advocates the distribution of goods and evils in whatever way will maximize total utility – with no regard for the character or the past behavior of the various recipients. Recipients of good and evil function merely as "vessels" into which value may be poured. The theory implies that the value should be poured out in whatever way will yield the greatest total. It should be clear, however, that this charge cannot be leveled against the axiology proposed here. The value of a given distribution of goods and evils depends crucially on the extent to which each recipient deserves his or her share. Past receipt and character play central roles in the determination of desert. Hence, the theory recognizes and pays careful heed to the morally relevant differences between persons.

Although I will not attempt to show it here, I believe that the other puzzle cases mentioned at the outset pose no special threat to C + JH. In each of those cases, C + H implied that some grave injustice should be committed. In some of those cases C + JH delivers normative results different from and more palatable than those delivered by C + H. In such cases, once we adjust utility for justice, it will turn out that the best consequence is the one in which no injustice is committed. Thus, as I see it, C + JH does not have the defect that Rawls had in mind in the passage cited.

It is important to keep in mind that the actual implications of the theory in these cases would depend upon details about the receipt levels and desert levels of the participants in all the outcomes. In some cases C + JH will imply that a serious injustice is required in order to assure the best outcome, and so (sadly) ought to be committed. The theory does not imply that justice must always be maximized; it implies that justice-adjusted intrinsic value must always be maximized.

6. SOME OBJECTIONS

A critic might object to C + JH, claiming that it is covertly circular. The circularity, it might be alleged, arises in this way: first we purport to explain the normative concept of *moral obligation* by appeal to the value-theoretic concept of *intrinsic betterness*. Then when it comes to give substance to the concept of intrinsic betterness, we appeal to the concept

25. Rawls, op. cit., p. 27.

171

of *justice*. Justice is explicated in terms of *desert*. And desert, finally, is explained by saying that a person deserves some pleasure or pain precisely when he *ought* to get it – and thus the circle is completed. We have made covert use of the concept of moral obligation in our attempt to explain moral obligation.

This objection turns on a misunderstanding of the proposal. The objection goes wrong at the final step, where it is alleged that we explain desert by appeal to moral obligation. I endorse no such explanation. The concept of desert is not defined by appeal to the concept of moral obligation. Indeed, it is not defined in any way here. It functions as a conceptual primitive for purposes of the present theory.

In my discussion of desert, I have made liberal use of evaluative terminology. Thus, I have spoken of "fair shares," "worthiness of receipt," "moral rights," and "fittingness." However I have tried to avoid use of the concepts of moral rightness, wrongness, or obligatoriness. The statement that a person *deserves* some pleasure must not be confused with the statement that *it would be morally right* for him to get that pleasure. In order for the theory as a whole to avoid circularity, it is important that the concept of desert is not explicated by appeal to the concepts of right and wrong. For, as I see it, desert plays a role in the determination of justice, and justice plays a role in the determination of the intrinsic value of outcomes, and the intrinsic value of outcomes plays a central role in the determination of right and wrong.

My approach involves a somewhat unorthodox view about the place of the theory of justice in moral philosophy. Traditionally, the theory of justice has been thought to belong in normative ethics. I have always been puzzled about its implications for action. Suppose the theory of justice firmly establishes that some sort of behavior is unjust. Is it supposed to follow that we should not engage in that sort of behavior? If so, the theory of justice seems to have invaded the turf of ordinary normative ethics. If not, the import of the theory of justice is obscure.

My approach firmly locates the theory of justice in axiology. Our axiology determines the value of each outcome, in part, by the justice or injustice of the distribution of pleasures and pains within that outcome. Justice and injustice, in turn, are understood to be determined by reflections on the quality of the fit between pleasures and pains received and pleasures and pains deserved in each outcome. Thus, as I see it, a full-blown axiological theory would have to include an account of justice. Normative ethics then takes the information provided by axiology, and generates prescriptions for right action. In my view, the prescription is very simple: behave in such a way as to make the world as good as you can.

I turn now to a second objection. It might be claimed that even if the theory presented here is acceptable, it cannot possibly figure in a defense of *consequentialism* – for the theory is not a form of *consequentialism*. The problem, according to the objection, is that my proposed axiology ascribes intrinsic value to complex states of affairs. The values of these states of affairs turn on normative features, such as desert and justice. No consequentialist theory, it might be claimed, makes use of normative features in this way.

In reply to this objection, I would first want to insist that C + JH is as much a form of consequentialism as the hedonistic utilitarianism of Mill and the pluralistic "ideal" utilitarianisms of Brentano and Moore. In each of these cases, the axiology is complex. In the case of Mill, the axiology is based on "higher" and "lower" pleasures, which allegedly have higher and lower intrinsic values. In the cases of Moore and Brentano, the axiology is based on such complex states of affairs as "the love of good" and "the hatred of evil." For Moore and Brentano, the value of a state of affairs turns crucially on normative features internal to that state of affairs. If Mill and Moore and Brentano are consequentialists, then so am I.

I can go beyond this merely historical point. I think the definition of "consequentialism" is a matter of great controversy. The literature is filled with incompatible (and sometimes idiosyncratic) definitions.[26] It would be hard to find any characterization that would meet with universal approval. Perhaps it would be interesting to consider a typical, and obviously relevant characterization. In *A Theory of Justice*, Rawls gives his own account. He says:

> The structure of an ethical theory is, then, largely determined by how it defines and connects these two basic notions [the right and the good]. Now it seems that the simplest way of relating them is taken by teleological

26. Moral philosophers have widely divergent views about the essence of consequentialism. Some say that consequentialist theories must require the *maximization* of some value; others permit mere *satisficing*; and others merely say that such theories claim that rightness depends in some way on the values of consequences. Some say that consequentialist theories all agree that the normative status of actions depends upon *intrinsic values* of consequences; others leave intrinsic value entirely out of account, and mention such things as preference satisfaction, or happiness. Some say that consequentialist theories must be theories about the moral normative status (rightness, wrongness, obligatoriness) of *actions*; others say that such theories may concern other sorts of value (rationality, goodness, justice, etc.) of other sorts of entities. Parfit goes so far as to say that a form of consequentialism might evaluate eye color, or even climate! ". . . the best possible climate is the one that would make outcomes best." (*Reasons and Persons*, p. 25.)

theories; the good is defined independently from the right, and then the right is defined as that which maximizes the good.[27]

Inspection will reveal that C + JH conforms to this characterization of teleological theories. I admit, of course, that in my "definition" of the good, I have made numerous references to matters involving justice. But, as I have already emphasized, my account of justice does not appeal to the central normative concepts of *right* and *wrong*. So far as I can tell, my characterization of the good is independent of my characterization of the right.[28]

27. Rawls, op. cit., p. 24.
28. Earlier versions of this paper were presented at Washington University, the Georgia Philosophical Society and the Universities of Connecticut, Rochester, West Virginia, and Missouri. It was discussed in faculty seminars at Arizona State University and St. Cloud State University. I am grateful to the participants in all these discussions for their valuable criticisms and suggestions. Especially useful comments were made by John Troyer, John Bennett, Ed Weirenga, Richard Feldman, Shelly Kagan, Ned Markosian, Sharon Ryan, David Blumenfeld, Peter Markie, David Cowles, Peter de Marneffe, and John Bahde.

   I am also grateful to Ted Sider, Owen McLeod, Ish Haji, Kevin Moon, Noah Lemos, Neil Schaefer, Bob Frazier, and two anonymous referees for *Philosophy and Phenomenological Research* for critical comments on earlier drafts. I have not had space to discuss all the objections these critics have presented. I hope to do so elsewhere.

   I first got the idea of presenting this sort of axiology by means of graphs many years ago in conversations with Michael Zimmerman. His paper "On the Intrinsic Value of States of Pleasure," *Philosophy and Phenomenological Research*, 41 (1980): 26–45 originally contained several very elegant, multi-colored graphs illustrating outputs of intrinsic value for various inputs of pleasure and value of object of pleasure. The published version of the paper does not contain the graphs, primarily because *Philosophy and Phenomenological Research* was, at the time, unable to reproduce them in print. In any case, I am grateful to Zimmerman.

Essay 9

Desert: Reconsideration of some received wisdom

INTRODUCTORY COMMENTS

In "Adjusting Utility for Justice" I proposed an axiology according to which the intrinsic value of each pleasure and each pain is adjusted by consideration of the extent to which the recipient deserves that pleasure or pain. My idea was that by thus adjusting the values of pleasures and pains for desert, I could make the axiology sensitive to justice. If this succeeds, we can maintain that our moral obligation is always to make the world as good as we can make it. We will not be open to objections based on the notion that utilitarianism ignores considerations of justice. For on the proposed view, considerations of justice play a central role in determining which world is best.

But it often happens that the suggested solution to one problem serves only to introduce further problems. In this case, the further problem concerns the nature of *desert*. Under what circumstances does a person deserve some pleasure or some pain? What factors might affect a person's desert of some good or evil?

Essay 9 does not contain anything like a thoroughgoing analysis of the concept of desert. My aims here are modest. I merely try to show that two deeply entrenched assumptions about desert are false.

The first assumption concerns the way in which desert interacts with responsibility. It has been assumed that desert is always based on actions *for which the deserving party is responsible*. Thus, if you deserve a reward for good behavior, you must be personally responsible for that behavior. If you deserve a penalty for some violation, you must bear responsibility for that violation.

The second assumption concerns the way in which desert interacts with time. It has been assumed that desert is always based on *past doings and sufferings*. Thus, if you deserve a reward for good behavior, you must have already performed the good behavior. If you deserve a penalty for some violation, you must have already committed the violation.

175

In Essay 9 I try to show how popular these assumptions are, and I try to show that they are both false. I also discuss some variants of the principles, and I show that they are false, too. The central conclusion of the essay is that there is much work to be done on the relations between desert (on the one hand) and such notions as time, responsibility, knowledge, and inevitability (on the other hand).

My claims about desert and responsibility were subsequently attacked by Saul Smilansky in *Mind* 105, 417 (January, 1996). I replied to Smilansky in the same issue of *Mind*.

9

Desert: Reconsideration of some received wisdom

According to an ancient and plausible view, the *justice* of an arrangement is the extent to which receipt of goods and evils corresponds to desert in that arrangement. John Hospers apparently had precisely this in mind when he said that "justice is getting what one deserves. What could be simpler?" (1961, p. 433). Mill said that ". . . it is universally considered just that each person should obtain that (whether good or evil) which he *deserves* . . ." (1957, p. 55).[1] Others have rejected this view as too simplistic (Feinberg 1963, p. 90, Sher 1987, p. 49, Slote 1973, p. 333, etc.) but have nevertheless maintained that there is an important conceptual link between justice and desert. Since justice is important, so is desert.

1. DESERT REQUIRES A BASE

It is natural to suppose that whenever a person deserves something, there is some answer to the question "Why does he deserve this?". For example, suppose a certain man deserves ten years in the penitentiary. There must be some explanation for this fact. Perhaps it is that he has been found guilty of a serious crime, and the most appropriate or fitting penalty would be ten years. Suppose another person deserves a reward. Perhaps she deserves it because she risked her life to save a drowning child. Whether we speak of desert in connection with prizes or grades, rewards or punishments, praise or blame, reparation or liability, it seems necessary that if a person deserves something, there is some "desert base"[2]: some fact to which we can appeal in order to explain this person's desert of this good or evil.

In his recent book on desert, Wojciech Sadurski affirms two general theses about desert and desert bases. Neither thesis is new. Each has been

1. Nicholas Rescher (1966, p. 83) says a similar thing, as does Sidgwick (1962, p. 280).
2. I believe that Feinberg (1963) introduced the term.

affirmed countless times by writers on desert. I think it is fair to say that they are part of the received wisdom about desert. Yet it also seems to me that each of these theses is false.

In this paper I first state the two doctrines about desert and say a few words about their popularity. I then explain why I think that each is false. I conclude with some speculations about the popularity of these views. I seek an explanation for the fact that they have been so widely believed.

2. A THESIS ABOUT DESERT AND RESPONSIBILITY

The first thesis links the concept of desert to the concept of responsibility. Sadurski states the thesis in this passage:

> When we are pronouncing judgments of desert we are inevitably making judgments about persons whom we hold responsible for their actions. It makes no sense to attribute desert, positive or negative, to persons for actions or facts over which they have no control. In particular, as people have no control over their natural assets . . . it would be unjust to consider those assets *per se* as relevant to any considerations of desert. (Sadurski 1985, p. 117)

Sadurski's point seems to be that a person cannot deserve anything in virtue of an action or fact unless she is responsible for that action or fact. James Rachels affirms the same thesis. He puts it this way:

> The concept of desert serves to signify the ways of treating people that are appropriate responses to them, *given that* they are responsible for those actions or states of affairs. That is the role played by desert in our moral vocabulary. (Rachels 1978, p. 157)

Similar remarks could be culled from the writings of many other philosophers.[3] It is part of the received wisdom about desert. Roughly, the idea is this:

DR: If S deserves x in virtue of the fact that S did or suffered y, then S is responsible for doing or suffering y.

3. In a widely cited passage Rawls (1971, p. 104) discusses the notion that people with "greater natural endowments" deserve the superior character that those assets make possible. Rawls says that the view is "surely incorrect". He explains his position by pointing out that such a person's ". . . character depends in large part upon fortunate family and social circumstances for which he can claim no credit". Rawls's view seems to be that no one deserves his character because no one is responsible for ("can claim credit for") something upon which his character depends. This is at least quite similar to DR.

There are very many positive instances of DR. Consider a typical case in which someone deserves punishment. Suppose a thug attacks a figure-skater. As a result of the attack, the figure-skater is unable to compete in the national championships. It would be quite natural for us to think that the thug deserves punishment in virtue of the fact that he attacked the figure-skater. But we would all retract this claim about desert if we learned that the thug bore no responsibility for the attack. Suppose, for example, that he had been hypnotized at the time, or that he had been coerced, or that he suffered from some mental impairment that made it impossible for him to control his actions. In any of these cases, the thug would not have been responsible for his action. If we thought he was not responsible for the attack, we would no longer think he deserved punishment for having done it. (Of course, under some of these imagined circumstances, we might continue to think it would be a good idea to lock him up. However, in such cases we would want him locked up for *treatment* or to put him out of circulation, not because he deserves *punishment*.)

The example involving the figure-skater concerns desert, according to the law, of punishment. But not all cases focus narrowly on desert of punishment. Consider desert of grades. Suppose a student submits an excellent paper. You think she deserves an A, and you think she deserves it in virtue of the fact that she wrote a paper that contains clear, accurate, and well-reasoned discussion of interesting arguments. Now you learn that the student did not write the paper; she paid a friend to write it for her. The student is not responsible for the content of the paper. Accordingly, you change your mind about her deserts. You no longer think she deserves an A. This is connected with the fact that you no longer think she is responsible for the clear and interesting arguments contained in the paper.[4] According to DR, it is always this way: if a person deserves something in virtue of some fact, then that person must be responsible for that fact.

3. A THESIS ABOUT DESERT AND TIME

Sadurski states a second thesis about desert. According to this thesis, desert base and desert necessarily stand in a certain temporal relation. Specifically,

---

4. When you discover that the paper was written by a hired hand, you may begin to think that your student deserves something else – expulsion. And you may think she deserves this in virtue of the fact that she paid someone else to write her paper. If you think this, you will probably also think that she is responsible for paying someone to write her paper.

desert base must always precede desert. Sadurski puts it this way: ". . . desert considerations are always past oriented. When talking about desert, we are evaluating certain actions which have already happened. That is why it is a confusion to base desert upon utilitarian grounds . . ." (1985, p. 117).

Again, the doctrine is part of the received wisdom about desert. Many philosophers have affirmed the same view. Rachels (1978, p. 154) expresses an extreme version of the principle when he says: ". . . the basis of all desert is a person's own *past* actions". According to this version of the thesis, desert bases are always actions, and they always precede the fact of desert. Joel Feinberg defends a somewhat weaker version: "If a person is deserving of some sort of treatment he must, necessarily, be so *in virtue of* some characteristic or *prior* activity" (1963, p. 72). Apparently, Feinberg would say that where a desert base involves activity, that activity must precede the fact of desert. John Kleinig endorses a similar view.[5] He says "Desert can be ascribed to something or someone only on the basis of characteristics possessed or things done by that thing or person. That is, desert is never simply forward-looking" (Kleinig 1971, p. 73).

In his article on "Rectificatory Justice" John Cottingham says this:

> The essentially backward-looking nature of justice-as-rectification seems hard to deny. Verbs like "to rectify" and "to correct" share with many other verbs (including "to punish", "to blame", "to thank", "to regret", "to renounce") what we might call an inherently "retrospective" logic: we cannot understand such verbs without grasping that their use involves an intrinsic and automatic reference back to some past event or state of affairs. (Cottingham 1992, p. 662)

Cottingham seems to be saying that an injustice can be rectified only *after the fact*. We cannot rectify an injustice prior to its occurrence. He apparently means to claim that this is an essential feature of the "logic" of justice as rectification.[6] If this is in fact what Cottingham means to say, then his

---

5. Brian Barry seems to commit himself to the same doctrine. He says, "Desert looks to the past – or at most to the present – whereas incentive and deterrence are forward looking notions . . ." (Barry 1965, p. 111). David Miller apparently means to defend precisely the same principle: "Desert judgements are justified on the basis of *past* and *present* facts about individuals, never on the basis of states of affairs to be created in the future. Desert is a 'backward-looking' concept . . ." (Miller 1976, p. 93).

6. Cottingham seems to be asserting that I cannot thank or blame you for doing something unless you have already done it. He seems also to be saying that I cannot regret doing something unless I have already done it. These claims seem to me to be clearly false. If you assure me that you will take care of my children after I am gone, I can thank you for this kindness that you will perform. If, as a result of your failure to drain the pipes, there is going to be damage to the plumbing later tonight when the temperature drops,

view is quite similar to Sadurski's view about desert and time. Where compensatory justice is involved, Cottingham presumably would say that a person is deserving of compensation only if he or she has already suffered some loss.

The second bit of received wisdom is this:

DT: If at t S deserves *x* in virtue of the fact that S did or suffered something at t', then t' cannot be later than t.

Many relatively clear-cut cases of desert conform to DT. Consider, for example, cases in which someone deserves some *prize*. In his discussion of prizes, Feinberg says that the prize ". . . is deserved by the contestant who has demonstrably satisfied the condition of victory . . ." (1963, p. 77). This may seem right. Certainly it would seem strange to say that one of the contestants already deserves the prize *before* the contest, in virtue of the fact that he will *later* perform so well. In such cases, desert arises only after the desert base has taken place.

Desert of *rewards and punishments* seems similarly rooted in the past. In the typical case, a person deserves a reward in virtue of the fact that he has performed some meritorious service, such as saving a life, or preventing an injury. Similarly, when a person deserves punishment, we naturally think it is because he has done some wrong. In the legal context, most of us would be outraged by the suggestion that someone deserves punishment today for the crimes that he will commit tomorrow (see Feinberg 1963, pp. 80–85).

The desert associated with *compensation and reparation* seems firmly rooted in the past, too. Commentators have pointed out that it hardly makes sense to say that someone already deserves "reparations" for the injuries he will suffer later. How can we "repair" that which is not already broken? If the point of such activities is "to restore the moral equilibrium" then it is no wonder that the desert base must precede the desert. One cannot "restore" an equilibrium that has not yet been upset. Equally, there is a puzzle about the notion that a person might already deserve compensation for work that she will perform tomorrow. (Of course, it might be

I can blame you for the damage that is going to occur. If I know that I will not be able to attend your party next week, I can already regret that I will not be able to attend. Indeed, if I am courteous, I will send you a note saying that I regret that I will not be able to attend. In all these cases, the thing for which I thank or blame you, or the thing that I regret, is still in the future at the time of thanks, blame or regret. If Cottingham's remarks about "inherently retrospective logic" mean what I have taken them to mean, then they are false.

181

generous or helpful or nice to pay someone in advance; and in some cases a worker might deserve the money before the work. But in these cases the desert base would most naturally be taken to be need, or prior injury, or some past injustice. The mere fact that I will work tomorrow seems not to justify the claim that I already deserve my paycheck.)

In some cases we say that someone deserves good fortune simply because he has suffered so much bad fortune. Again, bad luck in the past provides a basis for saying that I deserve better luck in the future.

In all these cases, and in many more like them, the desert base either precedes or is simultaneous with the fact of desert. In none of these cases is the desert base entirely in the future. Thus, the examples are consistent with DT.

4. THE REFUTATION OF DR

In spite of the fact that it seems to be part of the received wisdom about desert, DR is clearly false. There are countless perfectly ordinary cases in which we deserve things in virtue of facts for which we bear no responsibility. A familiar sort of case involves compensation for injury. Suppose, for example, that a fast food restaurant is careless with its hamburgers. Many customers become ill with food poisoning. Those customers deserve several things: an apology; some compensation for their illness; a refund of the money they spent on the bad hamburgers. The customers deserve these things in virtue of the fact that they are innocent victims of the restaurant's carelessness. Yet in any typical case the customers bear no responsibility for the fact that they were poisoned.

Consider again the case of the figure-skater and the thug (mentioned above in §2). The example was used to illustrate the fact that sometimes a person (the thug) deserves something (punishment) in virtue of something for which he was responsible (the attack). Yet the very same example also illustrates the fact that sometimes a person deserves something in virtue of something for which she bears no responsibility. For the figure-skater deserves an apology and some compensation in virtue of the fact that she was viciously attacked. Yet she bears no responsibility for the attack.[7]

---

7. Klenig, Sher and others have endorsed the view that we can deserve such things as compensation and apology in virtue of harms innocently suffered. These philosophers have at least implicitly recognised that DR is false. Kleinig (1971, p. 74) explicitly rejects it.

Perhaps it will seem that I must have gotten the principle wrong. The counterexamples are so obvious that it may seem that no one could seriously believe DR. Perhaps the intended principle is really this:

DR': If S deserves x in virtue of the fact that S did or suffered y, then *somebody* is responsible for the fact that S did or suffered y.[8]

In the hamburger case cited above, the innocent diners are not responsible for getting poisoned, and that's why the example refutes DR. However, the staff of the fast food restaurant *are* responsible for selling the spoiled hamburgers. Thus, the example does not run counter to DR'. A corresponding point holds in the case of the figure-skater and the thug. The skater is not responsible for the attack, but the thug is. Perhaps DR' is a better formulation of the received wisdom in question.

I think DR' is also false.[9] I think that there are familiar cases in which no one is responsible for a certain misfortune, and yet the person who suffers that misfortune deserves something in virtue of the fact that he has suffered. Consider, for example, a case in which a young child becomes ill with a painful disease. Suppose the child suffers for a while with this disease, and eventually dies. The parents are overwhelmed with grief. Surely no one bears any responsibility for their misfortune, and yet the grieving parents might deserve various things in virtue of enduring it. At the very minimum, they deserve some expression of sympathy from their friends and neighbors.

Many moral philosophers have endorsed the principle that each of us, merely in virtue of being a person, deserves a certain minimal amount of respect. If we do deserve anything in virtue of being persons, then we have further evidence for the independence of responsibility and desert. It is pretty clear that I am not responsible for the fact that I am a person. Although my parents may bear some responsibility for the fact that I exist, it is not clear that either they or anyone else is responsible for the fact that I am a person. If no one is responsible for this fact, and yet I deserve some

8. Sadurski hints at this idea when he says "To say 'I didn't deserve such a tragedy to happen to me' would make sense only under the condition that someone can properly be held responsible for what actually happened" (1985, p. 118).
9. Kleinig seems to be committed to the rejection of DR' when he affirms that the Niagara Falls deserve to be so famous (1971, p. 72). However, it is not clear that he takes such examples literally. In a footnote he says that it may be argued that the statement is true "only in a subsidiary sense". Furthermore, as Kleinig notes, the view is in conflict with his claim that deserved things must be pleasant or unpleasant for the one who deserves them.

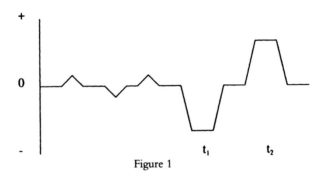
Figure 1

respect in virtue of being a person, then desert is further severed from responsibility.

Let us now turn to the evaluation of DT.

5. THE REFUTATION OF DT

We naturally say that if a person has been short-changed in the past, then she deserves some extra benefit now. Our talk of desert in such a case seems linked to the idea of "balance" or "fairness" or "appropriateness" in the allocation of good and evil. If this is so, then one wonders why it is not equally natural to say that if a person *will be* short-changed in the future, then she *already* deserves some extra benefit now. Future mis-allocations are surely as bad as past ones; present re-allocations surely serve to bring about balance and fairness just as much as future ones would; if desert in such cases is fundamentally a matter of achieving balance and fairness in allocations of good and evil, then it is hard to see how there can be any justification for insisting that harms be suffered before com-pensatory benefits are distributed. Why wait? Why not say that those who will be harmed later already deserve their compensation today? What justifies the alleged temporal asymmetry of desert and its base?

Imagine a graph showing the good and bad fortunes that befall a per-son, S, throughout his life. Suppose the graph looks like Figure 1. Suppose that the dip at t_1 represents a serious misfortune that S then suffers, and the rise at t_2 represents a compensating bit of good fortune that S enjoys at t_2. Since the size of the rise at t_2 is equal to the size of dip at t_1, we may want to say that the t_2 rise compensates for the t_1 fall. S may complain

184

that his life is pretty boring (only two dips; only three rises – and these pretty small) but (given obvious assumptions) it's hard to see how he can complain about unfairness. His misfortunes seem to have been compensated.

I have not told you the direction of time in the example. I did not say that t_1 is earlier than t_2. One wonders why it should matter which way time is flowing. If S suffers a misfortune at t_1, and enjoys a bit of good fortune at t_2, then, from the "extra-temporal perspective", the goods and bads of S's life pretty nearly balance out. Thus, there is a question about the relevance of temporal priority in DT.

I am convinced that DT is not true. Furthermore I think that there are familiar examples that show that it is not true. One fairly clear example concerns the sometimes extraordinary benefits that are given to children who have contracted fatal diseases. Organizations such as the Make-a-Wish Foundation provide very generous benefits (such as visits to Disneyland) for such children. It seems to me that the rationale for such benefits is clear: since the children are quite innocent, and are going to suffer terrible harms, they deserve extraordinary benefits. Since it will be impossible to provide these benefits to the children after they suffer the harms, the Make-a-Wish Foundation gives them the benefits in advance.

A second example concerns soldiers who volunteer for suicidal missions. In some contexts these soldiers are thought to be deserving of great honours. Celebrations may be held; they may be given medals or promotions. Then they go off to perform the actions in virtue of which they deserve to be so treated. Again, the desert base is rooted in the future, not the past.

If one wished to defend DT, one could of course try to force these examples into the requisite temporal shape. Thus, one could admit that the sick children deserve the benefits they receive from the Make-a-Wish Foundation, but could deny that they deserve these benefits in virtue of the harms they will later suffer. Rather, it could be insisted, such children are deserving in virtue of the fact that they *have contracted fatal diseases*, or the fact that they *have already suffered*. These are facts about the past, and are thus consistent with DT.[10]

In the case of the soldiers, one could say that they deserve their medals

---

10. One could insist that the children actually do not deserve any benefits; the Make-a-Wish Foundation gives them the benefits simply out of kindness and sympathy. I find this suggestion deeply implausible – perhaps even offensive.

in virtue of the fact that they *volunteered (or were chosen) for their suicidal missions*. Again, it could be claimed that the desert base is "properly" in the past.

I reject these desperate manoeuvres. It seems clear to me that the sick children do deserve special consideration, not only because they have already suffered, but also in virtue of the fact that they are going to suffer. Perhaps this can be made more plausible by appeal to a thought-experiment. Suppose there are two sick children in the hospital. Suppose each has a painful disease. The first has suffered for several months, and has been quite miserable. Yet the doctors are perfectly certain that she will soon become well, and in a short time will be fully recovered with no lingering effects. The second has also suffered for several months, and has also been miserable. In his case, however, the prognosis is different. The doctors are perfectly certain that he will soon die. There is no cure for his fatal affliction. In this situation, the Make-a-Wish Foundation offers a special treat for exactly one sick child. Imagine that this is an all-expense-paid trip to Disneyland. The Foundation stipulates that the treat is to be given to the most deserving child in the hospital.

It seems clear to me that, in the absence of any unusual and so far unstated factors, the child with the fatal disease would be the more deserving, precisely because he is going to suffer the greater misfortune. Though his past sufferings are no greater than the other child's, he is destined to suffer worse misfortunes in the future. This explains the fact that he is the more deserving of the two.

6. WHY DR HAS BEEN BELIEVED

It is hard to understand why so many philosophers have accepted DR. I have never seen an argument for it. My suspicion is that some may have accepted it simply as a result of failure to consider a sufficiently wide variety of examples. Perhaps these philosophers focused exclusively on a narrow range of cases involving desert of things like punishment and reward; perhaps in all these cases the one who deserves is also responsible for the desert base; perhaps these philosophers assumed without further reflection that all cases would be like these few. And yet, if we consider the class of cases involving desert of sympathy, condolence, and compensation for innocent suffering, we immediately see that there can be desert without responsibility.

Another possible explanation is that advocates of DR focused exclusively on cases in which the deserving person deserves in virtue of some action he or she performed. In such cases, the person is typically responsible for the action. Again, hasty generalization might be the culprit.

7. WHY DT HAS BEEN BELIEVED

DT seems rather more natural and plausible. Counterexamples are less common. But the counterexamples are fairly obvious. What accounts for the attractiveness of this principle?

For a time I thought that the plausibility of DT should be explained by appeal to a certain confusion. I thought that another principle was true, and that this other principle was easily confused with DT. I am no longer convinced by this explanation. Nevertheless, it may be useful to discuss it.

According to a popular view, ordinary facts about the past are entirely "settled": from the perspective of the present, there is nothing we can do to prevent them, or "undo" them. Thus, if I have already suffered an injury, the fact that I have suffered this injury is settled; it is an unalterable fact.

Determinists may hold that all facts about the future are already settled. This is a controversial position. A more moderate view is that at least some facts about the future are in this sense settled. Thus, for example, consider the fact that the sun will rise tomorrow, and the fact that the seasons will change at approximately their appointed times, and the fact that each of us will eventually die. It is reasonable to suppose that facts such as these are settled – though in some cases the precise dates are not yet settled. They are like facts about the past, since there is nothing we can do to prevent them. No matter what possible course of action we take, these things will happen.

However, certain other facts about the future seem still unsettled. Suppose a certain mugger is contemplating a mugging, and has not yet made up his mind whether he will mug me or whether he will mug another innocent victim. If this mugger's reflections have genuine point – if his choice of victim is really still "up to him" – then it is not yet settled that I will be injured by him in a mugging.

It might be thought that there is an important connection between desert and this sort of settledness. Specifically, it might be thought that this is true:

DS: If at t S deserves x in virtue of the fact that S did or suffered something at t', then the fact that S did or suffered that thing at t' is already settled at t.

Inspection will reveal, I think, that every example so far mentioned in connection with DT in fact conforms to DS. When the desert base is in the past it is already settled. All such cases conform to DS. Cases in which the desert base is in the future conflict with DT, but they may seem to conform to DS, since in all the cases so far discussed the desert base is settled at the time of desert. Consider, for example, the case involving the Make-a-Wish Foundation. I wanted to say that the child with the fatal disease deserved special treatment in virtue of the fact that he will later suffer a great misfortune. The example refuted DT. However, the example does not refute DS, since the child's suffering was described as inevitable, or settled, even though still in the future. DS (unlike DT) permits the child to be deserving in virtue of this future, but settled fact.

The account I formerly accepted goes like this: it is possible that the appeal of DT derives largely from its confusion with DS. DS is true; it's easy to confuse DS with DT. Perhaps some philosophers have confused DT with DS, and have for this reason erroneously thought that DT is true.

I am no longer quite so happy with this explanation, since I no longer think that DS is true. I think there are cases in which, at a certain time, someone deserves something in virtue of a certain fact but that fact is *not* settled at the time of desert. Consider this example: a customs inspector may realize that he is about to invade the privacy of a traveller. The traveller has done nothing wrong, and yet his bags are going to be searched. The inspector says "I'm sorry sir, but you will have to open all these bags, and allow us to search through them". The inspector is apologizing for something that is about to happen. It is reasonable to suppose that the innocent traveller deserves the apology even before his privacy has been invaded.

The crucial fact about this example is that, at the time of the apology, the customs inspector may recognize that he is under no *compulsion* to inspect the bags; he may recognize that it is still fully in his power to refrain from inspecting them. Thus, while it is a fact that he is going to inspect the bags, it is not yet a settled fact. It is something that he is going to do, but freely. The example thus shows that DS is false. Therefore, we cannot explain the plausibility of DT by saying that it has been mistaken for DS, which is the truth in these matters. In order to make use of this line of explanation, we must suppose that philosophers have made *two* mistakes. First, they mistakenly supposed that DS is true. Second, they confused DT with DS.[11]

So we are left with our question: why have so many philosophers accepted DT?

Perhaps a different confusion explains this mistake. A fundamental constraint on our system of criminal justice is that no one shall be punished for a crime he has not yet committed. In some cases, our commitment to this constraint is almost fanatical. Even when we know that a certain person will commit a crime, we maintain that he is legally innocent until he commits the crime, and is proven guilty. The police insist that their hands are tied – the man does not deserve to be punished until he has actually done what we all know he intends to do.[12]

There are of course lots of good reasons for insisting upon this policy. One is epistemic. Even when we have quite good evidence, we rarely know precisely what the future will bring. There is always (or almost always) the chance that the person will not commit the crime. Thus, it is safer to adopt the general policy of always waiting to see what the future brings. If he commits the crime, we can immediately step in and set the wheels of justice grinding. If he does not commit the crime, we will have avoided a terrible injustice.

There is a second important factor in such cases. Consider a typical case in which it seems quite likely that a certain person will commit some crime. We think he will deserve the legally mandated punishment only if he will be responsible for the crime; and we think he will be responsible

---

11. An interesting feature of the example involving the customs inspector is this: although the later invasion of the traveller's privacy is not *settled* at the time of desert, the inspector *knows for certain* that it is going to occur. This may suggest that the relevant fact is neither *being in the past* nor *being settled*, but is rather *being known for certain*. In other words:

    DK: If at t S deserves x in virtue of the fact that S did or suffered something at t', then the fact that S did or suffered that thing at t' is already *known for certain* at t.

    I am convinced that DK is false. I may deserve the prize for best essay in virtue of the fact that my essay was the best of those submitted. However, it may be that no one knows that my essay was the best of those submitted. I didn't read the other submissions; the judges were careless or inept – they didn't recognise that mine was best. If DK has any appeal, I suspect that it is due to a confusion of the fact that S deserves x with the fact that someone would be justified in claiming that S deserves x.

12. Christopher New tries to show that there is no moral argument against "prepunishment". He claims that ". . . there may be room in our moral thought for the notion of pre-punishment, and . . . it may be only epistemic, rather than moral, constraints that prevent us from practising it" (New 1992, pp. 35). New's paper is the only one I have ever seen in which there is an explicit attack on anything like DT.

189

for the crime only if he will commit it "freely"; and we think that if he will commit it "freely", then it cannot yet be quite certain that he will commit it. There must still be some possibility that he will decide not to commit it. So we insist upon a legal system that prohibits punishment-in-advance.

There is yet a third reason to avoid laws that permit punishment-in-advance. Suppose the law permitted punishment-in-advance. Surely there would be safeguards. Advance punishment would be permitted only in cases in which it is perfectly certain that the suspect is going to commit the crime. (That is, it is certain that he will commit the crime *unless the law steps in and prevents his doing so.*) But if we have such sure-fire knowledge that the suspect is going to commit the crime, it would make even better sense to step in and prevent that criminal behavior. However, if we lock the pre-criminal up, or otherwise prevent his crime, he will not commit the crime. In this case, he cannot possibly deserve punishment for committing it. Antecedent punishment, in such a case, would be deprived of its desert base. Thus, in order to be sure that those who are punished really deserve their punishment, we insist upon a system that permits punishment only after the crime has been committed.

There is a fourth reason. Suppose a person appears at the police station and offers to pay a fine for speeding. She says that she is going to speed later in the day, and wants to pay the fine in advance so as to avoid red tape and inconvenience. The police officer does not accept her check, and does not agree that she deserves the fine. Rather, he takes steps to ensure that she does not speed. To accept the money and agree that she deserves the fine would be to acknowledge that she is going to speed, and in effect to grant her permission to do so, and this the officer cannot do.

For all these reasons, and perhaps for others as well,[13] we are whole-heartedly committed to a judicial system that prohibits punishment-in-advance. Part of this commitment involves the principle that no judge or jury may determine that a certain person deserves punishment under the law at a time in virtue of the fact that he will later commit a certain crime. For the commission of a crime to serve as a desert base for punishment in a court of law, the crime must already have been committed.

I suppose it is possible that some philosophers may have confused this legal principle about desert of punishment with the much more general

---

13. Saul Smilansky (1994, pp. 50–53) argues against New's claim. His argument turns on his claim that pre-punishment violates certain Kantian views about respect for persons as autonomous agents, rather than as mere objects.

principle DT. It should be obvious that the truth of the legal principle (if it is true) implies nothing about the truth of DT.

8. CONCLUDING REMARKS

It is widely assumed that desert is intimately linked to responsibility and time. Principles DR and DT express elements of the received wisdom about this alleged linkage. Yet it is clear upon reflection that neither principle is true. A person may deserve sympathy or even compensation for injuries received, though neither he nor anyone else is responsible for those injuries. A person may deserve benefits for harms received even though she has not yet suffered those harms. If there is any connection between desert and responsibility, it is far more complex than the connections indicated by DR and DR'; if there is any connection between desert and time, it is far more complex than the connections indicated by DT and DS.[14]

REFERENCES

Barry, Brian 1965: *Political Argument*. London & New York: Routledge & Kegan Paul.

Cottingham, John 1992: "Justice; Rectificatory", in Lawrence Becker, ed., *Encyclopedia of Ethics*. New York & London: Garland Publishing Co.

Feinberg, Joel 1963: "Justice and Personal Desert", in C. J. Friedrich and J. W. Chapman, eds., *Nomos VI: Justice*. New York: Atherton Press.

Hospers, John 1961: *Human Conduct*. New York: Harcourt, Brace & World, Inc.

Kleinig, John 1971: "The Concept of Desert". *American Philosophical Quarterly* 8, pp. 71–78.

Mill, J. S. 1957: *Utilitarianism*. Indianapolis: Liberal Arts Press.

Miller, David 1976: *Social Justice*. Oxford: The Clarendon Press.

New, Christopher 1992: "Time and Punishment". *Analysis* 52, pp. 35–40.

Rachels, James 1978: "What People Deserve", in *Justice and Economic Distribution*, ed. John Arthur and William H. Shaw. Englewood Cliffs: Prentice-Hall.

Rawls, John 1971: *A Theory of Justice*. Cambridge: Harvard University Press.

Rescher, Nicholas 1966: *Distributive Justice*. Indianapolis: Bobbs-Merrill.

14. Earlier drafts of this paper were read and criticised by David Cowles, Richard Feldman, Ish Haji, Ned Markosian, Owen McLeod, Ted Sider, the Editor and referee for *Mind* and others. My thanks to all these friends and colleagues for their comments and suggestions. I am especially grateful to McLeod for extensive discussion and bibliographical assistance.

Sadurski, Wojciech 1985: *Giving Desert Its Due: Social Justice and Legal Theory*. Dordrecht: D. Reidel Publishing Co.

Sher, George 1987: *Desert*. Princeton: Princeton University Press.

Sidgwick, Henry 1962: *The Methods of Ethics*. London: Macmillan & Co.

Slote, Michael 1973: "Desert, Consent, and Justice". *Philosophy and Public Affairs* 2, pp. 323–347.

Smilansky, Saul 1994: "The Time to Punish". *Analysis* 54, pp. 50–53.

Essay 10

Justice, desert, and the Repugnant Conclusion

INTRODUCTORY COMMENTS

Each of the hedonistic axiologies that I described in "Mill, Moore, and the Consistency of Qualified Hedonism" is a form of "totalism." So is the desert-adjusted axiology of "Adjusting Utility for Justice." In the present context, we may understand totalism to be the view that the value of a whole possible world is the sum of the values received by the inhabitants of that world.

Totalism has great intuitive appeal. It may seem obvious that all the value of a world must be distributed among those who receive value in that world. How could the value of the world be different from the sum of the values received by those in the world who receive value?

However, a number of philosophers have recognized that problems arise when we compare worlds with populations of dramatically different sizes. If there are very many recipients of value in a world, then the sum of their receipts may be quite large, even if each recipient receives just a tiny share. The sum is large not because each lives such a good life, but because there are so many of them. Totalism declares such a world to be very good, but it may seem less good than a less populous world in which each recipient gets much more but the total is smaller. This would seem to show that totalism is false.

A particularly striking version of the problem was made famous by Derek Parfit. He calls it the "Repugnant Conclusion," and it goes roughly like this: Imagine a world, A, in which there are 10 billion supremely happy people. Each of them enjoys a life containing a hundred units of whatever makes life worth living. This world seems to be very good.

But consider now another world, Z. In Z each person has a life barely worth living. Let's say that each enjoys just one unit of whatever makes life worth living. It would appear that no matter how many people there are in Z, it can't be as good as the heavenly A. Yet, as Parfit points out, standard totalistic axiologies imply that if Z is sufficiently populous, it is better than A. Thus, for example, if are are more than a thousand billion people in Z, and each has a life barely worth living, then the total value of Z exceeds that of A. This seems deeply wrong.

In Essay 10, after introducing this puzzle, I explain some of the elements of the axiological view developed in the earlier papers in this volume. In the present context I call it "justicism" rather than "justice-adjusted hedonism."

The theory is here shown to be derived from some ideas originally suggested by Franz Brentano. As I indicated in Essay 9, the theory was developed in an effort to solve certain problems confronting utilitarianism – problems explicitly about justice. I think, however, that as a sort of happy by-product, justicism also generates a plausible answer to Parfit's awesome question. This is a remarkable result because justicism is a form of totalism, and it is widely thought that no totalistic theory can provide a satisfactory answer to Parfit's question.

My solution turns on a simple and plausible assumption: There is some modest level of happiness that people deserve merely in virtue of being people. If a person receives some happiness, but much less than this modest level, then though that happiness is good for him, it does not make the world better. If it is a small enough amount of happiness, it may make the world worse.

If this intuition is right, then we can see why the Z world is not better than the A world. Z contains a huge population of people each living a minimally happy life. But if each is getting much less than he or she deserves, then each life makes the world *worse* – even though it is a life that the recipient would view as better than no life at all.

10

Justice, desert, and the Repugnant Conclusion

I. INTRODUCTORY COMMENT

In Chapter 17 of his magnificent *Reasons and Persons*, Derek Parfit asks what he describes as an 'awesome question': 'How many people should there ever be?'[1] For a utilitarian like me, the answer seems simple: there should be however many people it takes to make the world best. Unfortunately, if I answer Parfit's awesome question in this way, I may sink myself in a quagmire of axiological confusion. In this paper, I first describe certain aspects of the quagmire. Then I introduce and explain some of the elements of a novel axiological view – 'justicism'. Justicism is derived from some ideas originally suggested by Franz Brentano. It was developed in an effort to solve certain other problems confronting utilitarianism – problems explicitly about justice.[2] I think, however, that as a sort of happy by-product, justicism also generates a plausible answer to Parfit's awesome question. This may come as a bit of surprise, since justicism is a form of totalism, and it is widely thought that no totalistic theory can provide a satisfactory answer to Parfit's question. After presenting and explaining my proposed solution, I address some objections.

I am grateful to David Cowles, Richard Feldman, Neil Feit, Noah Lemos, Ned Markosian, Jeff McMahan, Kevin Moon, Neil Schaefer, Ted Sider, and Michael Zimmerman for generous comments and criticisms of earlier drafts. I am especially grateful to Peter Vallentyne, both for his comments on this paper at the Greensboro conference, and for other extensive and valuable discussion. Another version of this paper was presented at a conference at the University of Illinois at Champaign-Urbana in May, 1995.
1. Derek Parfit, *Reasons and Persons*, Oxford, 1984, p. 381. Parenthetical page references in what follows are to Parfit's book.
2. I try to show how this can be done in my 'Adjusting Utility for Justice: A Consequentialist Reply to the Objections from Justice', *Philosophy and Phenomenological Research* LV, 3 (September 1995), 567–585, reprinted as Essay 8 in this present volume.

II. THE PROBLEM

Imagine some gods bragging about their creative powers. One god says he can create a really good world. 'I can create a world in which there are a million people, and each enjoys fifty units of whatever makes life worth living.' A second god is not impressed. 'Big deal,' he says. 'I can create a world in which there are ten million people, and each enjoys seventy-five units of whatever makes life worth living. So I can create a world that would be much better than the best world you can create.' A third god chimes in. 'I can create a far better world. I can create a world with ten billion people, each enjoying a hundred units of whatever makes life worth living.'

These gods seem to be presupposing what Parfit calls an 'impersonal total principle' about the evaluation of worlds (p. 387). They seem to think that one world is better than another if and only if the total net amount of whatever makes life worth living in the first is greater than the total net amount in the second. If we assume that all the value in a world is distributed among the residents, then a form of totalism says that the value of a world is the sum of the values enjoyed or suffered by the residents. Letting 'IV(x,w)' indicate the total net lifetime amount of intrinsic value received by a person, x, at a world, w, and letting 'IV(w)' indicate the total intrinsic value of a world, w, we can state this totalistic thesis in this way:[3]

T: IV(w) = the sum, for all x in w, of IV(x,w)

Imagine a fourth god. Suppose this god is unable to create people who enjoy large amounts of whatever makes life worth living. His very best effort would yield a person who enjoys one unit. Not very impressive.

---

3. A number of controversial assumptions are implicit in T. Some of these concern the arithmetic of intrinsic value. For example, that the intrinsic value of a life can be represented by a number; that interpersonal comparisons are possible; that the difference between a good life and a bad life corresponds to the difference between a positive number and a negative one; etc. Furthermore, I am assuming that all the recipients of value at a world will be people. On many standard axiologies, dogs, cats, ponies, and other sentient beings may also be recipients of value. I make this assumption here primarily to simplify the puzzle. In a fuller account, it would be rejected. Another assumption behind T is that talk of the 'sum' of the values of the lives at a world will make sense. If there are infinitely many lives at a world, simple summation will not work. Thus, what I say here must be restricted to cases in which there are finitely many lives at each world. For a discussion of some possible ways to extend this sort of treatment to other cases, see Peter Vallentyne and Shelly Kagan, 'Infinite Value and Finitely Additive Value Theory', *The Journal of Philosophy* **94** (1997): 5–26.

Such lives are barely worth living. However, the fourth god has other powers. He can create *lots of people*. In fact, he can create a world with a population of a billion billion if he so chooses. He speaks up: 'For any world you can create with ten billion people, each enjoying a hundred units of whatever makes life worthwhile, I can create a better world. For I can create a world in which there is a huge population – a billion billion – each member of which enjoys one unit of whatever makes life worth living. Since I can create so many more people, I can create a world that would be better than yours.'

It appears that if T is true, and the fourth god has the ability to create the populous world, then he is right – his world would be better. If T is true, the third god's world (which we can call 'A') would have a total value of a thousand billion units. (Each person enjoys a hundred units; there are ten billion people; one hundred times ten billion is a thousand billion.) But the fourth god's world (which we can call 'Z') would have a total value of a billion billion. (Each person enjoys one unit; there are a billion billion people; one times a billion billion is a billion billion.)

Perhaps the fourth god has the stated power. He can create the populous world, Z. However, his claim that Z would be better seems preposterous. Imagine Z (if you can). A billion billion people, each trudging wearily through a drab life – a life so drab that it is barely better than no life at all. Each person in this world might be saying to him- or herself, 'If it gets any worse than this, I will kill myself'. Surely, such a world is not supremely good. It is in fact a world of very low value. The thought of living in such a world is repugnant. The thought that some god might create it is equally repugnant.[4]

Parfit presents a statement that he calls 'The Repugnant Conclusion'. It is this:

> For any possible population of at least ten billion people, all with a very high quality of life, there must be some much larger imaginable population

---

4. Imagine that a fifth god is present at the discussion. This one has other strengths and weaknesses. His weakness is that he can produce worlds with populations of at most one person. But he has a compensating strength. He is capable of making these people enjoy huge amounts of utility. Suppose he speaks up: 'I can create a world in which there is just one person, but I can see to it that that one person enjoys slightly more than a billion billion units of whatever makes life worth living. So I can create a world far better than A, and slightly better than Z.' Again, if we calculate the values of worlds by appeal to the impersonal total principle, it would appear that this fifth god is right. His world would be the best of the worlds so far considered. Again, this seems preposterous. A world containing just one lonely 'utility monster' does not appear to be supremely good.

whose existence, if other things are equal, would be better, even though its members have lives that are barely worth living (p. 388).

Parfit goes on to remark, 'As my choice of name suggests, I find this conclusion very hard to accept' (p. 388).

What, precisely, is the problem of the Repugnant Conclusion? We have started with some innocent-looking assumptions: something makes lives worth living; whatever it is, it comes in various amounts; more of it is better than less; the value of a life is the total amount of this stuff in that life (minus the amount of evil in that life); the value of a world is the sum of the values of the lives lived in that world. But given these assumptions, we seem to be committed to saying that a very populous world (such as Z) in which everyone leads a life barely worth living is better than a less populous world (such as A) in which ten billion people lead lives of extraordinary happiness. But Z does not seem better than A. In fact, Z seems far worse than A. So we have a problem. Our assumptions seemed innocent, yet they apparently lead to a false conclusion.[5]

III. AVERAGISM

A natural hypothesis is that the source of the difficulty is totalism, represented here by T. Perhaps the value of a world should be calculated in some other way. One of the most popular proposals in that the value of a world should be taken to be the *average* amount of value enjoyed by its residents.[6] Those who accept this proposal may endorse the following principle, in which 'P(w)' indicates the population of w, or the total number of people who ever live in w:

Av: $IV(w) = $ the sum, for all x in w, of $IV(x,w)$ divided by $P(w)$.

In the case at hand, world-rankings based on Av accord better with intuition. The average amount of value enjoyed by the residents of the less populous world, A, is $+100$. The average amount of value enjoyed

---

5. Parfit, p. 388. In his dissertation, 'Ethical Theory and Population', University of Massachusetts, forthcoming, Kevin Moon points out that all the essential features of the puzzle of the Repugnant Conclusion appear in J. M. E. McTaggart, *The Nature of Existence*, Cambridge, 1927. McTaggart describes a pair of lives relevantly like those lived in A and Z, and points out that if the low quality life lasts sufficiently long, it would contain a total amount of value greater than that contained in the high quality life. He goes on to say that 'This *conclusion* would, I believe, be *repugnant* to certain moralists' (pp. 452–453, emphasis added).

6. Parfit discusses averagism in various places in chs. 18 and 19. He focuses especially on averagism in § 143, 'Why We Ought to Reject the Average Principle'.

by the residents of the more populous world, Z, is +1. Thus, according to averagism, A is much better than Z. This is consistent with my axiological intuitions.

Unfortunately, Av yields counterintuitive results in other cases. One fairly striking case is discussed by Parfit (pp. 401–2). It involves Adam and Eve. Imagine that Adam and Eve are living peacefully in the Garden of Eden. Each is enjoying a life containing 100 units of value. A serpent informs them of the joys of sex. If they procreate, and are fruitful, the world will eventually contain ten billion people, each enjoying a life containing 99 units of value. If Adam and Eve do not procreate, no other person will ever live.

The average level of value in the non-procreation world is +100 (200 divided by 2); the average level of value in the procreation world is just a shade above +99 (I leave the calculations to the interested reader). Averagism implies that the non-procreation world is better. This conflicts again with my axiological intuitions. In virtue of the fact that the procreation world contains ten billion people, each enjoying an extraordinarily large amount of whatever makes life worth living, it seems to be the better of the worlds available to Adam and Eve. In this case, it strikes me that a world containing ten billion happy people in vastly better than a world containing just two happy people.

Another very strange implication of averagism involves the ancient Egyptians (p. 420). Suppose a couple are contemplating having a baby. Suppose they know that this baby would have a life very much worth living. Let us say it would have a life worth +100. If there were very many ancient Egyptians, and they all led lives of low value, this couple's baby might *increase* the average value of lives lived. But if the ancient Egyptians were very numerous, and they all led lives of very high value, then this couple's baby might *decrease* the average value of lives lived. If averagism is true, the same baby, living a life of the same value, under some circumstances would make the world worse and under other circumstances would make the world better. This surely is absurd. As Parfit says, '[R]esearch in Egyptology cannot be relevant to our decision whether to have children' (p. 420).

A final difficulty for averagism involves 'mere addition' (ch. 19). Mere addition occurs when we add some people to a world without affecting the values of the lives of the people already there. Suppose a world with ten billion extremely happy people, each living a life very well worth living – let the value of each be +101. Imagine the mere addition of some people as happy as the happiest person you know. Each of the mere

199

additionals enjoys 100 units of whatever makes life worth living. If Av were true, this mere addition would make the world *worse*, since it would lower the average. Again, this seems preposterous. Adding a supremely happy person to a world, when it detracts from no one's happiness, surely must make the world better.

Totalism seems false. Averagism seems false. The literature contains a variety of other proposals. Some have suggested hybrid theories combining aspects of totalism and aspects of averagism.[7] Thomas Hurka once proposed that the goods enjoyed by members of large populations are worth less than similar goods enjoyed by members of small populations.[8] Others have suggested still other solutions. Many of these proposals have been discussed in the literature, and many of them (as I see it) have been refuted. This is not the place to attempt to review this large literature.[9] Instead, I will turn to a presentation of what I take to be the most promising approach.

IV. BRENTANO'S DISTINCTION

In his essay, 'Loving and Hating', Franz Brentano makes a profoundly important distinction. He attributes the distinction to Aristotle, and says that it can be found in the *Nicomachean Ethics*.[10] He draws the distinction in this way:

> We may distinguish between realizing what is good in general, a good in the whole world-order, and realizing a good in a particular individual. If at the Last Judgement a greater amount of bliss were given to a person who actually deserved it less, then he would have a greater amount of good than

7. T. M. Hurka discussed several forms of averagism in 'Average Utilitarianisms', *Analysis*, xlii (1982), 65–9, then discussed some more forms in 'More Average Utilitarianism', *Analysis*, xlii (1982), 115–119.

8. See, for example, Thomas Hurka, 'Value and Population Size', *Ethics*, xciii (1983), 496–507. Hurka's view was critically discussed by James L. Hudson, 'The Diminishing Marginal Value of Happy People', *Philosophical Studies*, li (1987), 123–137.

9. For a critical review of an important collection of papers on the Repugnant Conclusion and related issues, see Jefferson McMahan, 'Problems of population Theory', *Ethics*, xcii (1981), 96–127; McMahan's article is a review of *Obligations to Future Generations*, ed. R. I. Sikora and Brian Barry, Philadelphia, 1978. A much more comprehensive and up-to-date review of the literature can be found in Moon's 'Ethical Theory and Population'.

10. Franz Brentano, 'Loving and Hating', *The Origin of Our Knowledge of Right and Wrong*, ed. Oskar Kraus, English edn. ed. Roderick Chisholm, trans. Roderick Chisholm and Elizabeth Schneewind, London, 1969. Although Brentano does not cite the passage in which Aristotle draws the distinction, I suspect that he has in mind *Nichomachean Ethics*, V.1 (1129b). It seems to me that Aristotle's point is not quite what Brentano takes it to be.

he otherwise would have, but the good in the universe, considered as a whole, would be less.[11]

In this passage Brentano is discussing the intrinsic value of 'bliss'. He wants to distinguish between two different ways of assessing the amount of intrinsic value contained in an episode of bliss. If we assess it in one way, we ask how much intrinsic value the blissful person receives. This calls for an assessment of the amount of intrinsic value there is in the episode *for the recipient*. The other way of assessing intrinsic value involves the attempt to say how much better the world becomes as a result of the occurrence of that episode. To find this amount, we must consider not only how much bliss the recipient receives, but also the extent to which the recipient deserved his bliss. Undeserved bliss may be good for the recipient, but Brentano thinks such bliss does not make the world any better. Since in this case the recipient does not deserve this bliss, there is an injustice in his receipt of it. In virtue of its injustice, his receipt of the bliss does not make the world better. So the second way of evaluating episodes of bliss involves asking how much value the episode contains *for the world*.

A corresponding distinction could be made concerning episodes in which someone experiences misery. According to this view, deserved misery may be bad for the recipient, but such misery does not make the world any worse. The reasoning here would be just the reverse of the earlier reasoning. In virtue of the justice of his receipt of this misery, the world is not made worse.[12]

Clearly, Brentano's Aristotelian distinction will have dramatic impact on a number of standard cases involving justice.[13] Consider, for example, a case in which someone enjoys 'stolen pleasures'. Imagine that an art-loving thief steals a beautiful painting, and rationalizes his theft by appeal to the fact that he will gain great satisfaction (or 'bliss') from the possession of the work of art. Brentano might say that the thief is partly right. Possession of the painting will yield pleasurable experiences that are good *for him*; but these experiences will not be good *for the world*, since the thief does not deserve to have those pleasures. The injustice of his receipt mitigates the value for the world of his bliss.

Consider the other side of the coin. Suppose a man has been found

11. Brentano, p. 149.
12. I have not been able to find this view in Brentano, but G. E. Moore affirms something quite like it in *Principia Ethica*, Cambridge, 1962, in his discussion of retributive punishment. See pp. 214–216.
13. As I tried to show in 'Adjusting Utility for Justice'.

guilty of a nasty crime, and has been sentenced to five strokes of the cane. He points out that the caning will be very painful. He claims that it will make the world worse. But Brentano could say that the man has neglected the important distinction. The caning will of course produce experiences that are bad *for the man*; but if he deserves precisely that much pain, these experiences will not make the world worse. Justice makes the pain less bad *for the world*.

It should be obvious how Brentano's axiological point provides the basis for a way of dealing with problems about justice. In general, the idea is that deserved goods make the world much better; undeserved goods do not make the world better. Deserved evils do not make the world worse; undeserved evils make the world much worse. If we focus on these 'desert-adjusted values' when we rank possible worlds, we have a way to incorporate considerations of justice into our axiology. As a result, it may be possible to explain why it is sometimes wrong to maximize personal receipt of good; and why it is sometimes right to increase personal receipt of evil. In general, the view would be that the rightness of actions is determined by the *desert-adjusted value* of outcomes.

The central point of Brentano's view is that facts about *desert* affect the value for the world of various goods and evils. In order to give substance to this proposal, one would have to flesh out the concept of desert. One would also have to give some account of the things that make for desert, positive and negative. While I acknowledge the importance of these projects, I do not have the space to pursue them here.[14] Instead, I shall simply sketch some of my conclusions.

V. DESERT

I cannot provide an analysis of the concept of desert. That is, I cannot formulate an enlightening, non-circular analytical definition of 'S deserves p at t'. The concept functions here as a primitive.

However, the concept of desert is familiar. We often hear people say that a particularly vicious criminal 'deserves to have the book thrown at him'; or that a sick child 'does not deserve to suffer in this way', or that

---

14. For more extensive discussion of the concept of desert, see Joel Feinberg, 'Justice and Personal Desert', *Nomos VI: Justice*, ed. C. J. Friedrich and J. W. Chapman, New York, 1963, pp. 69–97; John Kleinig, 'The Concept of Desert', *American Philosophical Quarterly*, viii (1971), 71–78; Owen McLeod, 'On Being Deserving', dissertation, University of Massachusetts, 1995; Wojciech Sadurski, *Giving Desert Its Due: Social Justice and Legal Theory*, Dordrecht, 1985; George Sher, *Desert*, Princeton, 1987.

those who have laboured in the background 'deserve their day in the sun'. Roughly – and this is not intended as a definition – to say that a person deserves some good is to say that it would be 'distributionally appropriate' for him to get it. I assume that desert is a matter of degree, so that it makes sense to say that a certain person deserves a certain good or evil *to a certain extent.*

Let us consider some likely sources of desert, or 'desert bases'.

Suppose an innocent person comes into existence. In virtue of *being a person*, he deserves a certain amount of happiness. Suppose time goes by, and he does nothing wrong, but does not receive any happiness. As I see it, he thereby builds up a sort of 'desert credit'. He deserved to be happy during that time, but was not. In virtue of this *deficient past receipt*, he now deserves full compensation, perhaps with interest.

Suppose an innocent person is brutally attacked by a mugger. The innocent person suffers. This person did not deserve this suffering, and as a result of enduring it, now deserves some compensation. He deserves some extra benefit, perhaps in the form of compensatory damages. This may help to make right the injury he suffered. This illustrates the operation of another desert base – *innocent suffering*.[15]

In many cases, *conscientious effort* increases the extent to which someone deserves a good. If one student worked long and hard to succeed in a course, and another blew off the whole semester, then (other things being equal) the hard worker deserves more to enjoy the rewards of success.

A recipient's *moral worthiness* may have an impact on his desert level too. Suppose two potential recipients of good are alike in all other relevant respects, except that one of them has been good, whereas the other has been bad. Then the one who has been good has greater desert. If no other factors complicate the case, it would be more just for the good to be given to him.[16]

There are undoubtedly other factors that may influence the extent to which a person deserves some good or evil, and in a full exposition of the theory of desert, each of them would be described in detail.[17] Further-

15. I discuss some temporal features of this sort of desert in my 'Desert: Reconsideration of Some Received Wisdom', *Mind*, civ (1995), 63–77. I try to show that it is possible for a person to deserve compensation at a time in virtue of injuries he has yet to receive.

16. In n. 38, on p. 310 of *A Theory of Justice*, Oxford, 1972, Rawls quotes a passage from 'On the Ultimate Origination of the Universe' in which Leibniz seems to say that moral worth is the sole basis on which a person might deserve anything.

17. For further discussion of views about the main desert bases, see Feinberg, McLeod, Sadurski, and Sher. For a comprehensive review of the literature on desert, see McLeod's bibliography.

more, in real-life cases several of the factors may be jointly operative. The ways in which the factors clash and harmonize so as to yield an overall desert-level must also be investigated. However, since my aim here is primarily to show how a desert-adjusted axiology can provide the basis for a solution to Parfit's puzzle, I shall not pursue these lines of inquiry here.

VI. JUSTICE

The idea under consideration is that in order to find the value *for the world* of an episode in which someone receives some of whatever makes life worth living, we have to consider the extent to which the recipient deserved it. Following Brentano (and perhaps Aristotle) I want to say that desert affects the value *for the world* of receipt of goods.

In the passage I cited above, Brentano explicitly discusses just one sort of case, and suggests a view about another. The explicit case is that in which someone enjoys a good that he does not deserve. Brentano's comment is that in such a case, the world is not made better by the presence in it of this person's enjoyment. Brentano implicitly suggests that this sort of 'mitigation' of value does not occur if a person fully deserves a good that he receives. If a person fully deserves a certain good, and receives that good, then the world is made better in full measure. Unfortunately, Brentano does not discuss some other cases. He does not tell us what happens when a person deserves *more* good than he receives. Furthermore, Brentano does not tell us what happens when a person fails to receive a good that he deserves. Let us attempt to formulate some plausible principles.

i. An outstandingly good sort of case is the one in which desert and receipt match precisely. If a person fully deserves a certain good, and receives that good, then the value of the world is substantially increased. Two factors work in concert. In the first place, there is the fact that someone has received some good. In the second place, there is the fact that justice has been done – the recipient deserved precisely the good that he received. As a result, there is a sort of enhancement of value. The value *for the world* of his deserved receipt in this case is greater than the value received by the person, taken just by itself.

ii. A less good case is the one in which a person receives a certain good, but does not deserve it. Brentano's remarks suggest that in this case, the good is valuable *for the person*, but not *for the world*. The world is not

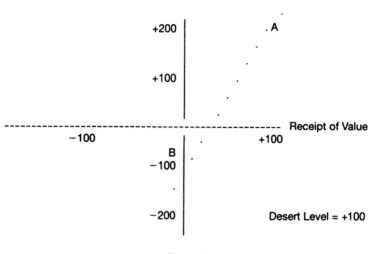

Value for the World

```
             +200  |         . A
                   |
                   |      .
             +100  |
                   |    .
                   |
                   |   .
----------------------------------------------- Receipt of Value
  -100            |       .   +100
             B     |    .
            -100  |
                   |  .
                   |
             -200  |         Desert Level = +100
```

Figure 1

made better by this person's receipt of that good, since he does not deserve
to be having it. Thus, lack of desert mitigates the value of a good.

iii. What shall we say about the case in which a person deserves a
certain good, but fails to receive it? Perhaps we should say that in this case
the injustice of the situation as a whole serves to make the world worse.
It would be better for the person to get just what he deserves, rather than,
as in this case, nothing.

iv. For present purposes one sort of case is especially important. This
is the sort of case in which a person receives some good, but less than the
amount he deserves. In this sort of case, it seems to me, the value for the
world of his receipt depends entirely upon how large a fraction he receives. If it is a very tiny fraction of what he deserves, then the case is
relevantly like the case (Case iii) in which a deserving person receives
nothing. It is then bad for the world. If the fraction is large enough, it
may be almost as good as the case (Case i) in which a person receives
precisely what he deserves.

We may illustrate the idea behind this view by appeal to a simple graph,
Figure 1. The graph concerns cases in which someone deserves a hundred
units of good. It depicts the functional relationship between various

205

amounts of receipt and values-for-world of this receipt. In the graph, the NS axis represents value *for the world*; the EW axis represents various personal receipt levels.

First consider Point A, which corresponds to Case i above. Point A indicates what happens when a person who deserves +100 units of value receives a hundred units of value. In this case we have an enhancement of value, since justice is done perfectly. I somewhat arbitrarily represent this phenomenon by saying that the value for the world of this case is +200. So if a highly deserving person gets precisely what he deserves, then justice is done perfectly, and the world is made much better.

Next consider Point B, which corresponds to Case iii above. This indicates what happens when a person who deserves +100 units of value receives nothing. In this case, the experience (or lack of experience) has no value *for the person*. However, in virtue of its injustice, it has negative value *for the world*. The world is made worse when a deserving person fails to receive what he deserves. I represent this value (again somewhat arbitrarily) as −50.

Note the curve connecting Point B to Point A. The points on this curve represent cases in which someone with positive desert receives less good than he deserves. In the area near Point B, we see that tiny receipts have negative value for the world, but at around +25 they cross over into positive territory. This illustrates the idea that receipt of much less than you deserve is not good for the world − it is almost as bad as receipt of no good at all. As the receipt levels increase, the value for the world increases steadily. In the area near Point A, the value of large receipts approximates the value of perfect match between receipt and desert. Receipt of just a little less than you deserve is very good for the world − almost as good as perfect justice would have been.

So far I have been considering some claims about the value for the world, adjusted for desert, of individual episodes of receipt. I want next to turn to some axiological principles concerning the values of more complex things. In particular, I want to focus on the values of *lives* and *worlds*. Once this is done, we can return to Parfit's population puzzle.

As we have seen, Brentano thinks that there are two ways to assess the value of an episode in which someone receives 'bliss', or whatever makes life worth living. I have already spoken of some likely views concerning value *for the world* of an episode of bliss. Let us consider value *for the person* of the episode. A very simple graph displays the most natural hypothesis (Figure 2).

The graph indicates that the value for the person of an episode of bliss

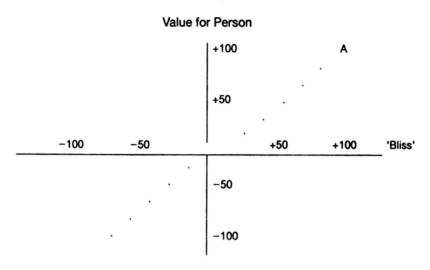

Value for Person

Figure 2

is a direct function of the amount of bliss in the episode. The graph contains further information about the disvalue of misery (or 'anti-bliss').

Although Brentano does not say this, I assume that he would accept several forms of totalism with respect to personal intrinsic value. One form of totalism says that the personal intrinsic value of a person's life at a world is the sum of the personal intrinsic values of the episodes of bliss and misery within that life at that world. Letting 'PIV(e)' indicate the value *for the person* of an episode of 'bliss' or misery, and letting 'PIV(x,w)' indicate the value for a person, x, of the life he or she lives at some world, w, I would formulate this totalistic principle about lives as follows:

PIV(1): PIV(x,w) = the sum, for all episodes, e, of good and evil in the life of x at w, of PIV(e).[18]

Although Brentano presumably would not be interested in this number, someone might want to know how much personal value there is in a world. Another totalistic principle gives the answer:

18. I acknowledge that there are a number of technical problems concerning the summation of value. For example, how are we to avoid 'double-counting' when several episodes of pleasure 'overlap'? How are we to find the sum in cases in which there are infinitely many episodes? These are serious and tricky problems that deserve careful attention.

PIV(w): PIV(w) = the sum, for every person, x, in w, of PIV(x,w).

Brentano is far more interested in what we have been calling 'value for the world'. The value for the world of an episode of bliss or misery is the value contained in that episode *adjusted for desert*. I illustrated the determination of this value (for a limited range of cases) in Figure 1. Let us use 'WIV(e)' to indicate the desert-adjusted intrinsic value, or what Brentano calls the value *for the world*, of the episode of bliss or misery, e. Brentano apparently is very interested in the total amount of this value in a world. I suggest that several sorts of totalism are true here, too. One of them concerns lives:

WIV(1): WIV(x,w) = the sum, for all episodes, e, of good or evil in the life of x in w, of WIV(e).

Finally, we may affirm the central totalistic doctrine of this axiology. It tells us that the worldly value of a world is the sum of the values *for the world* of the lives lived there:

WIV(w): WIV(w) = the sum, for every person, x, in w, of WIV(x,w).[19]

The fundamental thesis of the proposed axiology is that the relevant, or important value of a world, w, is the sum of the values of the lives lived there, *adjusted for desert*, or WIV(w). One implication of this view is that it permits us to say that w1 may be much better than w2 even though w1 contains no more personal value than does w2. The worldly value of a world depends not merely on the total amount of personal value experienced there, but also on details of the distribution: who gets to enjoy the goods? who gets to suffer the evils? to what extent do these recipients deserve these goods and evils when they receive them?

VII. APPLICATION TO REPUGNANT CONCLUSION

Now, at last, let us turn to the central question: What is the connection between the proposed theory and the problem of the Repugnant Conclusion?

According to Parfit's description, each person at the Z world enjoys a quality of life that is just slightly above the neutral level – a life just barely

---

19. Equivalently, one could say that the worldly value of a world is the sum of the worldly values of the *episodes* that occur there.

worth living. Let us say that each life in Z contains no evil but just one unit of whatever makes life worth living. According to PIV(1), each life in Z has a value *for the person* of +1. But because there are so many such lives being lived there, totalistic axiologies seem to imply that the total value of the Z world is very great. If there are a billion billion people at the Z world, the sum of their qualities of life would be a billion billion. The value of Z itself may therefore seem to be a billion billion.[20]

Given one very natural assumption, my proposed axiology yields a dramatically different result. The assumption concerns desert. Let us assume that the residents of Z are relevantly like us – each of them is a person, and starts out deserving a quality of life roughly equivalent to that which we deserve. To make the calculations simple, let us assume that each deserves a quality of life that rates +100.[21] Now, to find the *worldly* intrinsic value of Z, we may consult Figure 1 and perform some calculations.

When a person deserves a life worth +100, but receives a life worth just +1, then that person has suffered a grave injustice. His receipt level is painfully lower than his desert level. As a result, according to Figure 1, the pitifully small share of goods enjoyed by this person may be slightly good for him (his life has a PIV of +1), but it does not increase the value of the world at all. In fact, if the intuitions behind Figure 1 are correct, we can say that the world is *made worse* by the fact that he receives just this good, since his total receipt departs so dramatically from the amount he deserves. The value *for the world* of such a life is −49.[22]

According to WIV(1), the worldly value of each life lived in Z is approximately −49. There are a billion billion people living these low

20. Principle PIV(w) serves to define this value, which I take to be of little importance.
21. In saying that each person starts off deserving +100, I commit myself to versions of two important and controversial moral doctrines. The first is *egalitarianism*. On the view I have proposed, people are equal with respect to their initial desert levels. Until we do evil, or suffer harms, or receive more than our fair shares, we are all alike with respect to desert. This is a version of egalitarianism. The second doctrine is a version of the thesis of *moral considerability*. According to this view, merely being a person gives each of us some 'standing' or 'worth'. Under my interpretation, the impact of the thesis is that merely being human makes each of us deserve to enjoy some positive value.
22. Note that if a person receives substantially less good than he deserves, the value for the world of his receipt is negative. It might therefore appear that if a person is going to have such low receipt, someone should simply kill him, in order to prevent the evil from coming into the world. This line of thinking seems to me to be mistaken. The person is *already in the world*. If he is killed, he gets even less of the goods he deserves. The world would be *better*, not worse, if he were given the chance to receive his sub-par fraction of the good.

quality lives in Z. My totalistic principle WIV(w) then yields the result that Z has a worldly value of −49 billion billion. In short, Z is a horrible world. (Note that adding more similar people to Z will make it *worse*, not better.) So we must not think that a new version of the Repugnant Conclusion will emerge at some higher population level. World A, on the other hand, has a worldly value of two thousand billion.

Brentano's distinction enables me to locate the precise spot where the reasoning behind the Repugnant Conclusion goes wrong. The mistake is in assuming that the value of the world as a whole is the sum of the values *for the residents* of the lives lived there. Following Brentano, my view is that the relevant assessment of the world is an assessment in terms of value *for the world*. When evaluated in the proposed way, taking due account of desert, it turns out that Z is indeed far worse than A. Our axiological intuitions are preserved.[23]

I find the Z world repugnant. It does not seem to me to be an outstandingly good world, in spite of the fact that the residents of Z receive (collectively) an enormous amount of value. I think I can see the feature of the Z world that is responsible for this evaluation. It is closely related to the fact that each resident gets such a tiny share of value. People should not be forced to live such drab lives. They deserve better. The repugnancy of the Z world is primarily due to the fact that there is rampant injustice there. Each resident of Z gets far less good than he or she deserves. This is what makes Z bad. The axiology sketched in this paper is designed to take this factor into account when evaluating worlds for worldly value.[24]

23. Near the end of 'Problems of Population Theory', McMahan sketches (and rejects) a possible solution to the Repugnant Conclusion based on the notion that everyone has a right to at least a certain minimum amount of value. There are obvious affinities between the view sketched by McMahan and the approach defended here.

24. It should be clear that the approach I have sketched also provides the basis for rebutting the claim of the fifth god, mentioned above in n. 4. In my discussion of Z, I appealed to the notion that it may be bad for people to receive far less good than they deserve. In order to deal with the world of the fifth god, I appeal to the notion that it may be less good for people to receive vastly more good than they deserve. Another look at Figure 1 may serve to make the view clearer. Notice that the curve begins to flatten out as it moves northeast of Point A. The idea here is that as a person receives more than he deserves, the world begins to benefit less. In other words, receipts beyond the amount deserved have decreasing marginal value for the world. This explains why it is so much better for some value to be split equally among some equally deserving people, rather than giving some much more than they deserve, and others less. The distribution

VIII. AN OBJECTION BASED ON PARFIT'S REMARKS ABOUT JUSTICE

Parfit imagines an objector saying that the Z world should be given a lower evaluation because there is so much injustice there.[25] This is precisely what I have said. But Parfit rejects this sort of solution. He seems to think that there need not be any injustice in Z. He says:

> We are asking whether, if Z comes about, this would be better than if A comes about. We could imagine a history in which only Z-like outcomes occur. The people in Z would then be no worse off than anyone who ever lives. If we believe that Z would be worse than A, this would not here be because Z's occurrence would involve injustice (p. 390).

As I understand him, Parfit is saying that Z might contain no injustice at all – so my proposed Brentanist solution cannot be relevant. Parfit's argument seems to be this: all the people in Z get equal shares of good; each person is exactly as well off as anyone who ever lives. Therefore, there is no injustice in Z. Therefore, we cannot solve the puzzle of the Repugnant Conclusion by claiming that Z is worse because it is so unjust.

As should be obvious, I reject the underlying principle about justice. I deny the inference from the premise that all are equally deserving, and all are treated alike, to the conclusion that all are treated justly. I view this as a case in which everyone deserves an equal share, and everyone receives an equal share, but everyone receives a share smaller than he or she deserves. In this case there is equality of treatment, and equality of desert, but no justice. There is uniformly distributed injustice. Everyone in Z gets less than he or she deserves, and so everyone suffers an injustice.

of value is not a zero sum game, in part because excessive receipts have diminishing value for the world. Although Figure 1 does not show this, it would be reasonable to suppose that the curve gradually flattens out, and approaches some maximum value. If the curve has this shape, the implication is clear. Once we reach the region where some person is receiving vastly more good than he deserves, increasing receipts begin to have infinitesimal value for the world. Figure 1 explains where the fifth god goes wrong. He proposes to create a world in which one person receives slightly more than a billion billion units of value. This would undoubtedly be unimaginably good for the sole recipient of the value. However, the world thus created would not be very good. Depending upon the precise shape of the curve, it might be that the value of the world would be around +1000. All that personal value makes the world much better when it is distributed in smaller, equal amounts more closely approximating what people deserve.

25. Parfit, p. 390. In the passage I cite, Parfit is actually talking about *intergenerational* justice, but it seems to me quite natural to extend his comment so as to make it apply to any sort of injustice.

211

IX. AN OBJECTION BASED ON THE IDEA THAT THERE COULD BE A HIGHLY POPULOUS WORLD WHERE THEY DESERVE LESS AND GET WHAT THEY DESERVE

A critic might agree that the proposed axiology implies that Z is far worse than A. Thus, the proposed axiology is not refuted by the original example. However, it might be thought that a variant of the original example will prove just as repugnant.

The critic might ask us to imagine a world, Z', in which there are a billion billion people. He might go on to ask us to imagine that each of them deserves +1 and gets +1. Given the axiological principles stated earlier, the worldly value of this world is two billion billion. Therefore, the proposed Brentanist axiology implies that Z' is better than A. But it is not. So the new axiology is erroneous.[26]

Two sorts of reply seem to be in order. In the first place, it is not entirely clear that Z' ought to be considered horrible. Note that the residents of Z' are not like us. They deserve far less than we deserve. Each of them deserves just +1, and each of them gets exactly what he or she deserves. Since Z' is so incredibly populous, and since the total amount of good enjoyed by the residents is so huge, and since everything in Z' is said to be just as it ought to be, it is not clear that we should find Z' repugnant.

There is a further difficulty with Z'. It is not clear that the description of Z' is coherent. Allegedly, this is a world in which there are a billion billion people, and each deserves and receives +1. I stipulated that merely in virtue of being a person, each of us deserves +100. If we do nothing wrong, and fail to receive the goods we deserve, we continue to deserve +100. The people in Z' allegedly deserve much less. But why do they deserve less? It must be because they did something wrong. If they did something wrong, that would make Z' worse. The description of Z' is therefore incomplete. These people must have done some evil deeds (otherwise they would not have such low desert levels). Yet the evil of those deeds is neither described nor included in the calculations.[27]

---

26. Several friends have raised this objection. I believe the first of them was Neil Schaefer.
27. It might appear that even if people start out deserving +100, they could misbehave and thereby lower their desert levels to +1. Then they could receive +1 and enhance the value of the world. If there were enough people, it might seem that they could somehow manage to raise the value of the world to the point where it exceeds the value of the A world. Could this happen? If it could happen, would a world in which it happens be

better than the A world? What does the proposed axiology say about such a world? These questions are far more complex than they may at first appear to be. In order to make them somewhat more manageable, we can view the issue from the perspective of a little game. The game represents (in a very simplified form) the value-theoretic problem. Can the players behave in such a way as to make the value of their world very high, even though each of them has low desert and low receipt?

Rules of the game:

Any number of people can play. The play progresses in rounds. In each round, each player is permitted to make one move. A player can either (a) inflict some amount of pain on someone; or (b) inflict some amount of pleasure on someone.

Scoring: Each player has two scores – a receipt level (RL) and a desert level (DL). At the beginning of play, each player's DL = +100. Furthermore, the world has a score, or IV level. At the outset IV = 0.

Changing your score: there are several ways in which you can change your score.

a. If you inflict n units of pleasure on someone who has positive DL, your DL goes up by $n/2$ units; his RL goes up by n units; his DL goes down by n units; and IV goes up by $2n$ units.

b. I you inflict n units of pleasure on someone who has negative DL, your DL remains constant; his RL goes up by n units; his DL remains constant; and IV goes down by $n/2$ units.

c. If you inflict n units of pain on someone who has positive DL, your DL goes down by $n/2$ units; his RL goes down by n units; his DL goes up by n units; and IV goes down by $2n$ units.

d. If you inflict n units of pain on someone who has negative DL, your DL remains constant; his RL goes down by n units; his DL goes up by n units; and IV remains constant.

I think it would be very costly for the world's IV for players in this game to try to get their DL down to +1. Here is one way they could do it: in the first round each player could inflict 198 units of pain on a deserving person. Then (rule c) each person's DL would go down by 198/2, or 99. Thus each player would have DL = +1. The cost to the world would be (2 × 198 × the number of players). Suppose there are 10 players. Then at the end of round 1, IV = −5,960. In round 2, each player could inflict 1 unit of pleasure on someone who deserves 1 unit of pleasure. In this case, IV would go up by (2 × 1 × 10), or 20 pts. IV = −5,940.

At the end of round 2, each player would have DL = 0. Inflicting pleasure on others will be less valuable for the world in this case. [Sorry, no rules for this case.] Let us say it's worth $n/2$ for the world. If it makes their DLs go negative, then further inflictions of pleasure will start to make IV get *smaller* (rule b).

There is another way in which players could reduce their DLs to +1. They could enjoy deserved pleasures. Let us suppose that each player starts out with DL = +100, and then enjoys +99. Then (rule a) each player's DL goes down to +1. At that point, each player could receive +1. My theory then implies that IV is extremely high. (Suppressing certain complexities, we can see that each player started out deserving +100, and received +100. If there are a billion billion players, IV = two hundred billion billion.) However, it seems quite clear to me that the imagined world would in fact be extraordinarily good, and so I am delighted that the axiology gives it such a high IV.

Moral of this story: it is hard to see how there can be a world that strikes our intuitions as being very bad, in which each resident deserves +1 and receives +1, and IV is extremely high.

X. SUMMARY AND CONCLUSION

In this paper, I have sketched the problem of the Repugnant Conclusion. Totalism seems to imply that if it is populous enough, a world whose residents live lives barely worth living (the Z world) would be better than a magnificent world such as the A world. I then presented the elements of justicism, according to which the value for the world of someone's receipt of good or evil must be adjusted for desert. Justicism implies that the world is made *worse* when people receive just a tiny fraction of the good they deserve. For this reason, justicism implies that the populous world is worse than the magnificent world. The striking fact about this proposed solution is that justicism is a form of totalism. So we can see that not all forms of totalism imply the Repugnant Conclusion.

Index of subjects

Index of persons

Index of cases